D1525133

Let the Oppressed Go Free

EXPLORING THEOLOGIES OF LIBERATION

Marvin A. McMickle

Foreword by Eboni Marshall Turman

JUDSON PRESS
PUBLISHERS SINCE 1824
VALLEY FORGE, PA

Let the Oppressed Go Free: Exploring Theologies of Liberation
© 2020 Judson Press, Valley Forge, PA 19482-0851
All rights reserved.

Judson Press has made every effort to trace the ownership of all quotes. In the event of a question arising from the use of a quote, we regret any error made and will be pleased to make the necessary correction in future printings and editions of this book.

Unless otherwise indicated, Scripture quotations are from the New Revised Standard Version of the Bible, copyright © 1989 by the Division of Christian Education of the National Council of the Churches of Christ in the United States of America. Used by permission. All rights reserved. Additional quotations are from HOLY BIBLE, New International Version®, NIV®, copyright © 1973, 1978, 1984, 2011 by Biblica Inc. Used by permission. All rights reserved worldwide and from The Holy Bible, Berean Study Bible, BSB, Copyright © 2016, 2018 by Bible Hub. Used by Permission. All Rights Reserved Worldwide.

Interior design by Beth Oberholtzer Design.
Cover design by Wendy Ronga, Hampton Design Group.

Library of Congress Cataloging-in-Publication data

Names: McMickle, Marvin Andrew, author.
Title: Let the oppressed go free : exploring theologies of liberation / Marvin A. McMickle.
Description: Valley Forge, PA : Judson Press, 2021. | Includes bibliographical references.
Identifiers: LCCN 2020033367 (print) | LCCN 2020033368 (ebook) | ISBN 9780817018191 (paperback) | ISBN 9780817082208 (epub)
Subjects: LCSH: Liberation theology.
Classification: LCC BT83.57 .M385 2021 (print) | LCC BT83.57 (ebook) | DDC 230/.0464—dc23
LC record available at https://lccn.loc.gov/2020033367
LC ebook record available at https://lccn.loc.gov/2020033368

Printed in the U.S.A.

First printing, 2020.

Contents

Foreword

The first time I ever heard the Rev. Dr. Marvin A. McMickle preach was at the historic Abyssinian Baptist Church in the village of Harlem. At the time, I was a young assistant minister there—the youngest woman, in fact, to ever be ordained by the church and only the second woman to preside over its ordinances in its 212-year history. McMickle, a son of Abyssinian having served there as an assistant minister during the pastorate of the Rev. Dr. Samuel DeWitt Proctor, was at the time the senior pastor of the Antioch Baptist Church in Cleveland, OH. Although the precision of my memory of the occasion is fading, one thing I will never forget is the sermon that Dr. McMickle preached that Sunday morning.

Perhaps one of the most stirring sermons that I have ever heard, he preached from the Book of Acts on the subject of Christian stewardship. He exhorted the gathered fellowship of believers toward the amplification of their vision and practice of care for God's economy through the giving of their unique gifts for the strengthening of the church, the development of the community, and the transformation of the world. While his intellectual sophistication, rhetorical style, and prophetic power were on full display that morning, what was most remarkable about the sermonic moment was how the Word he proclaimed on that day—a word of care, commitment, offering, love, and grace particularly for the sake of the most marginalized among us—was precisely what he has given his life and ministry to over the years.

McMickle is an heir to the liberationist strand of Black social Christianity and in that homiletical moment his preaching was a clear manifestation of his own uncompromised lived witness that has—from the church house to the community house to the school house—endeavored to mobilize the saints toward caring for and transforming the realities of the marginalized. *Let the Oppressed Go Free* is further evidence of his rigorous stewardship and deep concern for the church, the academy, and the world. It is a record of theologian-activists who loved God with their minds to such an extent that they too proclaimed God's healing, deliverance, freedom, justice, and care for the oppressed with their very lives. The privilege of studying and digesting this narrative arc of theologies of liberation in the US serves to remind those who are struggling to survive and thrive in a MAGA-infested nation and world of the bountiful wisdom that emerges from the theological vision of the Black Church from which McMickle descends, that is, "trouble don't last always."

McMickle positions James H. Cone's late-twentieth century Black theological intervention and its concern for liberation from all forms of antiblackness in the church and public square as the genesis of theological liberation movements in the US. He explicitly signals that what society faces in this "trumped-up" contemporary moment is not new. We have seen the diminishment and subjugation of the poor, the racially minoritized, and gender subjugated before. With the help of God, we resisted then, and we can resist now. In the spirit of those abolitionist, feminist, protowomanist, and queer ancestors who, in the words of black feminist Barbara D. Savage, continue to "walk beside us"—Frederick Douglass, Sojourner Truth, Susan B. Anthony, Martin Luther King, Jr., Bayard Rustin, Pauli Murray, and Harvey Milk, among others. McMickle implicitly contends that if the church is serious about the ministry of the Palestinian Jew from the ghetto of Nazareth that it proclaims; the life of the One whose ministry was primarily concerned with letting [all] of the oppressed go free, then the significant complexities of antiblack racism must be interrogated and dismantled. Black lives *must* matter for the church. McMickle takes his cues from the intersectional concerns and methodologies of Black womanist theology. He further and most provocatively argues that the insidiousness of antiblackness cannot be fully addressed apart from attending to its interdigitation with other forms of oppression and subjugation that diminish the life chances of all of God's creation. In the name of Jesus, he maintains that the church is called to attend to sexism, classism, homophobia, and colonialism's enduring legacies.

This intersectional fight is what is before us. And in consummate form, *Let the Oppressed Go Free* takes its place among McMickle's vast intellectual corpus as its Christian ethic of stewardship. It meets us amidst the current surge of racism, fascism, sexism, queerphobia, economic injustice, and the medical apartheid accompanying the COVID-19 global pandemic, as a historical witness and very present testimony against all that threatens to diminish life for the most marginalized among us. Compelled by the words of Jesus as recorded in Luke 4:18, *Let the Oppressed Go Free* illuminates a genealogy of "hope against hope" (Rom. 4:18). Hope that has been born from the flesh and blood realities of those who have persisted in faith and action despite the brutal and seemingly unrelenting logic of genocide, slavery, and rape. To be sure, this is the best kind of intellectual preaching. It is a love offering that renders an abiding act of care for the church and theological academy. Herein McMickle decidedly proclaims with Cone, the father of Black theology, that indeed, "God is on the side of the oppressed." With conviction, McMickle propels his readers to the Gospel tasks of setting "at liberty them that are oppressed" that is so desperately needed in our world today.

Rev. Eboni Marshall Turman, PhD
Assistant Professor of Theology and African American Religion
Yale University/The Divinity School

Acknowledgments

There are many people who need to be acknowledged in relation to this book project. First, there is Judson Press, which has been supportive of my work for the last twenty years. This is the fourteenth book project on which we have collaborated. I began working with Randy Frame as the editor. Most of my work was been with Rebecca Irwin-Diehl. In the middle of this project she took on a wonderful new assignment within ABHMS, and Linda Triemstra Cook and Lisa Blair have carried on with the editorial work for this book. I tell all aspiring writers that your best asset in the development process for a new book are trusted and reliable editors. I have been blessed with some of the best, and for that I am thankful.

I want to express my thanks to several schools that hosted me and allowed me to share the substance of this book in the context of their academic communities. First, I want to thank Dr. Stephanie Sauve at Colgate Rochester Crozer Divinity School (CRCDS), who invited me to deliver the 2018 African American Legacy Lectures that focused on the work of James H. Cone and the rise of Black theology. I thank Dr. Quintin Robertson of United Lutheran Seminary of Philadelphia, Pennsylvania, for hosting me in 2019 for the Urban Theological Institute Lectures. Finally, I want to thank Dr. Clifford Chalmers of Westminster College in Missouri, who invited me to deliver the C. S. Lewis Lecture in 2018. Along with my classes at CRCDS, these lectureships allowed me to wrestle with the material that is found in this book.

I am grateful to the persons who previewed sections of this book and added their expertise to the arguments I have tried to make. I am especially grateful to Emilie M. Townes, who previewed the chapter on womanist theology. I wanted to be sure that an established scholar in that field had the chance to see the approach I took on that topic. I am also grateful to my colleagues in ministry who contributed their stories and struggles as found in the chapter entitled "Listen to These Women!" I am blessed to number among my friends such gifted persons as Traci Blackmon, Leslie Callahan, Sabrina Ellis, Zina Jacques, Suzan Johnson Cook, Carolyn Ann Knight, Gina Stewart, and Sharon Williams. The church and the world would do well to listen to these women.

My ministry has been enriched by my association with my sisters in ministry in Cleveland, Ohio, including Gloria Chaney, Tonya Fields, Monica Harmon, Courtney Clayton Jenkins, Christine A. Smith, and Mylion Waite. I sponsored or shared in the ordination of all these women in ministry, and I had the privilege of hiring and working with most of them. They have helped me broaden my understanding of the struggles of women seeking to honor their call to ministry. I had each of them in mind as I talked about *Let the Oppressed Go Free*.

Both James H. Cone and Gayraud S. Wilmore died while this book was being researched and written. Words alone cannot fully express my deep admiration for their scholarship, their courage in introducing Black theology as a new academic discipline, and their example as men who devoted themselves to a ministry of teaching and writing. While many are called to the pulpit, I pray that God will continue to call men and women to the classroom, the research library, and the often isolated and solitary work of the writer.

Along with James A. Sanders, who was my Old Testament professor at Union Theological Seminary in New York City, James Cone taught me the discipline of critical thinking. Holding strong opinions is one thing; submitting even one's own opinions to deep reflection, critical thinking, and the critique of one's peers in the church and the academy are necessary steps in the writing of a book. Sanders reviewed the first three chapters of this book, and as always "my teacher" challenges me to think and then think some more before I announce any conclusions.

As always, I am indebted to my bride of forty-five years. Peggy McMickle has read pages, listened to lectures, attended classes, heard sermons, and offered the kind of encouragement and advice that comes as a result of our partnership over the years. She did not know when we got married in 1975 how many hours I would spend being closed off in my study reading, writing, chasing down footnotes, and interacting with editors. This is my eighteenth book project, and each time she has handled the separation with grace, patience, and understanding. Nothing I have done over my career as a pastor, professor, seminary president, or public theologian would have been possible without her support.

Finally, to God be the glory! The Lord made it clear to me the path he wanted me to follow. My guiding verse has been Ephesians 4:11, which says God called some to be apostles, prophets, evangelists, and "pastors and teachers." That is the task to which I was called, pastor and teacher. Whether in a pulpit, a classroom, a political rally, a civil rights demonstration, a faculty meeting, a panel discussion by way of Zoom, or writing a book, I have tried to remember and remain faithful to the work to which I was called by God when I was sixteen years old. It has been a good journey; and as the songwriter Kenneth W. Louis says, "Jesus, you brought me all the way."

Introduction

A Reflection on Fifty Years of Liberation Theology

When James Cone released *Black Theology and Black Power* in 1969,[1] he was making the claim that the center of the gospel message was God's concern for and identification with the oppressed people of the world. This claim was based upon a reading of Scripture that focused on two primary sources. First, there was the Exodus story and the deliverance of the Hebrews from 430 years of captivity in Egypt. Second, there were the words found in Isaiah 61:1 and again in Luke 4:18 when Jesus quotes from Isaiah and declares that the mission of the coming Messiah was "to set the captives free."

If viewed through this lens, the heart of the gospel was not simply about the nature or the attributes or the names of God, topics that have occupied theologians, biblical scholars, Sunday school teachers, and preachers for nearly two thousand years. Rather, the heart of the gospel is seeing how God has entered human history to condemn those who oppress the poor and needy, and how God has acted in powerful ways to bring that oppression to an end. What difference does it make how baptism is performed or how the Lord's Supper is served, if the churches in which those rites and ordinances were practiced were segregated and if the people receiving or presiding over those rituals were at the same time participating in systems and policies that intentionally disadvantaged, disenfranchised, and dehumanized other human beings? God's sympathies reside with and among the oppressed.

James Cone made it clear in 1969 that to be a Christian was to work with God to end that oppression. No amount of conformity to religious ritual or denominational doctrine was an acceptable alternative to engaging in the work of justice that sets the captives free. This was the primary message of the biblical prophets; religiosity is not an acceptable alternative to doing the works of righteousness and justice. Micah 6:8, Amos 5:24, and Isaiah 58:6 make that point abundantly clear. Yet, generations of white scholars and church leaders never made the connection between that clear and consistent message in the Bible and the freedom struggle going on in the United States right before their eyes. The work of God, and thus the work of those who sought to be faithful to God, is to set the captives free.

Given his location as an African American theologian writing in the 1960s with the chants of "we want Black power" echoing from street corners and college campuses across the United States, with the Black Arts movement emerging in urban centers across the country,[2] and with the election of Black people to multiple offices at the local and congressional level resulting in part in the creation of the Congressional Black Caucus,[3] Cone made his claim about God even more specific. God was not just on the side of the oppressed in general terms. God was on the side of Black people in this country as they struggled for freedom and dignity against racism and the presumption of white supremacy. That was the birth of what came to be known as Black theology. It was and remains a theological formulation that must be considered within the framework of a particular context. Black theology is not theology for the ages; it is theology for this age in which we are living—with the problem of racism and white supremacy being as problematic now in 2020 as it was in 1969.

We need Black theology as a framework by which we can hear and respond to the tragic events in Charlottesville, Virginia, in 2017, when Nazi sympathizers and white nationalists marched through the streets of that city carrying swastikas and Confederate flags. We need Black theology to provide a biblically grounded and historically informed position from which to respond to Donald Trump, who responded to that rally by saying there were "very fine people on both sides."[4] It should be noted that Trump would return to those comments almost two years later, on April 26, 2019, when he said again, "His answer in 2017 was perfect, and that Robert E. Lee was a great general, and that he was the favorite general of many military leaders assigned to the White House."[5]

How was it possible that generations of white theologians had studied and written about the gospel but had never made this connection between what God had done through Moses, the prophets, and Jesus, and what the church should be doing in the world in every generation in terms of the work of justice? How could scholars be at work during the front-page-news days that was the civil rights movement of the 1950s and 1960s and not say a word about the brutality being employed every day in order to maintain white supremacy in the United States? How could white preachers and teachers not make the connection between what was happening in the streets across America in terms of racial violence and race-based policies that undergirded an inequitable social order, and what should be happening in their sanctuaries, their classrooms, their neighborhoods, and their personal lives as matters of being faithful to the gospel?

Fifty years after the emergence of Black theology, some white, conservative evangelical Christians still fail or refuse to see the connection between the message of the gospel and the freedom struggle for Black people in the United States. In 2019, Daniel Akin, who is president of Southeastern Baptist Theological Seminary in Fort Worth, Texas, said, "James Cone was a heretic and almost certainly not a Christian based on his teachings."[6] However, as Andre Henry points out in response, "The heresy that Cone is guilty of is denying white Christian leaders' authority to define what Christianity should look like for Black people."[7] Rather than allowing white theologians and church leaders to define singularly the frame of reference by which the Christian faith is to be understood, Cone sought to establish a new frame of reference, both for doing theology and for living as a Christian in American society. Henry continues, "Cone recognized that Black Christians needed to embrace a frame of their own. He said, rightfully, that Black people and other persecuted groups don't organize their faith around ruminating on theological propositions, but around encountering God in their struggle for freedom."[8]

Black theology provides an informed position from which to ask the question of why twenty-first-century white evangelical religion can be so outspoken on matters of abortion and the right to life for the unborn, but so silent on matters of criminal justice reform, affordable and accessible health care, quality public education, and paying a living wage to people who are trying to work their way out of poverty. Does the right to life pertain only to the womb and the unborn child? Should it not extend to the workplace, the schoolyard, the courtroom, and the dinner table in the homes of America's neediest families? These are just some of the policy actions that could be taken to set the captives free.

Given the way in which white conservative Christians have interpreted the gospel and tolerated, if not served as apologists for white supremacy, Cone faced a specific challenge as he was writing in 1969. Behind every word he wrote was the question of whether it even made sense for Black people to remain Christian. With the Black Power movement active on college campuses, and with the Nation of Islam (Black Muslims) active on street corners and well-placed mosques (Muhammad's Temples), the question was being raised as to whether Christianity was "a white man's religion." Those who were not alive during those years may be unfamiliar with the challenge these movements posed to the Black Christian church at that time.

I can remember during my late teen years in Chicago, spending far more time at a Black cultural center led by a jazz musician named Phil Coran than I did at the church where I had grown up. As will be discussed at much greater length later in this book, Cone was as focused on making Christianity relevant to the young, intellectually restless, budding Black nationalists like myself and my friends who crowded into that center every week, as well as those gathering on college campuses, in Nation of Islam mosques, and in various chapters of the Black Panther Party across the country, as he was on debunking and critiquing the theology of the white religious establishment. While teaching at Adrian College in Michigan in 1967, shortly after the uprising in Detroit,[9] Cone wondered to himself, "What, if anything, is theology worth in the Black struggle in America?"[10] He continued:

> I was fed up with white theologians writing about the gospel as if it had nothing to do with Black Power and Black people's struggle for cultural identity and political justice . . . I was fed up with conservative Black churches preaching an otherworldly gospel as if Jesus had nothing to say about how white supremacy had created a world that was killing Black people. . . . It was time for me to join

my Black brothers and sisters in the fight for justice using what I'd learned in graduate school . . . Militant Negro ministers needed a theology that could liberate their minds from any dependency on white theology.[11]

However, it quickly became apparent even to Cone that focusing on oppression related to the problem of race and racism would not set all the captives free. While his mission was clear as far as Black theology was concerned, there was also a need for and room for more than one contentious claim about God and about the gospel. Thus, Black theology must be viewed as one of the earliest forms of liberation theology to appear in the 1960s and 1970s and beyond. Other scholars began to write and speak as they sought to represent the concerns of other oppressed groups, not rooted solely in the experience of race and racism. That continuing expansion of the voices and communities clamoring to be set free from captivity is also a focus of this book. Indeed, fifty years after the release of *Black Theology and Black Power*, the notion of Black theology has melded into a broader theological framework now known as liberation theology.

Within a matter of two or three years, there emerged a rigorous discussion about God and the gospel through the eyes of (predominantly) white women. This led to the emergence of feminist theology. This movement raised objections to the fact that women, who represent the numerical majority in most local churches, were being prohibited from becoming ordained clergy and from exercising leadership in the church. In partnership with the feminist movement already at work in US society, feminist theology turned its attention not just to matters of grievance about reproductive rights or equal pay for equal work (and more recently to the problem of sexual harassment and assault as expressed through the #MeToo movement, which will be discussed at greater length later in this study. Rather, like Black theology, the leaders in feminist theology looked at the ways in which the Bible was being used and misused to justify and prolong women's oppression.

Black theology pointed out how slaveowners and segregationists regularly handpicked Bible verses to justify white supremacy and to give biblical credence to their claims about the inherent inferiority of Black people. Similarly, feminist theology pointed out the ways in which Scripture was being employed by some church leaders to reinforce the second-class status of women in church and society, a status they viewed as being consistent with God's intentions for the role of women in the world. The biblical scholar Phyllis Trible highlighted the use of biblical stories that she called "texts of terror,"[12] which—when overlooked, neglected, or read carelessly—reinforced the values of patriarchy and apparently endorsed "sacred violence" against women. Feminist theology proclaimed that women who have been captive to sexism also wanted to be set free.

It did not take long for African American women to realize that feminist theology and the feminist movement in general were not adequate to address their experiences of oppression since first-wave feminism covered matters of gender but not matters of race and class. Thus, by the 1980s, womanist theology, which will be discussed in full form in the relevant chapter, was birthed with a strong critique not only of feminist theology but also of James Cone, who, they said, had focused on racism but failed to address how gender issues cause African American women to experience racism differently from their male counterparts inside the church and in the broader society.

Jacqueline Grant set forth the heart of the problem for womanist theology with her use of the term "tri-partite oppression."[13] Her focus was on the triple, interconnected problems of race, gender, and economic status. White women found some shelter under the broad umbrella of white privilege. No such shelter had ever been provided to Black women whose work and whose wombs were exploited by men. Womanist theology preached the same biblical message, but these theologians defined and described the oppressed more broadly than either Black theology or feminist theology. Here again, God's desire was to set the captives free.

In Latin America, liberation theology was birthed by those who saw poverty and economic exploitation as the major challenge they faced. Writing from Peru, Nicaragua, El Salvador, and other countries in Central and South America, church leaders saw the oppressed were the victims of government policies and multinational corporate practices. They were poor workers and farmers who were overworked and underpaid by those who exploited the natural resources of their countries and created wealth for a few and massive wealth disparity for the majority in their countries. Rather than reacting to the four-hundred-year legacy of slavery and white supremacy in the United States, Latin American liberation theology was a reminder that while slavery had ended where it once existed in those nations, class distinctions and labor relations had changed very little.[14]

In other parts of the world, post-colonial theology was taking root in nations that were attempting to emerge from decades and even centuries of colonial rule by one of the European powers. Nations such as England, France, Spain, Portugal, Belgium, the Netherlands, and Italy had brazenly divided up the world among themselves and employed colonization of smaller and less-developed countries as a way to enhance their economies and to enlarge their global, territorial footprint. From South Africa north to Senegal, and from the Philippines in the Far East to the island nations of the West Indies, colonization was justified through what the French called "civilizing mission"[15] and what England disguised as "civilization, Christianity, and commerce."[16] Even the United States got into the business of colonial pursuits using "Christianization and civilization" as its justification for doing so.

The liberating challenge of post-colonial theologians has been to reclaim their traditional cultures, including aspects of their traditional religious practices that had been suppressed by their colonial overlords. What can the Christian church say to formerly colonized people, when the church through its missionary activity imposed a preferred form of Christianity on people who may not have been Christian before the colonizers arrived, and who may not wish to remain Christian once their colonial subjugation has ended? The reach of the Roman Catholic Church into places in Latin America and across Africa, and the influence of the Anglican Church in India and throughout the West Indies, continues to this day. Post-colonial theology has often emerged on the heels of some form of struggle, whether armed or nonviolent, by an oppressed and colonized nation that had gained its independence. The captives have been set free, and now these people had to redefine their religious and theological identity separate and apart from their former colonial status.[17]

When taken together, liberation theology emerging from Latin America and post-colonial theology emerging from newly independent nations all over the world presented a significant expansion in the work to set the captives free. It was now being made clear that ending oppression and establishing justice were a global challenge for the church, and not just a movement focused upon or limited to movements and issues of special urgency only within the United States. Just as feminist theology and womanist theology pushed the boundaries of the discussion about liberation beyond the issue of race that was the focus of Black theology, so Latin American liberation theology and post-colonial theology broadened the topics and the geography of the struggle to set the captives free.

The God of the Bible may have been at work to free the Hebrew people from slavery in Egypt. But the logic is as clear as the message of Moses; the God who sent Moses to demand that Pharaoh set the Hebrews free was thereby functioning as the sovereign Lord and creator over the whole world. The God of the Exodus was not merely a local deity whose interests resided within the borders of a single nation. Yahweh, the God who was first revealed to Israel, had authority and power that exceeded anything at the disposal of what was then the most powerful nation and the most powerful person in the world.

This point has special relevance for the United States in the twenty-first century. There are many Christians in this country who perpetuate the notion that the United States is the center of God's attention and the apple of God's eye. They cling to the eighteenth- and nineteenth-century idea set forth by Ernest Lee Tuveson that this country is "the redeemer nation" whose mission it was and is to spread its values and influence throughout the world.[18] What had failed in Europe was going to be perfected in the New World, and most especially in the newly formed and steadily expanding United States of America. Never mind that this redeemer nation depended upon legalized human slavery for its workforce, and upon the destruction of native inhabitants and the theft of their homelands to accomplish its expansionist desires captured in the phrase "Manifest Destiny."

This has resulted in bad foreign policy as the United States has sought to bully its way around the world while asserting its status of American exceptionalism. However, this has also resulted in bad theology, reducing God to a national totem whose sole purpose is to answer when people sing "God Bless America," while Donald Trump publicly refers to non-white nations as ****hole countries. This is the lingering effect of the redeemer nation syndrome. This is what lies at the heart of Make America Great Again. This is the tragic flaw at the heart of so much American Christianity. There is an equating of the best interests of the ruling elite of this country with what they project to be the will of God.

Latin American and post-colonial theology reminds us that it is far more appropriate to sing with my slave ancestors that "He's got the whole world in his hands." Poverty in El Salvador, gang violence in Guatemala, and sexual assault in Honduras are of as much concern to God as are any of the concerns and grievances being voiced by any group within the United States.

As the expansion of liberation theology has continued, another community with a global reach has spoken up about its oppression and harassment inside the church and throughout the broader culture. This time the issue was sexual orientation, and the movement that has arisen is called queer theology.[19] At stake is not whether homosexuality exists or is sanctioned by the church. There is nothing the church can do to disrupt or prevent same-sex activity. Such an approach would meet with no more success than previous attempts to curtail fornication or adultery. What happens in the privacy of the bedroom is not the issue for queer theology. The issue is what can happen at the marriage altar when a same-sex couple wants to get married. The issue is also what happens before a council authorized to ordain persons into Christian ministry when an openly gay, lesbian, or transgender person steps forward and claims that God has called them into ministry to serve alongside their heterosexual and cisgender colleagues.

No one seriously doubts there are LGBTQ people already active in the Christian ministry in every denomination, including the ones that have the strictest prohibitions about that identity or its lived expressions. Whether or not those churches are open and affirming of LGBTQ persons as members, such persons are almost certainly present in every local church across this country. Every church I have ever served has had members, musicians, and in some instances even ministers who were known to be gay or lesbian. The issue always was how open a person could be about their sexual orientation. The issue has been whether LGBTQ Christians should be restricted from serving as ordained clergy unless and until they swore to a life of celibacy that would exclude them from engaging in same-sex sexual activity.

Over the last few years, the issue has advanced beyond who can be ordained to the Christian ministry to who can be married by a Christian minister inside or outside a Christian church. Recently, the United Methodist Church announced a plan to split over this question of same-sex marriage, whether the actual officiant was heterosexual or homosexual.[20] Similar schisms have occurred within many other Protestant denominations, including my own American Baptist Church family. None of the African American Baptist denominations have even engaged in this discussion to any significant degree.

What does Scripture say about same-sex attraction or homosexual activity, and how should Christians respond to those biblical lessons? Can the discussion be limited to the tenth-century BC Holiness Code of Leviticus 18, while ignoring other purity taboos also listed throughout Leviticus? Can the discussion be limited to the words of Paul in Romans 1:26 while ignoring the other practices condemned in verses 29-31? What do we say if homosexual orientation is a biological predisposition rather than a behavioral choice? And even if it were a behavioral choice, should the church view it differently (more stringently) than it does any other biblically prohibited sexual activity?

What do we do as church leaders and members when the broader society becomes more and more accepting of the LGBTQ community, and when that community continues to abandon the church they see as being out of step with twenty-first-century scientific knowledge and social values around civil rights for all human beings? According to Public Religion Research Institute's 2017 survey, "Roughly two-thirds of Catholics, Orthodox Christians and mainline Protestants favor same-sex marriage. Among white evangelicals a huge change is happening. Twice as many young evangelicals favor same-sex marriage (53%) as those over 65 (25%)."[21]

The LGBTQ community intersects all the groups that have been listed above. It reaches into every country on earth. It involves people of all racial and ethnic groups. It includes persons of all age groups and generations. What queer theology does is raise to public view and public debate another constituency that embraces the central message of liberation theology, which is to set the captives free.

This book will discuss one last theological movement and one last call to set the captives free: namely, American Indian liberation or a theology of sovereignty.[22] What does it mean to set the captives free after more than four hundred years for Native Americans from Alaska and Canada in the north to Ecuador and Bolivia in the south? When looking solely within the history of the United States, this theology asks this nation to remember the Indian Removal Act of 1830, when President Andrew Jackson ordered all Southern tribes (Cherokee, Seminole, Creek, Choctaw, and Chickasaw) living on the east side of the Mississippi River to be forcefully relocated to what eventually became Oklahoma under the supervision of the United States Army. This resulted in the Trail of Tears, a phrase that refers "to the 800-mile journey of sickness, misery, and death. Some 18,000 Cherokee were removed from their homeland, and 4000 of them died along the way."[23]

Most Americans are aware of such places as Yorktown and Gettysburg and Pearl Harbor, where a great loss of life occurred during military conflicts. American Indian liberation theology asks the question, What about the massacre at Wounded Knee in South Dakota, where hundreds of Lakota Sioux women and children were massacred by soldiers in 1890? Most Americans mourn the death of General George Armstrong Custer and his Seventh U.S. Cavalry at the Battle of Little Big Horn in Montana in 1876. Few are aware that Custer and the same Seventh Calvary conducted a massacre of peaceful Cheyenne Indians living on a reservation at the Washita River near Cheyenne, Oklahoma, in 1868. No list of oppressed people and no call for justice can be fully told that does not include the near decimation of Native Americans.

It should be made clear that this oppression was not limited to a few tragic events in the mid- to late nineteenth century. The destruction of Native American life and culture began with the arrival of European conquerors, colonizers, and settlers as early as the first Spanish conquistadors who arrived in Mexico and Peru in the sixteenth century when the Incas and Mayas were decimated by disease and by gunfire. The horror continued at Plymouth, Massachusetts, and at Jamestown, Virginia, in the seventeenth century when English settlers forced the Wampanoag and Powhatan tribal groups out of their ancestral lands as part of English colonial expansion.

It continues into the twenty-first century primarily for groups on the Standing Rock Reservation near Bismarck, North Dakota. That area remains the center of a dispute over crude oil pipelines running through that region. The problem at Standing Rock is not just the issue of ancestral territory but also the environmental issue of oil spilling into the ground and endangering the water supply for several surrounding states.[24] President Barack Obama had stopped construction of those pipelines out of sensitivity to both issues, cultural and environmental. However, President Trump reauthorized that construction project. Since that time, 383,000 gallons of crude oil have leaked into the ground.[25]

Summary

What has been set forth in this introduction is the broad observation about the ways in which Black theology emerged as part of a quick succession of theological positions, all with the same objective: to set the captives free. Each form of liberation theology focused on a matter of urgency to a particular group of people who were experiencing oppression and discrimination based upon who they were, rather than anything they may have done to merit their experience of violence or marginalization or loss of opportunity.

The remainder of this book will look back at the rise of each of the liberation movements that have been identified here in an attempt to create a timeline from the release of *Black Theology and Black Power* in 1969 to the emergence of all the subsequent theological arguments that have been shaped and shared since that time. Again, the objective here is to make the case that while Black theology focused on issues of race and racism as those cruel realities affected the bodies and psyches of African Americans for hundreds of years, that form of captivity and oppression was not the only form from which people wanted to be set free. Thus, race quickly expanded to gender, class, economic status, sexual orientation, colonization, and finally near-total extinction and the highest demographics of suffering and deprivation of any group residing in this country.

"Me Too" is the underlying theme for setting the captives free. No sooner has one group stated their grievances and challenged church and society to respond to their predicament when another group emerges to say, "Me too." We too are the people of God, and we also have a story of suffering that needs to be heard. Liberation theology may have begun with a glimpse into the reality of being Black in a white supremacist society. However, it has steadily expanded its focus and its reach into a global effort to set the captives free. All of them!

This early use of the term "me too" became clear to me during my nearly forty years in theological education, both as a professor and as a seminary president. In my courses on various aspects of African American religious life and thought, I would make frequent reference to Black theology and to the issues of race and racism that have long been at work in the history and current practices of the United States at the policy and personal levels. While the non-African American students listened respectfully and never sought to minimize the experiences of African Americans, they were anxious to tell their own stories of oppression as well.

"Me too," said white female students who were frustrated by their denomination's unwillingness to honor their call to ministry and ordain them as readily as their male counterparts were being ordained. Even when they were being ordained, they were being assigned to staff positions or to the smallest congregations, positions from which their male counterparts were not being forced to choose. "Me too," said African American female students who affirmed Cone when it came to issues of race, but whose experience was equally influences by their gender and their economic condition. It was especially painful to listen to these African American women studying for careers in Christian ministry report that their own African American churches, and often the African American male students sitting next to them in class, were not supportive of their call to ministry and their vocational aspirations.[26]

"Me too," said the international students whose experiences with colonial rule and the physical occupation of their countries, or the crushing poverty brought on by the greedy practices of multinational corporations, made them anxious to frame the gospel in ways that spoke to their oppression and their desire for liberation beyond anything that Black theology seemed to offer them. "Me too," said the LGBTQ students who cut across all categories of the student body—male and female, Black and white, US citizens and international students on visas, physically able and physically challenged. Their experience had been that people who were committed to liberation on matters of race, gender, economic condition, or nationality and citizenship status were not necessarily as enthusiastic when it came to sexual orientation.

"Me too," said Native American students who wondered aloud how African American students could come to class wearing sports gear celebrating the Cleveland Indians, the Washington Redskins, the Atlanta Braves, or the Chicago Blackhawks. How could their classmates who professed liberation sympathies fail to see how such images were offensive to Native Americans? "How would you like for us to cheer for a team called the Cleveland Coons or the New York Niggers? You would not cheer for the New Jersey Jews, so why do you allow our people to be reduced to cartoon figures and comic caricatures?" This is as much a question of liberation theology as anything that applies to any of the other groups that have raised their voices to celebrate the Messiah whose mission is to set the captives free!

NOTES

1. James H. Cone, *Black Theology and Black Power* (New York: Seabury Press, 1969).

2. *African Americans: Voices of Triumph—Creative Fire* (New York: Time-Life Books, 1993), 162–64.

3. Henry Louis Gates Jr. and Donald Yacovone, *The African Americans: Many Rivers to Cross* (New York: SmileyBooks, 2013), 249.

4. Rosie Gray, "Trump Defends White Nationalist Protesters: 'Some Very Fine People on Both Sides'," The Atlantic.com, August 15, 2017.

5. Jordyn Phelps, "Trump Defends 2017 'Very Fine People' Comments, Calls Robert E. Lee 'a Great General'," ABCNews.com, April 26, 2019.

6. Andre Henry, "White Evangelicals' Attacks on James Cone are about Power, Not Truth," Religionnews.com, January 9, 2020.

7. Ibid.

8. Ibid.

9. Andre Henry, "White Evangelicals' Attacks on James Cone are about Power, Not Truth," Religionnews.com, January 9, 2020.

10. James H. Cone, *Said I Wasn't Gonna Tell Nobody* (Maryknoll, NY: Orbis Books, 2018), 1.

11. Ibid., 9.

12. Phyllis Trible, *Texts of Terror: Literary-Feminist Readings of Biblical Narratives* (Philadelphia: Fortress, 1984); B. Diane Lipsett and Phyllis Trible, eds., *Faith and Feminism: Ecumenical Essays* (Louisville, KY: Westminster/John Knox, 2014); Rosemary Radford Ruether, *Liberation Theology: Human Hope Confronts Christian History and American Power* (New York: Paulist Press, 1972).

13. "Womanist Theology," in Marvin A. McMickle, *An Encyclopedia of African American Christian Heritage* (Valley Forge, PA: Judson Press, 2002), 274–75; see Kelly Brown Douglas, *Sexuality and the Black Church: A Womanist Perspective* (Maryknoll, NY: Orbis Books, 1999); Courtney Pace, *Freedom Faith: The Womanist Vision of Prathia Hall* (Athens: University of Georgia Press, 2019); Katie Geneva Cannon, *Katie's Canon: Womanism and the Soul of the Black Community* (New York: Continuum, 2002); M. Shawn Copeland, *Enfleshing Freedom: Body, Race, and Being* (Minneapolis: Fortress, 2010).

14. Gustavo Gutiérrez, *A Theology of Liberation* (Maryknoll, NY: Orbis Books, 1973); Joseph E. Mulligan, *The Nicaraguan Church and the Revolution* (Kansas City, MO: Sheed and Ward, 1991); David Batstone, *From Conquest to Struggle: Jesus of Nazareth in Latin America* (Albany: State University of New York Press, 1991).

15. Harry Liebersohn, "The Civilizing Mission," University of Illinois in Champagne, September 27, 2016, found in muse.jhu.edu, September 2016.

16. "The Philosophy of Colonialism: Civilization, Christianity, and Commerce," scholarsblogs.emory.edu.

17. David A. Sanchez, *From Patmos to the Barrio: Subverting Imperial Myths* (Minneapolis: Fortress, 2008); Kay Higuera Smith, Jayachitra Lalitha, and L. Daniel Hawk, *Evangelical Postcolonial Conversations: Global Awakenings in Theology and Praxis* (Downers Grove, IL: IVP Academic Press, 2014).

18. Ernest Lee Tuveson, *The Redeemer Nation: The Idea of America's Millennial Role* (Chicago: University of Chicago Press, 1980).

19. Patrick Chen, *Radical Love: Introduction to Queer Theology* (New York: Seabury Books, 2011); Edward Batchelor Jr., *Homosexuality and*

Ethics (New York: The Pilgrim Press, 1980); Horace L. Griffin, *Their Own Receive Them Not: African American Lesbians and Gays in Black Churches* (Eugene, OR: Wipf & Stock, 2006).

20. Julie Zauzmer, "United Methodists Plan to Divide," *Plain Dealer*, January 4, 2020, A6.

21. Guthrie Graves Fitzsimmons, "Christianity's Future Looks More Like Lady Gaga Than Mike Pence," CNN.com, January 24, 2019.

22. George E. ("Tink") Tinker, *American Indian Liberation: A Theology of Sovereignty* (Maryknoll, NY: Orbis Books, 2008).

23. Robert V. Remini, *A Short History of the United States* (New York: HarperCollins, 2008), 102.

24. Sam Levine, "Dakota Access Pipeline: The Who, What, and Why of the Standing Rock Protests," TheGuardian.com, November 3, 2016.

25. Emily S. Rueb and Niraj Chokshi, "Keystone Pipeline Leaks 383,000 Gallons of Oil in North Dakota," NewYorkTimes.com, October 31, 2019.

26. Demetrius K. Williams, *An End to This Strife: The Politics of Gender in African American Churches* (Minneapolis: Fortress, 2004).

CHAPTER 1

Witness to the Birth
of Black Theology

It was fifty years ago, in the fall of 1970, that I began my studies as a master of divinity student at Union Theological Seminary
(UTS) in New York City. For earlier generations of UTS students,
the teachers and writers who might have drawn them to that school
were the German-born theologian Paul Tillich or the American-born
social ethicist Reinhold Niebuhr. However, by 1970, both had long
since left the faculty. Tillich died in 1965, and Niebuhr would follow
him from earth to glory in 1971. Neither of them was a factor in my
decision to attend UTS.

What drew me to Union, as would be the case for two successive
generations of African American students, was the presence of James
Hal Cone. His first book, *Black Theology and Black Power*, had
been released in 1969.[1] I enrolled at Union just in time to experience
the fallout of that landmark text. I was there in 1970 listening as
Cone challenged Union students and faculty about the major premise
of Black theology, namely, that the sin of racism had infected the
nation in general and the body of Christ in particular. Moreover, neither the church nor theological education had responded adequately
to the reality of racism or to white privilege and the assumptions and
institutional realities of white supremacy as the social arrangement
upon which the United States was founded.

In addition to being the babysitter for his young children and being
a regular presence in his apartment in McGiffert Hall, I was at Union
to hear the lectures and even read some of the galley proofs of what

would become his second book, *A Black Theology of Liberation*, and his third book, *God of the Oppressed*.[2] I was a doctoral student in a joint degree program with Union and Columbia University when Cone was elevated to the status of full professor with tenure, at which time his professorial lecture was the basis of what would become another book, *The Spirituals and the Blues*.[3]

It should be noted that our friendship lasted well beyond my years at Union. He participated in my installation as pastor of St. Paul Baptist Church in Montclair, New Jersey, in 1976. He came to lecture in a doctor of ministry seminar I was sharing in at Ashland Theological Seminary in 2009. Most recently, James Cone was the guest speaker when I was installed as the twelfth president of Colgate Rochester Crozer Divinity School in Rochester, New York, in 2012. In that presentation, he reminded the audience that his first lectures on Black theology had been delivered at CRCDS in 1968. Having him share in my installation as a seminary president brought our friendship full circle. I was scheduled to be part of a small group of his friends who were to gather in the apartment of Serene Jones, the president of Union, in February 2018. We were to meet there, because Cone said, "I have something to say to all of you." He never got a chance to say it, and worse, we never got a chance to hear it, because his health quickly worsened, and he died.

What is of most importance for this book is that despite his having advanced to the rank of full professor with tenure at one of the leading theological seminaries in the world, there was still the question of whether or not his frame of reference was of equal value to those that were being employed by many white scholars and many white church leaders as well. What most white theologians could not grasp, and what most Black preachers in the 1960s and 1970s should have grasped but did not, are the reasons why James Cone wrote *Black Theology and Black Power*.

The answer to that question cannot be found without first considering the social and political atmosphere that engulfed this country during the years when Cone's earliest books began to appear. One cannot fully grasp what James Cone was doing in 1969 and 1970 without taking a step back in time and considering the world in which he was at work. Biblical scholars and professional theologians would speak about the *Sitz im leben*, which is a German phrase that means the "setting in life." That is where this book begins, and that is where any discussion of James Cone and Black theology must begin; not with what he said, but what forces were at work that shaped the things he eventually said in his writings and lectures and interviews.

White resistance to the freedom struggle was brutal and relentless. It included church bombings such as the bombing of Sixteenth Street Baptist Church in Birmingham, Alabama, that killed four young girls who were attending Sunday school. In that same city, fire hoses and police dogs were used against people seeking an end to racial segregation in their hometown. It involved the burning of buses carrying freedom riders in Anniston, Alabama. There was the brutal beating of civil rights marchers on the Edmund Pettus Bridge in Selma, Alabama, on a day that came to be known as Bloody Sunday. on It included the murder of Medgar Evers, Jimmie Lee Jackson, Viola Liuzzo, and three civil rights workers in Neshoba County, Mississippi. What I was witnessing was an all-out defense of the premise, the power, and the prerogatives of white supremacy.

What was shocking for me to discover was that racism, segregation, and racially motivated violence were in no way limited to the states of the former Confederacy. In the summer of 1966, when I participated in Freedom Marches led by Martin Luther King Jr. through some of the most racially segregated neighborhoods of my hometown of Chicago, I saw both Confederate flags and Nazi swastikas being waved.

What were white preachers and theologians saying at that time that could make Christianity relevant to Black people struggling for freedom from random but repeated instances of violence and terror in locations ranging from the Delta region in Mississippi to the inner city of Detroit, Michigan? Any attempt to discuss James Cone and Black theology apart from this historical context will miss the problem he was facing and the solution he was offering.

Black Power, White Neglect, and Christian Faith

Black theology did not emerge out of a vacuum; it was entirely conditioned by the sociopolitical winds that were swirling across this country in the 1960s. As the title of Cone's first book suggests,

Black theology was fueled and formed in light of the emergence of the Black Power movement. The critical moment in the civil rights movement was not the March on Washington in 1963; it was James Meredith leading what he called "A March Against Fear," which was a one-man walk across the state of Mississippi. Meredith, who had earlier integrated the University of Mississippi, wanted to prove that a Black man could walk across the length of that state without being harmed. Meredith hoped that his march would give Black people in that state the courage to register to vote. Regrettably, he was wrong in his assumption, because he was shot on the first day of that march.

Other civil rights leaders rushed to Mississippi to resume the march that Meredith had begun. Among those who gathered were Martin Luther King Jr. of the Southern Christian Leadership Conference (SCLC) and Stokely Carmichael of the Student Non-Violent Coordinating Committee (SNCC). During a speech on July 28, 1966, near Greenwood, Mississippi, Carmichael repeatedly declared, "We want Black power."[4] When asked by a reporter what he meant by the term "Black power," Carmichael responded, "The only way that Black people in Mississippi will create an attitude where they will not be shot down like pigs, where they will not be shot down like dogs, is when they get the power where they constitute a majority in counties to institute justice."[5] King tried to soften the blow of what Carmichael had just said, but a clear schism had emerged between the older and more established forces of nonviolent protest in SCLC and the younger and more impatient members of SNCC.

In that critical hour, the church was failing us, because in most instances nothing was being said or done by church leaders about the struggle in which we were engaged. However, the Nation of Islam was offering its solution. Upon entering one of their mosques, one was immediately confronted with a mural that depicted the representation of the cross on which Jesus was crucified. Instead of the body of Jesus hanging on that cross, there was a hangman's noose dangling from one of the crossbeams. First through Malcolm X and later through Louis Farrakhan the reality of living in a racist society was being discussed.

At that time, the National Baptist Convention USA, Inc., with its five million members was the largest Black organization in the world. How sad to observe that, following its president, Joseph H. Jackson, the national church body seemed more interested in feuding with King over the tactics and techniques of nonviolent direct action than addressing the issues those tactics and techniques were meant to confront: racism and white supremacy. In 1968, when Dr. King was assassinated, the city council in Chicago, through the efforts of Jesse Jackson, renamed South Park Avenue to Martin Luther King Jr. Boulevard. South Park was the major thoroughfare through the heart of Chicago's Southside Black community. It was also the street on which Olivet Baptist Church was located, the church where Joseph H. Jackson served as pastor. Jackson changed the official address of the church to East 31st Street so King's name would not be on any letterheads, church bulletins, or advertisements. That is what the pastor of the largest church in America's second largest city and the president of that nation's largest Black organization was doing while the freedom struggle continued after the death of King.

Young people living in Chicago at that time like myself were left to wonder about the usefulness of the church. If it had nothing to say and could find nothing to do so far as the freedom struggle was concerned, then why should we still believe that it served any truly useful purpose beyond providing an occasional spiritual bromide? Part of my family belonged to the Church of God in Christ (COGIC). I loved them dearly, but they never got involved in any civil rights activism, because their focus was seeking holiness, and involvement in the freedom struggle might impede their quest for that spiritual goal.

My home church was part of the Disciples of Christ, a predominantly white denomination. I cannot recall a time when the issues being addressed by the civil rights movement were discussed by our youth group or explored in Sunday sermons. Could you be both Black and Christian at that point in history? That seems especially odd in retrospect, since there was an obvious racial divide within that Christian denomination. Not only were we an all-Black congregation on the Southside of Chicago, but there was an all-Black national body within the Disciples of Christ Church. From 1963 to 1966 I attended the annual sessions of the National Christian Missionary Convention. That was a gathering of all the Black congregations of the Disciples of Christ from across the country. I remember meeting in Brooklyn, New York, Detroit, Michigan, Rockford, Illinois, and other locations.

These annual sessions paralleled the most pivotal years of the civil rights movement from the March on Washington in 1963 to the passage of the Voting Rights Act in 1965. Perhaps there were discussions about civil rights and race relations going on at those gatherings. What is certain is that I was deeply aware of the obvious racial division within that national denomination. It seemed true for most of my formative years that being Black and Christian was something that I and most Black people were being called upon to do within all-Black churches and all-Black denominations. Except for a once-a-year exchange between our inner-city congregation and some affluent white congregation in one of the suburbs of Chicago, or a week at a summer camp attended by forty or fifty persons from various churches in that denomination, I had no interaction with white Christians where the issues of civil rights, Black power, or white supremacy that were front-page news in the country could constructively be discussed.

This is a good time to return to the summer of 1966 when Dr. King came to Chicago to address what he said was the most racially segregated city in the United States in terms of residential patterns. Like most Americans, I thought that racism and segregation was a Southern problem, because that was where all the news reports about racial violence were centered. We heard about Birmingham and Selma, Alabama. We heard about Jackson and Philadelphia, Mississippi. We heard about sit-ins in at Woolworth's lunch counters in Nashville, Tennessee, and Greensboro, North Carolina. We heard about segregationist governors like Lester Maddox of Georgia, George Wallace of Alabama, and Ross Barnett of Mississippi. We knew about US Senators like Harry Byrd of Virginia, James Eastland of Mississippi, and Herman Talmadge of Georgia, who built their careers on the promise of maintaining segregation as a way of life.

We were aware of the struggles involved in the integration of Central High School in Little Rock, Arkansas, in 1957. We followed the events that involved James Meredith integrating the University of Mississippi in 1962. The same was true for Autherine Lucey, who was the first Black student to attend the University of Georgia in

1956 before she was expelled by the trustees of that university. We had seen George Wallace stand in front of the administration building at the University of Alabama in an attempt to block the admission of that school's first Black students in 1963. Nothing that happened in those Southern states surprised us as we viewed those events from our television screens in Chicago.

All that changed for me in July and August of 1966. I found myself marching through all-white neighborhoods in Chicago where redlining by banks and racism by realtors had prevented Black people from buying homes. This was the kind of thing I read about and saw on television with the play *A Raisin in the Sun* by Lorraine Hansberry. In that play (later made into a movie), a Black family wanted to use the proceeds from an insurance policy to move out of slum housing and buy a home of their own. The problem was that they wanted to move into what was at that time an all-white neighborhood where they most definitely were not wanted.

What happened in Chicago in the summer of 1966, however, was not a play. The events were all too real. I saw with my own eyes the hatred and scorn heaped upon us as we peacefully marched along. I heard with my own ears the shrieks of "niggers go home" and "why don't you monkeys go back to Africa." I saw the Confederate flag being waved in Chicago; part of a state that fought for the Union against the Confederacy. I saw members of the American Nazi Party led by George Lincoln Rockwell displaying the swastika; the emblem of Hitler and Nazi Germany. Black people in Chicago were not prevented from voting, or eating at a lunch counter, or sitting in any available seat on a bus or an elevated train. We could do all those things so long as we were content to reside in the Southside and Westside neighborhoods where the Black population was clustered.

Two aspects of housing-related injustice in Chicago must be shared here. The first involves the total dislocation of the neighborhood where I spent my earliest childhood years so that the Dan Ryan Expressway could be built. For a distance of ten miles long and two miles wide, Black communities were claimed by eminent domain so that a mostly white workforce could build a highway and light rail system that would allow mostly white people to access downtown locations as quickly as possible. What happened to the people who once lived in the neighborhoods uprooted by the expressway? Many of them ended up in Robert Taylor Homes and Stateway Gardens, a long row of sixteen-story public housing projects that were built alongside the expressway. Vibrant Black communities were lost to asphalt on the highway and concrete buildings that were the breeding ground of the gangs and drugs and crime that haunt Chicago to this day.

The second housing-related story involved my immediate family in the fall of 1966. While I was away at college, my mother and her sister, who lived together in an area called Garfield Park, moved into a house in Foster Park. That was an all-white area at that time, but it would not remain so for very long. By the time I had come home for the Christmas break, For Sale signs were popping up on almost front yard on our block. White residents had been convinced by realtors that the presence of Black people would undercut the value of their property. So, what came to be known as "white flight" began to occur. Within one year an all-white neighborhood had become predominantly Black. Within three years, all the white families had moved out of Foster Park and settled in neighborhoods further to the west. Today, there are towns and communities that did not exist fifty years ago. They were created as places where white families could continue to flee in their endless effort to move away from me and from people like me.

This was the atmosphere that prevailed in Chicago when Dr. King came there is 1966 to make the case that racism and segregation were a national, and not just a regional problem. This is what fueled the passions of the people who lined the streets with their hate-filled speech and actions as we marched along.

I assumed that many of the white people hurling insults and projectiles toward us were members of some church body. Given the ethnic makeup of many of those neighborhoods, it could easily be assumed that a great many Roman Catholics or Orthodox Christians were in those crowds. It did not matter to them that we were usually dressed as if we had just stepped out from a church. It did not matter to them that we were singing certain Christian hymns and engaging in prayer as we passed along. All that mattered to them was that we were Black and that we were not wanted in their neighborhood. I do not recall the leader of the Roman Catholic Diocese of Chicago condemning the violence being exhibited by his fellow Roman Catholics. I do not recall our Irish Catholic mayor, Richard J. Daley, offering any words of comfort to the marchers or any words of condemnation to the whites who were assaulting us.

I also remember that Daley and Joseph Jackson collaborated to keep as many Black clergy as possible in Chicago from participating in those marches or showing any support for what King and the local leaders like Al Raby were trying to accomplish. Those who defied the Daley/Jackson mandate faced severe consequences. One of those who dared to support King was Clay Evans of Fellowship Missionary Baptist Church. He was in the midst of a building project for that church during the summer of 1966. However, when he showed unwavering support for what King was doing, he discovered that all of his building permits were revoked, all the union laborers walked off the job, and his building project was stalled by order of City Hall.[6]

All of this was on my mind during 1966 when I kept asking myself if you can be Black and Christian in this country with all that was going on, and with the silence coming from the white church and the pettiness coming from many leaders of the Black Baptist church. What I was able to find at the heart of Cone's work was the answer to what had become for me an urgent and existential concern: Can one be both Black and Christian at that precise moment in history? That was precisely the question that Cone himself was attempting to address. Writing in *The Cross and the Lynching Tree*, Cone said, "My initial challenge was to develop a liberation theology that could be both Black and Christian—at the same time and in one voice. That was not easy because, in the Black community the public meaning of Christianity was white. Martin Luther King, Jr. and Malcolm X gave me intellectual resources and spiritual courage to attack white supremacy."[7]

With Black power rising on one side with its dismissal of Christianity as a force for social transformation, and with the Nation of Islam rising on the other side with its critique of Christianity as "the white man's religion," the critical question for me and for many of my generation was whether Christianity had anything to say about or offer to the Black freedom struggle that was raging in the country.

James Cone offered an answer to the question. With a resounding "yes" he assured us that we could be both Black and Christian in 1969 and in the turbulent years that followed. His reading of the gospel led him to the conclusion that the heart of the gospel message lined up perfectly with the aspirations being expressed in the Black freedom struggle: God's care and concern for the poor and the oppressed. If God was on the side of the oppressed, and if Black people in the United States were an obvious example of people living under oppression, then God was identified with the Black freedom struggle. To be a Christian, argued Cone, was to be engaged in the struggle for Black liberation.

The years of 1965 to 1970 were no time for religious activities if they were devoid of any engagement with God's concern for the poor, the oppressed, and the marginalized. No new forms of worship and praise; no reworked Christian education curriculum; no new denominational programs; no fundraisers for new buildings were an adequate response to what was happening in this country at that time. The church had to speak out on these matters of race and racial violence. Those who used religion to justify the status quo had to be called out. Those who used religion as a way to explain away their refusal to get involved had to be exposed.

A New Understanding of the Gospel Message

For me, Black theology was the equivalent of the 1933 Barmen Declaration in which the Confessing Church in Germany sought to assert the heart of the gospel while the established German Lutheran Church was being coopted by Hitler and the Nazis.[8] The gospel of Jesus Christ had long since been coopted by slaveholders, slave traders, preachers who were defenders of the slave regime, and their descendants who grew complacent about or wholly accepting of the system of white supremacy and Black degradation. Cone was trying to assert that more than two hundred years of American Christianity was standing on an illegitimate foundation. Christianity could not be used to justify racism or white supremacy, because the God revealed in Scripture was on the side of the oppressed and not the oppressor.

If that was the case, if God was on the side of the oppressed and wanted to set the captives free, than those themes ought to have been echoed in the sermons heard in local churches, in the lectures heard in college and seminary classrooms, and in the writings of the leading theologians whose views tended to influence the thinking of scholars across the country and around the world. However, when he looked around the landscape of the American theological establishment, and when he noted the content of the sermons in many pulpits, Black and white across the country, the message of liberation was rarely if ever seen or heard. There was little in the way of a critique of racism in its individual or its systemic forms. There was little or nothing about the calls for racial justice, civil rights, voting rights, and the right not to be lynched or harassed by the Ku Klux Klan.

Even the voices that were so outspoken on other forms of social injustice were silent when it came to racism and the rights of African Americans. Take Walter Rauschenbusch as an example. He is credited with shaping what came to be called the social gospel. Beginning with his ministry among the impoverished immigrants in the so-called Hell's Kitchen section of New York City, Rauschenbusch argued passionately and persuasively that the gospel message demanded justice for people impacted by poverty.[9] Yet, by his own confession he never expressed any concern about people impacted by racism. Rauschenbusch confessed, "For years the problem of the two races seemed to me so tragic, so insoluble that I have never yet ventured to discuss it in public."[10] Talking about the years when lynch mobs were murdering Black people on a regular basis, Cone says about Rauschenbusch, "White theologians and ministers at that time were silent, as if the meaning of the Christian gospel had nothing to do with segregation and lynching."[11] He continued by saying about every white theologian dating back to Jonathan Edwards in the mid-eighteenth century, "None of America's greatest theologians made the rejection of white supremacy central to their understanding of the gospel."[12]

According to Christopher Evans, one of his biographers, Rauschenbusch tended to think of the plight of African Americans as a matter of economics rather than racism. Evans writes, "Like many northern Progressive Era leaders, Rauschenbusch largely saw race as a problem of the rural south that could be solved through economic means. Writing at a time preceding the great migrations of African Americans to urban centers in the north, he called for the abolition of the sharecropping system in the south, decrying how this system kept African Americans in a state of economic serfdom."[13] It would not have been hard to trace the origins of the sharecropping system in the United States to the deeply embedded racism in Southern society that sought to impose a form of labor on Black workers that resembled as much as possible the slavery that had been abolished by the Thirteenth Amendment.

Yet, Rauschenbusch, the leading progressive theologian of his generation, did not make that connection. Rather than focus on racism as the cause of Black suffering, Rauschenbusch "shared the social gospel's larger tendency to absorb African-Americans into other 'unregenerate' ethnic, non-Protestant groups that required 'Christianization.'"[14] Thus, the problem was not that white people should abandon their racist economic practices. The problem was that Black people were in need of hearing and accepting the gospel. Rauschenbusch, who often referred to Black children as "pickaninnies," believed that African Americans could be transformed if they "embraced the wisdom and example of the white middle class."[15] Of course, the white middle class was as insistent on maintaining a rigidly segregated society as any other demographic within white society at the turn of the twentieth century when Rauschenbusch was at work.

As Cone pointed out in *The Cross and the Lynching Tree*, things did not improve when the baton for leadership among Progressive Christians passed from Walter Rauschenbusch to Reinhold Niebuhr.[16] Cone said, "Niebuhr had eyes to see Black suffering, but I believe he lacked the heart to feel it as his own."[17] Referring to Atticus Finch in Harper Lee's novel *To Kill a Mockingbird*, Cone said of Niebuhr: "He failed to step into Black people's shoes and walk around in them. It was easy for Niebuhr to walk around in his own shoes, as a white man, and view the world from that vantage point, but it takes a whole lot of emphatic effort to step into those of Black people and see the world through the eyes of African Americans."[18]

Given Cone's attempt to link the Roman cross and the lynching tree in the United States as tools used to "strike terror in the subject community,"[19] Cone pointed out, "Between 1880 and 1940, white Christians lynched nearly five thousand Black men and women in a manner with obvious echoes of the Roman crucifixion of Jesus. Yet, those Christians did not see the irony or contradiction in their actions."[20]

What was the response of Reinhold Niebuhr to this American tragedy that took place precisely at the time when he was considered the leading theologian in the United States? Cone makes that clear when he says, "During most of Niebuhr's life, lynching was the most brutal manifestation of white supremacy, and he said and did very little about it. Should we be surprised then, that other white theologians, ministers, and churches followed suit?"[21]

This was the theological mindset on matters of race and racism that prevailed in most of white America in general, and in the white churches and academic institutions as well. The challenge for Cone was to get his colleagues in the theological academy and those who occupied pulpits across the country to come to a new and radically different understanding of the gospel message. Rather than needing Christianization at the hands of white preachers and missionaries, as Rauschenbusch and his social gospel adherents asserted, what African Americans need is liberation from the oppressive grip of white supremacy and the racialized society that whites have built to protect and maintain their position.

Black theology intended to make the case that setting the captives free was the central work and will of God. It did not matter what else people were saying or doing in the name of being religious; if they were not working to end racial injustice in this country, they were not fully engaged in doing the will of God. Like the biblical prophets of the eighth century BCE, to whom I will refer in chapter 2, Cone was asserting that religion that was devoid of working for justice and righteousness was unacceptable to the God revealed in Scripture.

I vividly remember that the debate that began in 1970 not only involved the Union community and other white seminaries and church bodies. It also involved Black church circles that wondered aloud whether there could be such a thing as Black theology. I remember attending the Baptist Ministers Conference of New York City, where most Black pastors, including the ones who had attended seminary, refused even to consider what Cone was attempting to say about the message of the gospel being God's concern about the victims of oppression. These preachers and pastors were so enamored with a gospel focused solely on human sin as defined by personal conduct, and on personal salvation as evidenced by confessing and repenting of those personal practices, that they could not comprehend a theology that reached beyond drinking alcohol or engaging in sexual misconduct and focusing instead on structural racism and racial violence.

That problem was not localized among Black preachers in New York City. I remember sitting with Cone at a session of the Progressive National Baptist Convention held in Chicago in 1980, when he was to give a lecture on Black theology before that group. Bear in mind, this was the Black Baptist convention that had been birthed in 1961 to provide a spiritual home for Martin Luther King Jr. This was the Black Baptist convention that was intended to make civil rights and racial justice the hallmark of its existence. If ever there was a group of Black preachers that should have resonated with what Cone was saying in 1980, this was that group.

A popular preacher delivered a rousing sermon at 11 a.m. that was met with a tumultuous response from the more than two thousand delegates packed into the ballroom of the Chicago Hilton Hotel. Cone was scheduled to speak in that same room at 1 p.m. after a one-hour lunch break. When the hour came for his presentation, fewer than one hundred delegates returned to hear about Black theology from the man who had brought that concept into existence.

Speaking about the PNBC and its connection to the legacy of Martin Luther King Jr., I was at Union when courses taught by many of the non-Black professors never mentioned the racial turmoil that still gripped the country two years after the assassination of King. Indeed, there was great focus given to the evils of the Vietnam war that was raging at that time. However, there was little attention given by many Union professors to the strong condemnation of that war by King in the now famous speech "A Time to Break Silence," which was delivered in 1967 at Riverside Church, located next door to and across the street from the buildings of Union Theological Seminary.[22]

In that speech, King set forth seven reasons why he opposed the war in Vietnam. The first three of those reasons reflected directly on the issues raised by Cone about the struggle between Black freedom and the forces of white supremacy. First was the fact that money used to fight the war in Vietnam was being drained away from funds set aside for the War on Poverty that President Lyndon B. Johnson had initiated in 1965. King said:

> I watched the program broken and eviscerated as if it were some idle political plaything of a society gone mad on war, and I knew that America would never invest the necessary funds or energies in rehabilitation of its poor so long as adventures like Vietnam contin-ued to draw men and skills and money like some demonic destruc-tive suction tube. So, I was increasingly compelled to see the war as an enemy of the poor and to attack it as such.[23]

King's second reason involved the composition of the fighting force being sent to Vietnam. He said:

> The war was doing far more than devastating the hopes of the poor at home. It was sending their sons and their brothers and their hus-bands to fight and die in extraordinarily high proportions relative to the rest of the population. We were taking the Black young men who had been crippled by our society and sending them eight thou-sand miles away to guarantee liberties in Southeast Asia which they had not found in southwest Georgia and East Harlem.[24]

King's third reason focused on the rising urban violence occurring in this country during the mid to late 1960s. Part of the rhetoric of the Black Power movement coming from Stokely Carmichael and H. Rap Brown was a move away from the nonviolent tactics that King had employed since the 1955–1956 Montgomery bus boycott. That was what led King to say:

> As I have walked among the desperate, rejected, and angry young men I have told them that Molotov cocktails and rifles would not solve their problems . . . But they ask—and rightly so—what about Vietnam? They asked if our own nation wasn't using massive doses of violence to solve its problems, to bring about the changes it wanted. Their question hit home, and I knew that I could never again raise my voice against the violence of the oppressed in the ghettos without first having spoken clearly to the greatest purveyor of violence in the world today—my own government.[25]

Then King concluded, using the male-dominant language of his generation, "Beyond the calling of race or nation or creed is this vocation of sonship and brotherhood, and because I believe the Father is deeply concerned especially for his suffering and helpless and outcast children, I come tonight to speak for them."[26] That phrase from King was and is at the heart of all forms of liberation theology beginning with Black theology; God is deeply concerned especially for God's suffering and helpless and outcast children. As King did in 1967, Cone did again in 1969 and urged others to do as well with the release of *Black Theology and Black Power*. Someone needs to follow the leading of the Holy Spirit and speak on behalf of those who have no voice in this society. Someone has to stand up and speak out and work to set the captives free.

Union was across the street from Columbia University, where students staged a protest about the war in Vietnam and took over the office of the president of that university. However, no such fervor seemed to grip the seminary community even when Father Daniel Berrigan, a leader of the anti-war movement, came to preach in James Chapel. The campus of the seminary was within walking distance of Harlem, that major Black population center in New York City. However, there was more interaction with the white churches on Madison Avenue and Fifth Avenue in midtown Manhattan than in the Black churches that were located just outside its doors.

If Black theology was not being warmly received at Union when the concept was first presented, then what was of interest within that theological community? I was there when there was far more interest in what was called process theology, which was an idea rooted in the thought of Alfred North Whitehead and further developed by John Cobb asserting that life was always in motion, that nothing was finally resolved, and that history was shaped by significant events that moved life in one way or another. Yet, none of those process theologians were able to see that such racially charged issues as the trans-Atlantic slave trade, the creation of the separate but equal doctrine" the practice of lynch mob justice, or the civil rights movement beginning with the Montgomery bus boycott in 1955 were, in fact, the kinds of events that process theology should have been considering.

To make this oversight even more glaring, process theology did focus on the struggle for women's rights, a struggle contemporaneous with the struggle against racism in the United States.[27] As Cone would later point out as regards Reinhold Niebuhr's failure to say anything about the struggle for racial justice in any of his writings,[28] process theologians appear to have similarly overlooked or ignored the racism going on all around them as they were at work on matters of "life shaping events." To quote Cone again, "It was easy for Niebuhr (and other white theologians) to walk around in his own shoes, as a white man, and view the world from that vantage point, but it takes a whole lot of emphatic effort to step into those of Black people and see the world through the eyes of African Americans."[29]

I was at Union when Lawrence Jones tried to focus on African American church history,[30] and when C. Eric Lincoln was focusing on religious practices within the African American community that included a look at the emergence of the Black Muslim movement.[31] I was at Union when Cone attempted to introduce Black theology as a legitimate addition to the traditional theological canon. All those initiatives were initially tolerated as electives in the curriculum. It seemed that learning about Karl Barth and Paul Tillich was considered essential. Learning about the way in which the God of the Exodus and Jesus of Nazareth was a valuable way to think about both biblical studies and systematic theology was considered optional. Of course, that made as much sense to African American students at that time as having a curriculum where Hebrew and Greek language studies were required, but where courses in preaching and pastoral care were relegated to secondary status, thus giving the impression that exegesis was far more important than proclamation or pastoral ministry.

Speaking of Karl Barth and Paul Tillich, I have long been taken by a quote from Tillich in a book by Barth entitled *The Preaching of the Gospel*. Tillich states that "Preaching must always be done with an awareness of the present moment." Barth continues by saying, "The words of the preacher must be relevant to immediate preoccupations of his [or her] hearers."[32] What James Cone was attempting to do was to interpret the gospel with an awareness of the present moment that was 1969 in the United States. What he was also doing, hearkening back to the words of Dr. King in his speech about the Vietnam war, Cone was also addressing the immediate preoccupations of his hearers, people engaged in the Black freedom struggle.

I was at Union at a time when the writings of German scholars like Jürgen Moltmann and Wolfhart Pannenberg were being treated as if they were a third testament to the Bible. I was happy to learn about the theology of hope and the idea that God suffers with humanity, and that suffering people can take hope for a better future through the hope of the resurrection. I was greatly enlightened by Moltmann's focus on eschatology and "believing hope" and how God is at work in history in ways that provide hope for those enduring an oppressive situation at the present time.[33]

While I did not expect a theologian located in Germany to address the issue of racism or the struggle for racial justice in the United States, what did amaze me was how the American-based theologians who taught us about Moltmann could not or would not connect suffering humanity with the suffering of African Americans or Native Americans in this country, or find a way to incorporate eschatology as something that might encourage those groups in their ongoing struggle against suffering rooted in racism. That was exactly what Cone, Lincoln, and Jones were attempting to do at Union in the early 1970s, but their message was having a hard time breaking through the traditional Eurocentric curriculum of most American theological seminaries.

It should be said at this point that if liberation theology was having a hard time being received at liberal-progressive theological schools like Union in New York City, one can only imagine how it was being ignored or dismissed at the more theologically conservative and even fundamentalist schools across this country such as Southern Baptist Theological Seminary in Louisville, Kentucky, or Southwestern Baptist Theological Seminary in Fort Worth, Texas, or Dallas Theological Seminary in Dallas, Texas, where Black faculty were largely nonexistent. Yet, the total student enrollment at any one of those schools was very likely larger than the combined enrollment at all the schools even attempting to talk about Black and liberation theology.

My point here is that I was something of an eye and ear witness to the birth pangs of Black theology as it was being worked out before my eyes by James Cone. As such, I was shaped and influenced by a reading of Scripture that placed God at the center of the struggle for liberation of oppressed people rooted in the Exodus story in the Old Testament, as well as the closely related passages in Isaiah 61 and Luke 4 where God's interest in the poor, the imprisoned, and the oppressed is set forth. It should be noted that Moltmann in his discussion of the theology of hope made a useful reference to the Exodus as a basis for understanding the mission of what he calls the Exodus Church. He writes:

> The coming lordship of the risen Christ cannot be merely hoped for and awaited. This hope and expectation also sets its stamp on life, action and suffering in the history of society. Hence, mission means not merely propagation of faith and hope, but also historic transformation of life . . . The hope of the gospel has a polemic and liberating relation not only to the religions and ideologies of men, but still more to the factual, practical life of men and to the relationships in which this life is lived.[34]

This is what James Cone was doing in 1969 with *Black Theology and Black Power*. He was linking the message of the gospel to the "factual, practical life of men and women and to the relationships in which this life is lived." The birth of a Black theology was a profoundly contextual event shaped by forces at work in this country during the civil rights movement and in the years that followed the assassination of Martin Luther King Jr. For me, it was an existential question that needed an answer: Can you be both Black and Christian at that time in the nation's history? James Cone provided me with an answer to that question, and the answer was a resounding "yes." The gospel points us to a God whose desire it is to set the captives free. That realization has fueled my ministry for the last fifty years.

NOTES

1. James H. Cone, *Black Theology and Black Power* (New York: Harper & Row, 1969).

2. James H. Cone, *A Black Theology of Liberation*, 40th anniversary ed. (Maryknoll, NY: Orbis Books, 2010); James H. Cone, *God of the Oppressed*, rev. ed. (Maryknoll, NY: Orbis Books, 1997).

3. James H. Cone, *The Spirituals and the Blues: An Interpretation* (Maryknoll, NY: Orbis, Books, 1992).

4. Taylor Branch, *At Canaan's Edge: America in the King Years 1965–1968* (New York: Simon & Schuster, 2006), 486.

5. Ibid., 487.

6. Zach Mills, *The Last of the Blues Preachers*: *Clay Evans, Black Lives, and the Faith That Woke the Nation* (Minneapolis: Fortress, 2018), Kindle chapter 5, notes 28 and 32.

7. James H. Cone, *The Cross and the Lynching Tree* (Maryknoll, NY: Orbis Books, 2011), xvii.

8. Barmen Declaration (1934), available at United Church of Christ, https://www.ucc.org/beliefs_barmen-declaration.

9. Walter Rauschenbusch, *A Theology for the Social Gospel* (New York: Macmillan, 1917).

10. Cone, *The Cross and the Lynching Tree*, 62.

11. Ibid., 132.

12. Ibid., 159.

13. Christopher Evans, *The Kingdom Is Always but Coming: A Life of Walter Rauschenbusch* (Grand Rapids, MI: Eerdmans, 2004), 254.

14. Ibid., 255.

15. Ibid.

16. Cone, *The Cross and the Lynching Tree*, 62.

17. Ibid., 41.

18. Ibid., 40.

19. Ibid., 31.

20. Ibid.

21. Ibid., 45.

22. Martin Luther King Jr., "A Time to Break Silence," in *A Testament of Hope: The Essential Writings of Martin Luther King Jr.*, ed. James M. Washington (New York: Harper & Row, 1986), 231–44.

23. Ibid., 233.

24. Ibid.

25. Ibid.

26. Ibid., 234.

27. John B. Cobb Jr. and David Ray Griffin, *Process Theology: An Introductory Exposition* (Louisville, KY: Westminster/John Knox, 1976), 132ff.

28. Cone, *The Cross and the Lynching Tree*, 40–41.

29. Ibid., 40.

30. Lawrence N. Jones, *African Americans and the Christian Churches: 1619–1860* (Cleveland, OH: Pilgrim Press, 2007).

31. C. Eric Lincoln, *Black Muslims in America* (Boston: Beacon Press, 1973).

32. Karl Barth, *The Preaching of the Gospel* (Philadelphia: Westminster Press, 1963), 54.

33. Jürgen Moltmann, *Theology of Hope* (Minneapolis: Fortress, 1993), 19–20.

34. Ibid., 329–30.

CHAPTER 2

A New Theology Is Born

Since this book marks the fiftieth anniversary of my first encounter with James Cone and Black theology, I want to look back at the birth of a new theological paradigm. Not many people can say that they introduced to the church an entirely new way of thinking about God and the gospel and the message of Jesus. Most theologians that I have encountered over the years were experts in a way of thinking about God and faith that someone before them had created. They were stewards of the legacy of Martin Luther, John Calvin, John Knox, Paul Tillich, or Karl Barth. Indeed, James Cone began his career in precisely this way; teaching courses on Karl Barth based upon the doctoral dissertation he had written on that approach to doing theology.[1]

Contemporaries and Context for James Cone and Black Theology: Learning from My Teacher

To be fair, Cone emerged as a result of several preceding events of great significance. One of those events was the release of a collection of sermons by Albert Cleage Jr. of Detroit called *The Black Messiah*. Cleage began his book by asserting that "Jesus was the non-white leader of a non-white people struggling for national liberation against the rule of a white nation, Rome."[2] A second event that should be considered involves James Forman, a leader of the Student Non-Violent Coordinating Committee (SNCC) ,who marched into the Riverside Church in New York City on April 26, 1969, and presented what he called the Black Manifesto that involved a twelve-point program of reparations and economic development totaling five hundred million dollars to be funded by white churches and Jewish synagogues across the country.[3] The third important event was the statement on Black theology issued by a group called the National Committee of Black Churchmen (NCBC) on June 13, 1969. Cone himself was part of the so-called theological commission of NCBC, along with Henry Mitchell, Preston N. Washington, and J. Deotis Roberts. The statement from that group revealed the clear outlines of Cone's *Black Theology and Black Power*. It read in part: "Black Theology is a theology of Black liberation. It seeks to plumb the Black condition in the light of God's revelation in Jesus Christ so that the Black community can see that the gospel is commensurate with the achievement of Black humanity . . . The message of liberation is the revelation of God as revealed in the incarnation of Jesus Christ. Freedom IS the gospel. Jesus is the liberator."[4]

Even though the context in which James Cone emerged was already alive with discussions about the link between the gospel and the Black freedom struggle, it was Cone who put flesh on the skeletal frame and breathed intellectual clarity into the concept of a Black theology of liberation. Unlike most academicians and scholars, Cone did not rely on the accepted form and formula for advancement in his field. He did not spend his life quoting from the established canons of theology as a way to gain academic rank and then tenure on the faculty of a school. Instead, he critiqued that academic tradition largely embodied by white male scholars for failing to address themselves in any of their writings to the urgent issue of racism as a tool of white supremacy.

It must be understood how power operates within any and all academic disciplines including theology. It includes which students are admitted into a school or into an elite academic program. It involves which professors are not merely hired but which ones receive promotion culminating in tenure, become heads of departments and deans of a faculty. As powerful as all those things are in an academic setting, real power is also wielded by those who determine the canon—the sanctioned and approved books, courses, and intellectual assumptions that underlie a school's curriculum.

Writing in a *New York Times* editorial entitled "The Academic Apocalypse," Ross Douthat talks about "the forces that have undermined strictly Western and white-male approaches to canon-making."

With English departments at universities being the point of reference, Douthat wonders "whether it is possible to teach an American canon and a global canon all at once . . . This should, by rights, be a moment of exciting curricular debates over which global and rediscovered post-colonial works belong on the syllabus with Shakespeare." Failing to embrace this debate, Douthat points out, many people committed to the established canon create a "false choice between 'dead white males' and 'we don't transmit values.'[5]

In the minds of many white religious scholars and church leaders, James Cone was creating an academic apocalypse. He used Black theology as the lens through which to assess the courses his colleagues had carefully shaped, the reading lists they had assembled, and the curriculum they had constructed. From that perspective, he pointed out, in the words of Daniel 5:27, "You have been weighed on the scales and found wanting." He contended that if one was not addressing the urgent issues of racial prejudice and race-based oppression, one was not being true to the message of the gospel.

Not surprisingly, his work was initially met with wide cynicism and ridicule from the white theological establishment. As Douthat hinted in his article about an academic apocalypse, Cone was not writing for the approval of that white establishment. Writing in 1969 with the Black Power movement displacing the nonviolent civil rights movement as the talking point in American society, it was not tenure or rank that was his first concern. As he put it:

> Nothing was at stake for me with European theology. It did not matter whether Barth or Harnack were right in their debate about the meaning of revelation. I wasn't ready to risk my life for that. Now with Black Power everything was at stake—the affirmation of Black humanity in a white supremacist world. I was ready to die for Black dignity. I was fed up with white theologians writing about the gospel as if it had nothing to do with Black Power and Black people's struggle for cultural identity and political justice . . . Black Power is the gospel of Jesus in America today.[6]

What should not go unnoticed is that Cone not only ignited a debate among white theologians concerning the message of the gospel. He also set in motion a debate among Black scholars who were wrestling with the same question about what the gospel had to say to Black people dealing with racism and oppression. Among those who entered this debate were Cone's brother, Cecil Wayne Cone, and J. Deotis Roberts.[7]

In a sense, both were responding to what James Cone had already set forth. Cecil Cone contended that the starting point for Black theology should not be in response to the Black Power movement that was his brother's point of departure. Instead, he asserted that Black theology should emerge out of a clear understanding of the Black religious experience dating back to the slave era in the United States.[8] With the work of his brother clearly in mind, Cecil Cone stated:

> The problem of identity in Black Theology therefore is located at two points: its identification with the academic structure of predominantly white seminaries and with the Black Power motif of Black radicals . . . Black religion is the only appropriate point of departure. Whenever a Black theologian starts from another place or alternates between two starting points, the result is confusion and distortion. I contend that such a result is evident in the work of the major Black theologians.[9]

Roberts took a different approach in his response to and critique of James Cone. He insisted that while liberation was an important first step in the freedom struggle, there had to be a second step that involved reconciliation with those whites who are willing to turn away from the structural racism that has shaped this country and "work at full potential in their community to prepare their white neighbors for accepting Blacks as people in a pluralistic or multi-cultural society."[10] For Roberts, liberation and reconciliation must be held in tandem, because they are consistent with the example of Jesus in the Bible. "We must be liberated—Christ is the Liberator. But the liberating Christ is also the reconciling Christ. The one who liberates reconciles and the one who reconciles liberates."[11]

In addition to Cecil Cone and Roberts, there was Gayraud Wilmore, who was as much a collaborator with James Cone as he was a theological contemporary. While Cecil Cone and Roberts were trained systematic theologians, Wilmore came at his work more from the perspective of a commentator on the history of the Black religious experience. That was the focus of his most notable book, *Black Religion and Black Radicalism*.[12] However, he also served as co-editor with James Cone on a two-part collection of essays about Black theology.[13]

What Cone began doing in 1969 was not an approach to theology that anyone in that field at that time had ever encountered. To borrow from the title of the book by Walter Fluker, the ground shifted[14] in theological education with the release of *Black Theology and Black Power*. Almost immediately, the esoteric discussions about the nature of God and the reliability of the Bible as a historical document were being supplanted by a new focus. As Cone stated, "There was a desperate need for a Black theology, a theology whose sole purpose is to apply the freeing power of the gospel to Black people under white oppression."[15]

In one book, Cone had launched a decades-long discussion about the connection between the gospel of Jesus Christ and the global struggle for liberation from various forms of oppression. *The Christian Century* offered this assessment of Cone's first book: "It manages to kick theology off its pedestal of irrelevant, abstract rhetoric and to make it functional to the end of Black liberation."[16]

James Cone as Part of Black Intellectual Tradition

That quote from *The Christian Century* is a reminder that James Cone as the intellectual and conceptual architect of a new theological tradition serves as part of a continuing repudiation of the claim by Thomas Jefferson, who stated in 1781 that "African Americans had never produced great art or rhetoric—how could they possibly be considered equal citizens?"[17] This false claim about the absence of any creativity of mind or imagination has served as one of the linchpins of white supremacy for more than two hundred years, and as one of the assumptions by many whites concerning what they viewed as inherent Black inferiority.

Jefferson seems to have overlooked the fact that the conditions of human slavery of which he was a practitioner hardly contributed to an atmosphere for creative intellectual expression. However, when "left alone," as Frederick Douglass often observed and encouraged,[18] African Americans have demonstrated over and over again their ability to contribute in significant ways to every arena of intellectual and artistic expression.

Consider the link from Phillis Wheatley to Ta-Nehisi Coates in literature. Think of the determination that ties Bessie Coleman, who earned her airplane pilot's license in France in 1921, to the unmatched heroism of the Tuskegee Airmen of World War II, to the fourteen African American astronauts who flew on NASA-sponsored missions into space. Think about the global impact of artists from the Shakespearean actor Ira Aldridge to the majesty of Kathleen Battle and Jessye Norman in classical music. It is difficult to imagine the sheer genius that links W. E. B. DuBois, who was the first Black person to earn a PhD from Harvard University, to Henry Louis Gates Jr., who is the director of the W. E. B. DuBois Institute for Afro-American Research at Harvard. Consider the gallantry and devotion to country exhibited from the United States Colored Troops, including my own great-great-great grandfather Elijah Alford, who served during the Civil War, to General Colin Powell, who served as chairman of the Joint Chiefs of Staff and later as Secretary of State. Thomas Jefferson could never have imagined Hiram Revels, who in 1869 was the first African American to serve in the United States Senate, much less Barack Obama, who was serving in the United States Senate when he was elected in 2008 to become the forty-fourth president of the United States.

That legacy of intellectual advancement and creativity also extends from Richard Allen, who gave shape and substance to a new African American church (African Methodist Episcopal Church), to James Cone, himself a member of the AME Church, who gave shape and substance to a new theological tradition. In fact, as early as 1794, Richard Allen was reflecting on what we now call liberation theology.[19] He wrote that "God sided with oppressed people . . . Allen reminded slaveholders that God almighty had obliterated unrepentant Egyptian slaveholders."[20]

What is of equal importance are the subsequent theological traditions that emerged in the 1970s and 1980s on the heels of Black theology. It must not go unnoticed that after Cone shattered the formula for doing theology in this country and in Europe, other groups representing other forms of oppression being felt in other parts of the world began to emerge and make their voices heard.

The Biblical Foundations for Setting the Captives Free

The essence of Black theology, as Cone was presenting it for the first time in 1970, was that white biblical scholars, professional theologians, and pastors and preachers seem to have ignored or overlooked the fact that the message of the Bible, running from the Exodus of the twelfth century BCE, to the eighth-century BCE prophets, to the life and teachings of Jesus in the first century CE, was a message of the liberation of the oppressed. More precisely, Cone was arguing that the liberation of the oppressed was God's primary mission on earth, and the only way to be faithful to God was to join in the work of liberating oppressed people. Given his own context and the issues at work in the United States at that time, Cone concluded that African Americans constituted the group that most notably embodied the dilemma of being oppressed as a result of enacted laws and cultural norms rooted in racial bias.

How was it possible that so many people who had studied and written about the Christian faith for so long could have failed to see this more than one-thousand-year-long message that weaved its way through the biblical story from the Exodus of the people of Israel from Egypt to the birth of Christ and the mission of the early church? This storyline is unmistakable. God has long since declared that there is no accurate reading of the gospel of Jesus Christ and no accurate assessment of the will of God on earth that does not include the work of setting the captives free.

It begins with Moses, who was sent by God "to bring my people the Israelites out of Egypt" (Exodus 3:10). Moses then went before Pharaoh for the first of many times declaring, "Thus says the LORD, the God of Israel, 'Let my people go'" (Exodus 5:1). The story of the Exodus culminates with God reminding Moses of what God had done to secure the liberation of a people that had been enslaved for 490 years: "You have seen what I did to the Egyptians, and how I bore you on eagles' wings and brought you to myself" (Exodus 19:4).

That message continues with the biblical prophets of the eighth century BCE who make the case that religion that does not include justice and righteousness is unacceptable to God. In a choice between engaging in the rites of worship and other temple practice or engaging in doing what is right so far as caring for the needy is concerned, God always chooses right over rites. Consider Micah 6:6-8:

"With what shall I come before the LORD
   and bow myself before God on high?
Shall I come before him with burnt offerings,
   with calves a year old?
Will the LORD be pleased with thousands of rams,
   with ten thousands of rivers of oil?
Shall I give my firstborn for my transgression,
   the fruit of my body for the sin of my soul?"
He has told you, O mortal, what is good;
   and what does the LORD require of you
but to do justice, and to love kindness,
   and to walk humbly with your God?

Amos 5:21-24 continues this theme that God prefers doing what is just and right over offering rites as an end in themselves. So, God says through this eighth-century-BCE prophet:

I hate, I despise your festivals,
   and I take no delight in your solemn assemblies.
Even though you offer me your burnt offerings and grain offerings,
   I will not accept them;
and the offerings of well-being of your fatted animals
   I will not look upon.
Take away from me the noise of your songs;
   I will not listen to the melody of your harps.
But let justice roll down like waters,
   and righteousness like an ever-flowing stream.

The message extends to the sixth century BCE in Isaiah 58:3-6. There the issue shifts from offering sacrifices to God as a sign of devotion to engaging in extended periods of fasting as a way to win favor with God. In this oracle, God seems to be speaking directly to the people in the role of a prosecuting attorney laying out the case against the defendant, Israel.

> "Why do we fast, but you do not see?
>> Why humble ourselves, but you do not notice?"
> Look, you serve your own interest on your fast day,
>> and oppress all your workers.
> Look, you fast only to quarrel and to fight
>> and to strike with a wicked fist.
> Such fasting as you do today
>> will not make your voice heard on high.
> Is such the fast that I choose,
>> a day to humble oneself?
> Is it to bow down the head like a bulrush,
>> and to lie in sackcloth and ashes?
> Will you call this a fast,
>> a day acceptable to the LORD?
> Is not this the fast that I choose:
>> to loose the bonds of injustice,
>> to undo the thongs of the yoke,
> to let the oppressed go free,
>> and to break every yoke?

In Isaiah 61:1, the work of the Messiah is linked to the work of liberation:

> The spirit of the Lord GOD is upon me,
>> because the LORD has anointed me;
> he has sent me to bring good news to the oppressed,
>> to bind up the brokenhearted,
> to proclaim liberty to the captives,
>> and release to the prisoners.

Jesus himself picks up that same theme in his appearance at his home synagogue in Nazareth when he takes the mantle of the Messiah upon himself and references parts of Isaiah 61 by saying,

> "The Spirit of the Lord is upon me,
>> because he has anointed me
>>> to bring good news to the poor.

He has sent me to proclaim release to the captives
   and recovery of sight to the blind,
      to let the oppressed go free,
to proclaim the year of the Lord's favor." (Luke 4:18-19)

If justice and liberation are where the ministry of Jesus began, then it should be noted that it comes to an end on the same themes as recorded in Matthew 25:31-46. In that passage, God's pleasure and affirmation belong only to those who act in ways that address the needs of those facing some physical hardship. Likewise, God's judgment falls on those who see human suffering and do not respond to what they have seen with their own eyes. The categories are clear: "'for I was hungry and you gave me food, I was thirsty and you gave me something to drink, I was a stranger and you welcomed me, I was naked and you gave me clothing, I was sick and you took care of me, I was in prison and you visited me.' . . . 'Truly I tell you, just as you did [or did not do] it to one of the least of these who are members of my family, you did [or did not do] it to me.'"

It is fitting to end this chapter with a variation of this biblical text found in a document circulated at a poor people's rally in Albuquerque, New Mexico, and used by James Cone in an essay:

I was hungry, and you formed a humanities club and you discussed
   my hunger.
Thank you.

I was imprisoned, and you crept off quietly to your chapel in the cellar
And prayed for my release.

I was sick, and you knelt and thanked God for your health.

I was homeless, and you preached to me of the spiritual shelter of
   the love of God.

I was lonely, and you left me alone to pray for me.
You seem so holy; so close to God.

But I'm still very hungry and lonely and cold.
So where have your prayers gone? What have they done?
What does it profit a man to page through his book of prayers
when the rest of the world is looking for his help?[21]

NOTES

1. James H. Cone, *Said I Wasn't Gonna Tell Nobody* (Maryknoll, NY: Orbis Books, 2018), 1, 17.

2. Albert Cleage Jr., *The Black Messiah* (New York: Sheed and Ward, 1968).

3. "The Black Manifesto," in *Black Theology: A Documentary History, 1966–1979*, ed. James H. Cone and Gayraud Wilmore (Maryknoll, NY: Orbis Books, 1979), 84.

4. "Black Theology—A Statement of the National Committee of Black Churchmen," *The Christian Century*, October 15, 1969, 1310.

5. Ross Douthat, "The Academic Apocalypse," NewYorkTimes.com, January 11, 2020.

6. James H. Cone, *Black Theology and Black Power* (Maryknoll, NY: Orbis Books, 1997), 8–9.

7. Cecil Wayne Cone, *The Identity Crisis in Black Theology* (Nashville: African Methodist Episcopal Church Press, 1975); J. Deotis Roberts, *Liberation and Reconciliation: A Black Theology* (Philadelphia: Westminster Press, 1971).

8. Cone, *Identity Crisis in Black Theology*, 143.

9. Ibid., 18.

10. Roberts, *Liberation and Reconciliation*, 28.

11. Ibid., 48.

12. Gayraud Wilmore, *Black Religion and Black Radicalism: An Examination of the Black Experience in Religion* (Garden City, NY: Doubleday, 1972).

13. Gayraud S. Wilmore and James H. Cone, *Black Theology: A Documentary History, 1966–1979* (Maryknoll, NY: Orbis Books, 1979), and *Black Theology: A Documentary History*, vol. 2: *1980–1992* (Maryknoll, NY: Orbis Books, 1993).

14. Walter Fluker, *The Ground Has Shifted: The Future of the Black Church in Post-Racial America (Religion, Race, and Ethnicity)* (New York: NYU Press, 2016).

15. Cone, *Black Theology and Black Power*, 31.

16. Cf. the quote from *The Christian Century* on the back cover of the 1997 edition of *Black Theology and Black Power*.

17. Thomas Jefferson, *Notes on the State of Virginia in 1781*, quoted by Richard S. Newman, *Freedom's Prophet: Bishop Richard Allen, the*

AME Church, and the Black Founding Fathers (New York: NYU Press, 2008), 23.

18. David W. Blight, *Frederick Douglass: Prophet of Freedom* (New York: Simon & Schuster, 2018), 425–26.

19. Newman, *Freedom's Prophet*, 9.

20. Ibid.

21. James H. Cone, "The Servant Church," in *The Pastor as Shepherd*, ed. Earl E. Shelp and Ronald H. Sunderland (New York: The Pilgrim Press, 1986), 63–64.

Set the Captives Free
from Poverty

While James Cone had fixed his attention on matters of race and racism within the United States, Latin American liberation theologians were at work expanding the focus of the church to consider the global problem of poverty and wealth disparity. Without denying the impact of racism on people in this country and around the world, the fact is that racism and the assumptions of white supremacy have a twin sibling named poverty whose capacity to inflict suffering on human lives is just as cruel and just as calculated. This message came from theologians such as Gustavo Gutiérrez of Peru and Leonardo Boff of Brazil, and David Batstone in the United States.

Latin American Liberation Theology

James Cone himself recognized and affirmed the rise of liberation theology in its Latin American context in his final book, *Said I Wasn't Gonna Tell Nobody*. He wrote in the book that was released just after his death in 2018, "Traditionally, theology has been 'written with white hands' wrote Leonardo Boff, a leading Latin American liberation theologian. But in the second half of the twentieth century, many marginalized voices broke their silence and revolutionized the teaching of theology as Christians engaged the Bible through the eyes of those who are poor and oppressed."[1]

The work of these theologians had been going on in Latin American countries through conferences and Spanish-language publications that were being disseminated as early as 1965, largely in response to concerns raised during the Second Vatican Council under Pope John XXIII between 1962 and 1965.[2] Gustavo Gutiérrez helps to frame the central message of Latin American liberation theology and its connection to the issue of poverty when he states, "All theological inquiry is contextual. Our context today is characterized by a glaring disparity between the rich and the poor. No serious Christian can quietly ignore this situation. It is no longer possible for someone to say 'Well, I didn't know' about the suffering of the poor. Poverty has a visibility today that it did not have in the past. The faces of the poor must now be confronted." Gutiérrez continues, "An active concern for the poor is not only an obligation for those who feel a political vocation; all Christians must take the Gospel message of justice and equality seriously. Christians cannot forego their responsibility to say a prophetic word about unjust economic conditions. Poverty poses a major challenge to every Christian conscience and therefore to theology."[3]

While Gutiérrez was the first Latin American theologian to publish a book on liberation theology, he acknowledges that his work built on the efforts of others who were already hard at work for liberation. He says:

> This book is an attempt at reflection, based on the gospel and the experience of men and women committed to the process of liberation in the oppressed and exploited land of Latin America. It is a theological reflection born of the experience of shared efforts to abolish the current unjust situation and to build a different society, freer and more human. Many in Latin America have started along the path to liberation, and among them is a growing number of Christians.[4]

It should be noted that in addition to Vatican II, which focused on changes in the Roman Catholic Church globally, Latin American liberation theology was especially influenced by the Latin American Episcopal Conference (CLEM) held in Medellin, Colombia, in 1968. With all the bishops present from all the diocese throughout Latin America, they resolved that the tragic social, economic, and political conditions affecting the majority of people in Latin America should be a central concern for the ministry and theology of the church, and "to be certain that our preaching, liturgy, and catechesis take into account the social and community dimensions of Christianity."[5]

Beginning with *A Theology of Liberation*, Gutiérrez puts a face on poverty so that the issue cannot be discussed as an abstraction. He says, "To be poor means to die of hunger, to be illiterate, to be exploited by others, not to know that you are being exploited, not to know that you are a person."[6] He goes on to describe the various words used in the Bible to describe people living in poverty, such as "indigent, bent over, weak, the beggar, the poor of the land, and the wretched."[7] He contends that from a biblical perspective, "poverty is a scandalous condition inimical to human dignity and therefore contrary to the will of God."[8]

More importantly, he reminds the reader that God's desire concerning poverty is to set the captives free. To that end, he talks about Moses leading the Hebrew people from slavery to freedom. He begins by asserting, "Poverty contradicts the very meaning of Mosaic religion. Moses led his people out of the slavery, exploitation, and alienation of Egypt so that they might inhabit a land where they could live with human dignity . . . To accept poverty and injustice is to fall back into the conditions of servitude which existed before the liberation from Egypt. It is to regress."[9]

Gutiérrez makes it clear that poverty is not a term to be defined. Rather, it is a way of being forced to live because of various cruel and unjust practices that are clearly set forth in Scripture. He says, "The prophets condemn every kind of abuse, every form of keeping the poor in poverty or creating new poor. They are not merely allusions to situations; the finger is pointed at those who are to blame. Fraudulent commerce and exploitation are condemned . . . as well as hoarding of lands . . . dishonest courts . . . the violence of the ruling classes . . . slavery . . . unjust taxes . . . and unjust functionaries . . . oppression by the rich is also condemned."[10]

While Gutiérrez, a Peruvian, speaks in biblical and theological terms about poverty, two Brazilian theologians, Leonardo Boff and Clodovis Boff, speak in much starker demographic and numerical terms concerning the reality of poverty in Third World nations across the planet. They state, "According to conservative estimates there are in those countries held in underdevelopment; five-hundred million persons starving; one billion, six-hundred million persons whose life expectancy is less than sixty years; (when a person in one of the developed countries reaches the age of forty-five, he or she is reaching middle age; in most of Africa and Latin America, a person has little hope of living to that age . . .)." They continue by pointing out the following: "One billion persons living in absolute poverty, one billion, five hundred million persons with no access to the most basic medical care; five hundred million with no work or only occasional work and a per capita income of less than $150 a year; eight-hundred-fourteen million who are illiterate two billion with no regular, dependable water supply."[11]

After describing the severity of the problem of poverty around the world, they offer their challenge to the church and to those who write theologically about the mission of the church. They use the word "com-passion," which they translate as "suffering with" as their point of departure. They assert that poverty cannot be reduced or eliminated by discussing or describing its many forms. Rather, "Without a minimum of suffering with this suffering that affects the great majority of the human race, liberation theology can neither exist nor be understood. Underlying liberation theology is a prophetic and comradely commitment to the life, cause, and struggle of these millions of debased and marginalized human beings, a commitment to ending this historical-social iniquity."[12]

What Gutiérrez and the Boffs make clear is that liberation theology is a call to the Christian church to act on behalf of those who are living in poverty. Gutiérrez invokes the phrase "preferential option for the poor" as the way to frame how the church should go about its work.[13] He continues, "Commitment to the poor is not optional in the sense that the Christian is free to make or not make this option or commitment, just as the love we owe to all human beings without exception is not optional."[14]

To make his point even clearer, Gutiérrez names several groups whose cause must be embraced if the scourge of global poverty is to be eliminated. He refers to "dominated peoples," "exploited social classes," "despised races," and "marginalized cultures." He makes two additional references to groups in Latin America that are also victimized and marginalized within that culture. First, he refers to the marginalization of Amerindian and Black populations and the contempt in which they are held. Then he talks about the conditions in which women live. He says, "We in Latin America are only beginning to wake up to the unacceptable and inhumane character of their situation."[15] Thus, Gutiérrez is reminding us that racism as it is manifested in the United States in all its ugly and oppressive forms is not the only "historical-social iniquity" that should concern us as Christians.

The Boffs supports this analysis by Gutiérrez that "the poor" take on many forms and faces. They state:

> We cannot confine ourselves to the purely socio-economic aspect of oppression, the "poverty" aspect, however basic and determinant this may be. We have to look also to other levels of social oppression such as:
>
> • racist oppression: discrimination against Blacks
>
> • ethnic discrimination: discrimination against indigenous peoples or other minority groups
>
> • sexual discrimination: discrimination against women . . .
>
> We have to go beyond an exclusively "classist" concept of the oppressed, which would restrict the oppressed to the socio-economically poor. The ranks of the oppressed are filled with others besides the poor.[16]

Latin American Theology and the Least of These

Latin American liberation theologians invite the church to use Matthew 25:31-44 as a point of reference for identifying the oppressed and then for responding to those various forms of oppression. A portion of that passage is worth revisiting here. Jesus said:

> "'For I was hungry and you gave me something to eat, I was thirsty and you gave me something to drink, I was a stranger and you in-

vited me in, I needed clothes and you clothed me, I was sick and you looked after me, I was in prison and you came to visit me.'

"Then the righteous will answer him, 'Lord, when did we see you hungry and feed you, or thirsty and give you something to drink? When did we see you a stranger and invite you in, or needing clothes and clothe you? When did we see you sick or in prison and go to visit you?'

"The King will reply, 'Truly I tell you, whatever you did for one of the least of these brothers and sisters of mine, you did for me.'" (Matthew 25:35-40 NIV)

To set the captives free is not merely a discussion to be engaged in or a policy paper to be adopted. Setting the captives free involves people physically, financially, emotionally, politically, and spiritually working by the power of the Holy Spirit to lift the bonds of human oppression.

I concur with Gutiérrez (as referenced above) that all theological inquiry is contextual.[17] That the major voices of liberation theology came first from the context of Latin America is not an accident. They were writing about their experience of poverty and economic injustice in places like Peru, Brazil, El Salvador, Nicaragua, and other Central and South American countries. The Boffs provide further categories by which to discuss and define poverty which, while true in Latin America, are no less true in the United States and around the world.

They reference "the socioeconomically poor,"—those who are deprived of the necessary means of subsistence such as food, clothing, medical care, and decent housing. There are victims of "the exploitation of labor," which involves unfair wages, high interest rates on loans, and not paying a fair price to produce raw materials. Then there are victims of "multiple levels of discrimination," such as Blacks by reason of their race, native tribes by reason of their culture, and women by reason of their sex.[18] They take a closer look at this third category when they say, "The poorest of the poor are often to be found among such groups, for they incur the whole gamut of oppressions and discriminations. In one base community a woman described herself as oppressed and impoverished on six counts: as a woman, as a prostitute, as a single parent, as Black, as poor, and because of her tribal origin."[19]

Christ and the Conquistadors

Latin American liberation theology is not limited to talking about or describing the issues related to poverty in that region of the world. If the oppressed are truly to be set free, then the root causes of poverty and economic disparity must be named and addressed. That means there must be a discussion about the history of conquest, colonization, and cultural genocide that has been intentionally inflicted upon large sectors of the people living in Central and South America. In short, it is not possible to talk about poverty and suffering in Latin America without taking a step back in history and considering the ways in which a theology of empire and conquest contributed to the present dilemma in that region.

In some respects, the nations of Latin America, indeed most of the Western Hemisphere from Canada to the Carolinas to Cuba to the Caribbean nations to Colombia to Chile, were greatly shaped and influenced by the twisted and perverted partnership of Christianity and the conquest of indigenous people and their lands. The patterns seemed to be that Roman Catholic missionaries came from Spain and Portugal to spread the gospel and convert the people of the New World to Christianity. While the people were praying to God, the conquistadors were preying on the people of those countries by extracting and exporting every valuable natural resource they could discover. In many instances, that included exporting the people themselves back to European capitals as slaves.

This discussion about Christ and conquest is the contribution of David Batstone to our understanding of Latin American liberation theology. In *From Conquest to Struggle*, Batstone argues that the liberation needed by the people of Latin America is not only from poverty as it currently exists in countries like Honduras, Guatemala, or El Salvador. To let the oppressed go free, he argues that there must be an accounting of the lingering effects of hundreds of years of economic exploitation, beginning with the conquest of that region largely by Spain and Portugal. He begins his book with this statement:

> Every discussion of Jesus Christ in Latin America must take into account an inescapable contradiction. On the one hand, the history

of Christian theology in Latin America is inextricably bound to the development and formation in the countries of the North Atlantic. The birth of Christianity in Latin America was itself essentially a product of the Spanish conquest of the continent which began in the sixteenth century and which was consolidated by means of the subsequent colonization of the culture by the church and the crown—the great two-headed Spain of the faith and the conquista.[20]

To dramatize his point, he refers to a 1932 book by John Mackay that muses on how Christianity and conquest became so entangled in Latin America. Mackay wrote:

Methinks the Christ, as he sojourned westward, went to prison in Spain, while another who took his name embarked with the Spanish crusaders for the New World, a Christ who was not born in Bethlehem, but in North Africa. This Christ became naturalized in the Iberian colonies of America, while Mary's Son and Lord has been little else than a stranger and sojourner in these lands from Columbus' day to this.[21]

I can recall hearing about the Spanish conquistadors in my elementary school classes on history and geography. I learned the names of the Spanish explorers who were in search of the New World and perhaps a sea route to India and the other side of the world. I learned about Vasco Da Gama, the Portuguese navigator who charted a sea route to India around the horn of Africa in 1497. I learned about Amerigo Vespucci, an Italian explorer who landed in what is now Brazil in 1499. I even learned about Leif Erikson, the Norwegian (Viking) explorer who was said to have arrived in what is now North America five hundred years before any other explorer. I learned about Ferdinand Magellan, a Portuguese navigator who in 1519 sailed from Spain to Africa and then on to Brazil in search of a route to the Spice Islands of Indonesia. What I did not know at that time was the true purpose(s) of those voyages or the lasting impact they would have on the indigenous people whose lands and people we were taught in school in the 1950s had been "discovered."

Of course, I learned about Christopher Columbus, the Italian-born explorer whose journey was funded by Spain. Beginning in 1492, he made four separate voyages to the New World where he first landed at a place he named Hispaniola, which is modern-day Haiti and the Dominican Republic. There was no pretense about converting the indigenous people to Roman Catholicism, which was among the reasons Ferdinand and Isabella supported his voyages. Batstone discusses Columbus in the context of this intersection of Christianity and conquest. He says, "Although *Cristobal* (translated literally, "Christ-bearer"), Columbus was clearly convinced that he was carrying out his mission of evangelization with the blessing of God, the extension of Spanish power and wealth were never far from his mind. Unfortunately, it was the might of the sword which was wielded to carry out both objectives."[22]

Believing there were large amounts of gold to be found and returned to Spain, Columbus set out to subjugate the native Taino population. Within sixty years of his arrival at Hispaniola, the native population had been decimated by disease and working conditions to the point that only a few hundred survived from what may have been a population of 250,000 people.[23] Batstone states:

> Historians estimate that when the first explorers reached the Pacific hemisphere the combined population of the Aztecs, Mayas, and Incas—the three major races of pre-Columbian Latin America—numbered somewhere between 70 and 90 million people. Only a century and a half later that number had been reduced to approximately 3.5 million; the majority of the native inhabitants had been massacred, while some were taken back to Europe as slaves.[24]

Thus began the conquest and exploitation of the people and lands of the New World, something that would continue for another four hundred years. The most notable act of conquest involved the robbing and eventual destruction of the Inca Empire of Peru by Spanish conquistadors led by Francisco Pizzaro beginning in 1530 until the entire nation was subdued by the Spanish in 1572. That region stretched for 2,175 miles along the Atlantic coast from Ecuador in the north to Chile in the south and encompassing all of Bolivia and Argentina as well.[25]

Whatever suffering the people of Latin America would endure in the decades and centuries to come, it was the destruction of this massive empire, along with the similar exploitation and then decimation of the Aztec empire in what is now Mexico,[26] that set the process in motion. The Roman Catholic monarchs of Spain and Portugal, seeking the expansion of the Christian faith and the expansion of their empires and all the wealth that such expansion might produce, set in motion the economic disaster that would eventually befall Latin America.

Slavery Is Also Part of the Latin American Story of Oppression

Many people living in the United States may be under the mistaken impression that the enslavement of African people during the trans-Atlantic slave trade affected only the economy and development of this country. They are unaware that many more slaves were brought to various locations in Latin America and the Caribbean than were ever imported into the United States. Thus, for many people living in that region to this day, the lingering impact of slavery and the class divisions created by that system can still be felt and seen. When Leonardo Boff talked about oppression rooted in racial discrimination against Black people as well as indigenous persons, this is what he had in mind.[27]

Henry Louis Gates Jr. reports on the number of enslaved persons from Africa who were brought to various locations in the New World. He states:

> It is difficult to comprehend the enormity of the slave trade; incredibly, no fewer than 12.5 million Africans were shipped to the New World between 1501 and 1866 . . . fewer than a half million of these became slaves in the United States . . . Almost half went to Brazil alone; Cuba received 779,100, far more than the United States did. Jamaica received just over one million, while Haiti received 773,700. Our neighbor Mexico received about 550,000 . . . Peru received approximately 150,000.[28]

A more through discussion of the impact of slavery on Latin America can be found in the work of Herbert S. Klein, who argues that the main reason why Spain in particular started the use of slave labor in its colonies was a combination of the growth of the agricultural plantation system around the production of sugar, and the fact that indigenous groups were either able to escape from the plantations and avoid capture and return, or they were nearly obliterated by the virulence of diseases brought by the Spanish for which they had no immunities.[29] Enslaved Africans seemed less affected by the effects of disease and were unfamiliar with the geography in which they now lived, which greatly reduced any likelihood of a successful escape.

Along with the Spanish, other Europeans, including the Portuguese, the French, the English, and the Dutch, were colonizing parts of Latin America. All of them were enriching their countries through the forced production of such commodities as tobacco, indigo, timber, coffee beans, and especially sugar. Slavery in Latin America began in 1513, one hundred years before the first Black indentured workers arrived at Jamestown, Virginia, in 1619. The trans-Atlantic slave trade that ended in the United States in 1807 remained in full force in Brazil, the largest slave importing country in the Western Hemisphere, until 1888.[30]

As in the United States, the end of slavery did not bring with it equal opportunity for an improved life. Klein points out, "Ex-slaves found themselves still living in the areas of the old plantation regimes and mostly at the lowest level of their respective socio-economic systems. Entering free society with little or no capital—often with skills only adaptive to a now declining plantation economy—and faced by continuing discrimination based on their color, most found it difficult to rise from the working class."[31]

Klein continues:

Even for those who obtained the skills, education, and capital needed to rise above the working class, they found that mobility was not as open to them as to the poor whites. The Black color was considered a negative identity, and that "whitening" of skin color was held a prerequisite for successful mobility . . . What distinguished the Latin American and Caribbean world was not so much the lack of prejudice as it was the subtle differentiations which that prejudice would create. Class was such a powerful determinant of position that the attributes of class would often influence the definition of color, whatever the phenotypic characteristics shown by the individual.[32]

In light of the more than three-hundred-year legacy of the enslavement of African people in Latin America, the call to let the oppressed go free comes from many directions. It comes from the legacy of the indigenous people whose lands were conquered by various European armies. It comes from the legacy of slavery and the continuing practice of racial discrimination. It comes from the class divisions that emerged after both national independence and the abolition of the slave trade. These are the cultural, economic, and political challenges that were being confronted by Latin American liberation theology.

Bishop Oscar Romero and Twentieth-Century Political Oppression

While the problems facing Latin America were set in motion in the fifteenth century with the arrival of Spanish conquistadors and with the importation of enslaved persons from Africa, the oppressed and impoverished people of that region of the world were not delivered from their sufferings even after their respective nations gained independence. The country of El Salvador serves as an example of the oppression, poverty, and even death that impacted so many people for the last fifty years.

El Salvador is the smallest in size of any nation in Central or South America, but it is the densest in population. It is surrounded by Guatemala to the northwest, Honduras to the northeast, and the Pacific Ocean on the south. At first, El Salvador was part of the Spanish empire, then in 1821 it gained independence and became part of the Federal Republic of Central America. It became a sovereign nation in 1841.

For most of its existence as a nation, El Salvador has endured chronic political and economic instability. It has suffered at the hands of authoritarian leaders who presided over a widening gap in income between the richest and poorest persons in the country. This resulted in the Salvadoran civil war (1979–1992), which was fought between the military-led government and a coalition of guerilla groups. It should not be forgotten that this tiny Latin American nation gained a great deal of attention from the news media and the government of the United States. There were two reasons for that attention in 1980: One was Oscar Romero, and the other was Ronald Reagan.

During the 1980s, the United States supplied the government of El Salvador with financial and military aid. *The Atlantic* magazine describes the sequence of events this way:

> It was a civil war of the 1980s, one that pitted leftist revolutionaries against the alliance of countries, oligarchs, and generals that had ruled the country for decades—with U.S. support—keeping peasants illiterate and impoverished. It was a bloody, brutal, and dirty war. More than 75,000 Salvadorans were killed in the fighting (most of them non-combatants that were victims of the military and its death squads). Peasants were shot en masse, often while trying to flee. Student and union leaders had their thumbs tied behind their backs before being shot in the head, their bodies left on roadsides as a warning to others. . . . Reagan was pouring billions of dollars of economic and military aid into the tiny country . . . For Reagan, El Salvador was the place to draw the line in the sand against communism.[33]

One of the most outspoken critics of the Salvadoran government was Roman Catholic Archbishop Oscar Romero, who was appealing to the soldiers in the army not to kill civilians randomly and rampantly in that country.[34] Batstone tells the story of various people in El Salvador whose lives dramatize this problem. Those persons remind us that poverty is neither accidental nor unintentional. Rather, poverty for some and prosperity for others is the result of policies and practices implemented by governments and often maintained by use of force.

In El Salvador, the National Guard was frequently deployed to arrest and assassinate persons who resisted the established order put in place by the government. That was clearly the case when several priests in the Diocese of San Salvador were machine gunned by army tanks and soldiers inside a Catholic retreat center because they were suspected of housing and supporting guerilla forces. Romero was influenced by liberation theology and was using it to speak out and stand up for the impoverished people of his country. He said, "Fr. Grande's death and the death of other priests after his impelled me to take an energetic attitude before the government . . . I support all of the priests in the communities. We have managed to combine well the pastoral mission of the Church, preference for the poor, to be clearly on the side of the oppressed, and from there to clamor for the liberation of the people."[35]

Romero gave voice to the voiceless people of El Salvador who were the victims of violence at the hands of their own government. In the truest spirit of liberation theology, he was identifying God with the struggles and sufferings of the poor. In the spirit of the 1968 Medellin Catholic Conference, he was connecting his pastoral ministry to the human rights abuses he was observing every day. His sermons and radio broadcasts became one of the few ways that government conduct was being reported and condemned. Romero's work was defined as being an archbishop not only for the Roman Catholic members of his diocese but also for all the people of his country.

> During Oscar Romero's three years and one month as archbishop, the role of the church in the political life of the country expanded with each succeeding crisis. At the same time, under increasing difficulties brought about by waves of persecution against the priests, religious, and CEB (ecclesial base communities) members, the focus increasingly was on the diminutive archbishop of San Salvador, both within and outside the country.[36]

Oscar Romero paid with his life for his attempts to put liberation theology into practice in El Salvador. He essentially signed his own death warrant when, during a Sunday morning homily on national radio, he ordered soldiers to disobey their commanding officers whenever they were told to murder civilians, whom Romero referred to as "your brothers and sisters." The next week, March 24, 1980, he was shot and killed by government soldiers while he was serving the Mass at a hospital chapel in San Salvador.

Later that same year, on the night of December 2, 1980, three Roman Catholic nuns and a lay worker were abducted, raped, and then shot to death in El Salvador. In the spirit of our times in 2020, I want to "call their names": Maura Clarke, Jean Donovan, Ita Ford, and Dorothy Kazel. The *New York Times* reported:

> After 17 years of silence, all four former national guardsmen con-victed of killing three American nuns and a lay worker in 1980 have said for the first time that they acted only after receiving or-ders from above . . . The next day, peasants discovered their bodies alongside an isolated road and buried their remains in a common grave . . . The killings came as the United States was beginning a decades-long, $7 billion aid effort to prevent left-wing guerillas from coming to power.[37]

To make matters worse, the two men responsible for trying to cover up what one State Department official called "an act of bar-barism" have been granted residence in the United States and now live in Florida.[36]

Batstone tells the story of one family impacted by the brutality of the government toward their own people in El Salvador, and how that experience was shared with their local bishop. He begins the story by describing Bishop Urioste: "He has seen more suffering than one would care to see in a lifetime. He was a close advisor to assassinated Archbishop Oscar Arnulfo Romero and has personally ministered to his country in a time when corpses littered El Salvador's streets and fields."

Then the bishop shared this story:

> The woman visited him [Bishop Urioste] after she had found her nephew and his wife dead alongside one of the roads which lead out of the capital of San Salvador. The National Guard had arrived at their home late one night, charging that the two young people were part of the guerilla movement. They were forcibly removed from their home and nothing was heard about them until two days later, when their mutilated bodies were found at the edge of town. The head of her nephew had been decapitated; a common style of execution used to intimidate.[39]

The woman who had lost so much sought to comfort the bishop by reading to him words from Psalm 22:24-26 (paraphrased): "For God has not hidden God's face from the poor one, but has answered when the poor have called . . . the poor will eat and be satisfied, they who seek the Lord will praise God." Here again is the spirit of liberation theology at work not only among the religious leaders but among some of the people as well. God is on the side of the poor and oppressed, no matter how bad things may seem at any point in time. That is the faith that has sustained people not only in El Salvador but in other countries in Latin America that have faced similar forms of oppression, violence, and poverty.

A New Christology for the Latin American Church

Having discussed the historical and political contexts in which Latin American liberation theology emerged, attention will now be given to the content of this theological formulation. Using both Gutiérrez and Batstone as points of reference, the content of this theology is both a new Christology that places God on the side of the oppressed communities and a new and expanded role for the church in the fight against poverty.

We begin with David Batsone and the issue of Christology. He employs the work of George Casalis to set forth a two-dimensional form of Christology: one for the ruling elite comprised of the religious and political authorities of Latin America, and another for the poor, the peasants, the powerless.[40] The first of these forms of Christology was "to baptize and justify the newly established social order as representative of the reign of Christ over creation . . . Jesus Christ of Latin America was a figure designed to legitimate the presence of colonial rule and to justify the structures of privilege and power which remained intact after the arrival of national independence."[41] In short, Christ was a conquering figure whose power had allowed first Spain and then all successive political regimes to rule and maintain power in Christ's name and by Christ's will. Casalis states, "Obedience to the great king of Spain and submission to the King of Heaven were deemed as one single act."[42]

The second form of Christology, the one that was offered to the poor people of Latin America, presented Jesus as a suffering Christ who was passive and not resistant to his place in the broader world of Roman conquest, and who was ultimately killed by the decree of that political regime. The message in this Christology is that social structures and power distribution are established by God. Social change was not possible, because the current conditions were consistent with God's design. This theology precluded the possibility of any meaningful change. Batstone then offers this assessment from the Brazilian liberation theologian Hugo Assmann: "The Christ of oppressive Christologies really has two faces. On the one side are all the Christs of the power establishment, who do not need to fight because they already hold a position of dominance. On the other are all the Christs of established impotence, who cannot fight against the dominion to which they are subject."[43]

This approach to Christology is reminiscent of the way in which Christianity was presented to African Americans during the days of slavery in the United States. There was the use of Colossians 3:22–4:1 and Ephesians 6:5-8 that encouraged slaves to be obedient to their masters and encouraged masters to be kind to their slaves. Along with Romans 13:1-7, which asserts that "the authorities that exists have been established by God," (NIV), it was regularly reinforced that white authority and Black submission to that authority was God's design. It was the repeated use of these verses in the Bible that caused Howard Thurman's grandmother, who had been a slave in Florida, to instruct him not to read anything to her from the writings of Paul because those were the verses the slave owners kept repeating in order to reinforce the legitimacy of the slave regime.[44]

It is also consistent with a point made by Isabel Wilkerson in *Caste*, in which she discusses three caste systems and how they were created and maintained: African Americans in the United States, Jews in Nazi Germany, and Dalits or the "untouchables" in India. She reports on a conversation she had with a man from India who asked his parents why it was that in that country some people had so much while others had so much less. Her answer to that question could have come straight from the mouth of any leader of a totalitarian regime that was attempting to use religion to justify their entrenched power: "Don't discuss about these things. Do your studies. Caste is created by God."[45]

The solution to the dual Christologies in Latin America that allowed for suffering and oppression among the poor and powerless throughout that region and the continued authority and prosperity of the ruling elite was the introduction of a liberation theology in which the God of the Exodus as discussed in Scripture is at the heart of the church's mission and message. Batstone states:

> The significance of the Scriptural testimony of God's acts of salvation and liberation, leading from the exodus of God's people from Egypt to the good news preached and lived by Jesus Christ, has been continually compromised and tempered by an established church more interested in stability than vitality . . . Liberationists contend that the various forms of escapist religion which ignore the crises of the human drama—and yet nevertheless predominate in contemporary society—are false distortions of a living faith which realizes itself in concrete activity in the world. Thus, they conceive of their task as a reclamation and fulfillment of Biblical revelation and Christian praxis.[46]

In short, God is on the side of the poor and the oppressed, and that is where the church of Jesus Christ must be at work challenging any and all systems of power that perpetuate injustice and inequity in society. The church must be at work to let the oppressed go free.

Gutiérrez reinforces this point about the church in Latin America working in support of the poor by using Scripture and theology as the basis for attacking the unjust systems that created and maintain the poverty experienced by so many people throughout Latin America. He writes:

> The theology of liberation attempts to reflect on the experience and meaning of the faith based on the commitment to abolish injustice and to build a new society. This theology must be verified by the practice of that commitment, by active, effective participation in the struggle which the exploited social classes have undertaken against their oppressors. Liberation from every form of exploitation, the possibility of a more human and dignified life, the creation of a new humankind—all pass through this struggle.[47]

Thus, not only is God on the side of the oppressed as revealed in the Exodus and in the life and teachings of Jesus, but "the Church must also be on the side of the oppressed classes and dominated peoples, clearly and without qualifications."[48] In paraphrasing Blaise

Pascal he ends by saying, "All the political theologies, the theologies of hope, of revolution, and of liberation, are not worth one act of genuine solidarity with exploited social classes. They are not worth one act of faith, love, and hope, committed—in one way or another—in active participation to liberate humankind from everything that dehumanizes it and prevents it from living according to the will of the Father."[49]

Let the church say Amen!

NOTES

1. James H. Cone, *Said I Wasn't Gonna Tell Nobody* (Maryknoll, NY: Orbis Books, 2018), 115.

2. Leonardo Boff and Clodovis Boff, *Introduction to Liberation Theology* (Maryknoll, NY: Orbis Books, 1986), 69.

3. Daniel Hartnett, "Remembering the Poor: An Interview with Gustavo Gutiérrez," *America: The Jesuit Review*, February 3, 2003, 1.

4. Gustavo Gutiérrez, *A Theology of Liberation* (Maryknoll, NY: Orbis Books, 1971), xiii.

5. From the Medellin document "Peace," September 6, 1968.

6. Gutiérrez, 164.

7. Ibid., 165.

8. Ibid.

9. Ibid., 168.

10. Ibid., 167.

11. Leonardo Boff and Clodovis Boff, *Introducing Liberation Theology* (Maryknoll, NY: Orbis Books, 1976), 8.

12. Boff and Boff, *Introducing Liberation Theology*, 10.

13. Gutiérrez, xxvi.

14. Ibid.

15. Ibid., xxii.

16. Boff and Boff, *Introducing Liberation Theology*, 29.

17. Hartnett.

18. Boff and Boff, *Introducing Liberation Theology*, 47.

19. Ibid.

20. David Batstone, *From Conquest to Struggle: Jesus of Nazareth in Latin America* (Albany: State University of New York Press, 1991), 13.

21. John Mackay, *The Other Spanish Christ: A Study in the Spiritual History of Spain and South America* (New York: Macmillan, 1932), 41, quoted in Batstone, 13.

22. Batstone, 14.

23. History.com editors, "Christopher Columbus," History.com, September 3, 2019.

24. Batstone, 15.

25. "Inca," *The Oxford Desk Dictionary of World History* (New York: Oxford University Press, 2006), 301–2.

26. "Aztec," *The Oxford Desk Dictionary of World History* (New York: Oxford University Press, 2006), 50.

27. Boff and Boff, *Introducing Liberation Theology*, 29.

28. Henry Louis Gates Jr., *Life Upon These Shores: Looking at African American History 1513–2008* (New York: Knopf Publishing, 2011), 4–5.

29. Herbert S. Klein, *African Slavery in Latin America and the Caribbean* (New York: Oxford University Press, 1986), 25.

30. Ibid., 257.

31. Ibid., 266.

32. Ibid., 267.

33. Raymond Bonner, "America's Role in El Salvador's Deterioration," The Atlantic.com, January 20, 2018.

34. Batstone, 93.

35. Tommie Sue Montgomery, interview of Oscar Romero, December 14, 1979, in *Revolution in El Salvador: Origins and Evolution* (Boulder, CO: Westview Press, 1982), 111.

36. Ibid.

37. Larry Rohter, "4 Salvadorans Say They Killed U.S. Nuns on Order of Military," TheNewYorkTimes.com, April 3, 1998.

38. Ibid.

39. Batstone, 24.

40. George Casalis, "Jesus—Neither Abject Lord nor Heavenly Monarch," in Jose Miguez Bonino, *Faces of Jesus: Latin American Christologies* (Eugene, OR: Wipf & Stock, 2002) 72–76, quoted in Batstone, 16–17.

41. Batstone, 16–17.

42. Ibid., 17.

43. Hugo Assmann, "The Power of Christ in History: Conflicting Christologies and Discernment," in Rosino Gibellini, *Frontiers of Theology in*

Latin America (Maryknoll, NY: Orbis Books, 1979), 149, quoted in Batstone, 18.

44. Howard Thurman, *Jesus and the Disinherited* (Boston: Beacon Press, 1976), 30–31.

45. Isabel Wilkerson, *Caste: The Origins of Our Discontent* (New York: Random House, 2020), 165.

46. Batstone, 21.

47. Gutiérrez, 174.

48. Ibid.

49. Ibid.

CHAPTER 4

The Intersection
of Race and Poverty in
the United States

In the previous chapters, attention was first given to Black theology and the need for the oppressed to be set free from the terror of racism and the racial violence that has been used to maintain a society in which African Americans have been denied many of the human rights they should have been able to enjoy. Then there was a discussion of Latin American liberation theology and the need for the oppressed to be set free from the grip of poverty and the government-sanctioned violence that is used to maintain massive wealth disparity in that region of the world.

In this chapter, I would like to consider the intersectionality of race and poverty and focus on the ways in which many African Americans have been the simultaneous victims of racism and poverty during most of the history of this country. That is the central premise of *Origins of the Civil Rights Movement* by Aldon Morris.[1] In that book, Morris describes what he calls "the tri-partite system of oppression" that locked African Americans into the margins of American society. The first part of that tri-partite system is maintaining people in abject poverty with no chance of escape through education, promotion, or the establishment of one's own business. The second part of the system involves the denial of voting rights so that no legislative solution to the problem of poverty could be pursued. The third and most brutal part of the system involved the regular use of physical intimidation and even death by the most torturous means imaginable for those in the African American community who dared to break out of their assigned and prescribed place in society.[2]

What is important to note is that despite that tri-partite system of oppression, some African Americans have been able to escape the grip of poverty. They have managed to achieve middle-class status or higher. They have achieved home ownership, which is a central component of the American dream. They have followed a path that has led from slavery in the eighteenth and nineteenth centuries to economic success in the twentieth and twenty-first centuries. What many economically successful African Americans have learned is that the oppressed have not yet become fully free. They have discovered that a job on Wall Street, a seat in a classroom at an elite college for their children, or a comfortable home in the suburbs for their families does not allow them to escape fully the implications of being Black in the United States.

In working to let the oppressed go free, the intersection of race and poverty must be considered as both of those oppressive forces work on the lives and psyches of some people. It must be asserted, however, that even if one manages to escape poverty, one never seems to escape fully racism in the United States if one is an African American. Nothing better illustrates that fact than the notorious attack on what was then called "Black Wall Street" by a white mob in Tulsa, Oklahoma, between May 30 and June 2, 1921. The *New York Times* recounts those events:

> On May 30, 1921, the Greenwood district of Tulsa, Okla., was a thriving Black community; a rarity in an era of lynchings, segregation, and a rapidly growing Ku Klux Klan . . . By sunrise on June 2, Greenwood lay in ruins; burned to the ground by a mob of white people, aided and abetted by the National Guard, in one of the worst acts of racial violence in American history. The death toll may have been a high as 300, with hundreds more injured and an estimated 8,000 or more left homeless.[3]

Drawing the link between race and poverty at that time, Maggie Astor continues:

At the time of the massacre, the Greenwood neighborhood had a population of nearly 10,000 including descendants of slaves as well as people who, according to the 2001 report of a commission that investigated the massacre, had come because Oklahoma seemed to offer a chance to escape the harsher racial realities of life in the Deep South . . . Thirty residents owned grocery stores. There were restaurants, hotels, theatres, and transportation services run by Black entrepreneurs.[4]

Oklahoma State Senator Kevin Matthews, who represents Tulsa in the state legislature today, reflected on his district in 1921. "That's what people don't know. We had that kind of prosperity in 1921. That was Black Wall Street for a reason, and it was burned down and destroyed for a reason."[5]

Like so many brutal attacks by white mobs against Black people, the events in Tulsa were set off by an allegation that a Black man had assaulted a white woman. The man, Dick Rowland, was arrested and taken to the Tulsa County Courthouse, where the sheriff had allowed a lynch mob to kidnap another Black man the year before. When a group of armed Black men showed up at the courthouse to guard against Rowland being treated in a similar fashion, "many white people went off to get their own weapons, and the crowd grew to more than 2,000."[6]

It bears remembering just how ferocious the attack by the white mob was in Tulsa. Astor describes the scene:

The morning of June 1, the mob rushed into Greenwood and opened fire, including with machine guns; led Black people out of their homes and businesses at gunpoint; looted valuables and set the buildings on fire. Black residents tried to defend themselves but were overpowered. The mob stopped firefighters from reaching much of the burning neighborhood, while the police and National Guard arrested Black people instead of the white rioters. In some cases, members of the Guard joined the rioters.[7]

Rather that rush to correct the wrongs that were done in Tulsa, Astor reports, a massive cover-up began to keep the rest of the state and the country from learning about what happened to Black Wall

Street. "Victims were buried in unmarked graves. Police records vanished. The inflammatory Tulsa *Tribune* articles were cut out before the newspapers were transferred to microfilm."[8] The fact that most Americans know nothing about the events in Tulsa in 1921 is explained this way by Scott Ellsworth from the University of Michigan: "What happens fairly rapidly is this culture of silence descends, and the story of the riot becomes actively suppressed."[9]

What can be learned from the Tulsa attack in 1921 is that race and poverty were integrally connected; and when Black people sought to break that connection and pursue the American dream for themselves, they were met with fierce resistance and blatant hostility. I state it this way in *Preaching to the Black Middle Class*, in which I caution African Americans who have managed to achieve a level of economic success that they are still vulnerable to the constant assaults of racism:

> Our relative economic security does not exempt us from the re-alities of racism. Black people living in the most affluent regions of the suburbs are still treated contemptuously by their white neighbors. The forms of discrimination may be more conspicu-ous in the inner-city regions than they are in suburban areas. But the intent remains the same: to assign Black people to a "place" within society beyond which they are not permitted to go with-out white approval.[10]

I wrote that book after my wife and I moved into a home in Mont-clair, New Jersey, in 1976. None of our white neighbors would even speak to us—even though we greeted them every time we passed in our driveways. That went on for three years. Then there came a day when one of my seminary classmates, Tom Leutner, and his wife and newborn child came to visit us. They set up a play pen for the baby in the back yard of our house, and Tom, who is white, stayed outside to watch over the baby. At one point I looked out the window and saw Tom involved in an animated conversation with our next-door neighbor.

Tom eventually came into the house and asked me if I had ever met my neighbors, because things said during their conversation sug-gested to him that they did not know us at all. Tom then invited me to go back outside with him, and at that point my white seminary classmate introduced me to my white next-door neighbor. It required a white man to vouch for me before my next-door neighbor was willing to speak to me. The fact that my wife and I were able to purchase that home at the age of twenty-seven, or that we were able to maintain it both inside and outside for the previous three years, did not matter to any white family in that neighborhood. All they saw was a Black couple living in "their neighborhood." I was not limited by poverty, but I was certainly being targeted by racism.

More than three decades later, Henry Louis Gates of Harvard University found himself in the same position. He begins by noting how quickly a Black middle and upper middle class has arisen in the United States. He says:

> One of the most dramatic shifts to the structure of the African American community has been the doubling of the Black middle class and the quadrupling of the Black upper-middle class since 1970 . . . My colleague Lani Guinier once said that affirmative action initially was a class escalator, but now it is a class perpetuator. Many Black students admitted to Ivy League universities are the children of the upper middle class—the very people whose class status was transformed by affirmative action.[11]

It should not be forgotten that Henry Louis Gates is a reminder of how often one's racial identity overwhelms or renders temporarily useless one's economic status. After all, it was Henry Louis Gates, professor at Harvard University and frequent host of television shows about African and African American history on the Public Broadcasting System (PBS), who was arrested by a white police officer named James Crowley after a white female neighbor in that community called the police because she thought Gates was breaking into what later proved to be his own house in Cambridge, Massachusetts. The door was stuck, and Gates used his shoulder to push it open. When Gates asked the police officer why he was proceeding with the arrest even after Gates had established that it was his own house he was trying to enter, Gates answered his own question: "Why, because I'm a Black man in America?"[12]

At that moment, Gates was experiencing what millions of Black men and women have experienced, and continue to experience every day, living while Black in America. However, that similarity quickly vanishes when social class and economic status enter the picture. Not all Black men who are suspected by their white neighbors or harassed by white police officers can call on Charles J. Ogletree, a Harvard Law School professor, to represent them in court. Even less likely is that Black men suspected of a crime would have President Barack Obama vouch for them during a nationally televised press conference or invite them and their arresting officer to the White House to have a beer and talk about how to improve police/community relations.

Millions upon millions of African Americans face the sting of racism every day in one form or another. In my own case, it never fails that when I enter an elevator where a white woman is present or walk past a white woman on a city street that she will double-wrap her purse around her wrist or drape it over her shoulder just in case I should attempt to snatch the purse from her. It did not matter that I was the president of Colgate Rochester Crozer Divinity School, or one of the three alumni recognized by Princeton Theological Seminary during its bicentennial celebration as being a distinguished alumni, or that I hold two earned and two honorary doctoral degrees. The only thing that mattered in those moments was that I was a Black male who was being profiled as a robber and perhaps as a rapist as well.

Speaking of being president of one of the oldest theological seminaries in the United States, I experienced racial profiling on the campus of that school by a part-time, weekend security guard who did not know why I was there. I was walking from the President's House to the main academic building, Strong Hall, on a Saturday afternoon. A young white male rushed out from the security office to intercept me and ask me if I "needed some help." He wanted to know where I was going. Mind you that the CRCDS campus at that time was a park-like setting where people in the neighborhood walk all the time. They walk their dogs across the campus. There is an outpatient medical facility on the campus, which means that patients and their families often walk around the campus. The Colgate Memorial Chapel was a regular site for weddings involving people with no other connection to the seminary except that one-day use of the chapel. There was never a report of anyone being stopped by a security guard to see if they "needed some help."

I told that young man that I knew exactly where I was going—to the office of the president where I, as the president of the school, go to work every day. That alone was not enough to reassure him that I should be where I was, since in his mind a Black man had no reason to be there even though many Black male students resided on the campus at that time. He was not a regular security guard. He did not know the faces that moved freely across the campus. He was a young, white male who brought his worldview with him to work that day. I was a Black man with a PhD who has had eighteen books published and who had been president of that school for several years by the time this event occurred. He was a white man with a security badge, a flashlight, and a strong suspicion that I was in a place where I did not belong.

At that moment, I became Trayvon Martin, a Black teenager in Florida walking home with a bag of candy and a soft drink, and that security guard became George Zimmerman, the self-appointed guardian of the mostly white neighborhood who called the police because he thought Trayvon Martin "was up to no good." At that moment, I became Ahmaud Arbery, who was stopped and ultimately shot and killed by two self-appointed security officers who decided that he was in a place where he did not belong.

I could recount dozens of instances when the reality of racism and racial profiling touched my own life. Multiply my stories hundreds of millions of times, as Black people have endured the indignity and inhumanity of racism and the assumptions of white privilege and white supremacy since the first indentured persons from Africa arrived at Jamestown, Virginia, in 1619. Consider the moment on September 9, 2009, when Congressman Joseph Wilson of South Carolina shouted out "you lie" while Barack Obama was delivering a televised speech before a joint session of the Congress of the United States. While he was reprimanded by the Congress for his actions, he has been reelected by his mostly white constituents in the Second Congressional district of South Carolina five times since that event. It is impossible to imagine what the reaction of white America would have been if an African American member of Congress had publicly said "you lie" to Ronald Reagan or either George H. W. Bush or George W. Bush.

I have no doubt that many white Americans held President Obama in contempt simply because he was elected president of the United States. Donald Trump built his political image around the so-called birther narrative, claiming that Obama was not born in this country and thus was not qualified to serve as president. No Black person in American history has achieved as high a position of power and influence as Barack Obama. Yet, in the eyes of the Joe Wilsons of the country, he was still viewed as a Black man undeserving of the decency and decorum he has undoubtedly shown to every white president, even when that president was lying. According to the *Washington Post*, Donald Trump has done so twenty thousand times since he was elected in 2016.[13] This is the legacy of racial animus and contempt faced by African Americans even when they have achieved great success in this country.

Eddie Glaude Jr. provides an interesting way to describe the challenges that confront this country today:

> We have to rid ourselves, once and for all, of this belief that white people matter more than others, or we're doomed to repeat the cycles of our ugly history over and over again . . . We need and America where "becoming white" is no longer the price of the ticket . . . So much of American culture and politics today is bound up with the banal fact of racism in our daily lives and our willful refusal to acknowledge who benefits and suffers from it. [14]

Working to rid the nation of the banal fact of racism in our daily lives is part of what Black theology was at work to address and to achieve. In the face of racism and the assumptions of white privilege and white supremacy the cry must go forth to let the oppressed go free.

Poverty Intensifies the Effect of Racism

While it is true that African Americans never fully escape the oppressive force of racism despite their level of economic success, it must be noted that racism does not sting quite as much, or its victims can more easily endure racial slights when they have a level of economic security that provides them with the security of good housing, a steady income, access to medical care, the ability to invest in the lives of their children, and to plan for and later enjoy a secure retirement. Racial bias may never be eliminated in the United States. However, not all victims of racism are the same. For some, racism is exacerbated by poverty that limits their daily options in terms of access to housing, education, employment, and health care.

For some, like myself and hundreds of thousands of other African Americans, racism can be brushed aside and sometimes ignored as we pursue professional careers, enjoy home ownership, send our children off to college, dispense our discretionary income, and pursue hobbies and personal interest while being less concerned than many about making ends meet at the end of every month. In many respects, persons like myself are the beneficiaries of the civil rights movement and of various forms of affirmative action. The challenge for people who are not the victims of poverty is to be sensitive to, supportive of, and allied in struggle with those for whom racism and poverty remain daily struggles.

W. E. B. Du Bois on Race and Poverty

In 1903, in *The Souls of Black Folk*, W. E. B. Du Bois observed that the problem of the twentieth century is "the problem of the color-line, the relation of the darker to the lighter races of me in Asia and Africa, in America and the islands of the sea."[15] While many people may be familiar with that phrase from Du Bois, what may not be as widely known is that within twenty years of this observation about race being the problem of the twentieth century, Du Bois was acknowledging that racial issues alone were not a sufficient way to address the issues facing the nation and the world.

He traveled through Europe and the Soviet Union in the years following World War I and observed the economic deprivation of people who lived in racially and culturally homogenous countries where race and racism was not an issue. In David Levering Lewis' biography of Du Bois, Lewis says, "The teleology of global class revolution now began to vie powerfully with the superordinate power of race in Du Bois' thinking. If race was the problem of the twentieth century, after his first encounter with the Soviet Union he also began to regard class as a dilemma of comparable magnitude."[16]

More than one hundred years ago, Du Bois was exploring the intersectionality of race and class (poverty) especially as it affected African Americans in the United States. Racism was not just an assault on the social or political status of African Americans. Racism was often the cause of programs, policies, and prejudices that resulted in generational poverty within African American communities across the country.

Through a farming system known as sharecropping, white landowners kept Black farmers perpetually in debt by fixing the value of the crop they had produced as less than the amount those farmers owed to the landowners for rent, seed, tools, and other necessities. That same practice remained in force year after year. Since it was against the law to attempt to leave the farm while still owing an unpaid debt to the landowners, Black people were reduced to a state that was as close to slavery as could be achieved.

Some Black families were able to escape the poverty of the South, and they made their way north during the Great Migration, which was a period of time roughly between the start of World War I in 1917 and the years following the end of World War II in 1945. Instead of poverty that was fueled by sharecropping and low wage jobs as domestic workers in the homes of white families, African Americans encountered collusion between banks and real estate companies that involved redlining, which essentially determined entire areas of a city where banks would not issue mortgages to purchase homes, something which has always been the first step out of poverty for most American families. If a Black family had the means to purchase a home without the need for a bank-issued mortgage loan, they often ran into restrictive real estate covenants that prohibited a white homeowner from selling their home to Black and often to Jewish families as well.

One of the biggest economic boosts ever provided to white people in this country came with the various programs introduced by Franklin Delano Roosevelt during the years of the Great Depression, starting with the stock market crash in 1929, and the Dust Bowl that devastated agricultural land from Texas in the south all the way to the Canadian border beginning in 1930. Much has been said about such programs as the Civilian Conservation Corps (CCC) or the

National Works Administration (NWA). What is less known is the systematic way in which African Americans were denied the benefits and opportunities of those programs. In *Caste*, Isabel Wilkerson sheds light on the economic impact of being shut out of so much of that programming when she notes, "Many may not have realized that the New Deal reforms of the 1930s, like the Social Security Act of 1935 (providing old age insurance) and the Wagner Act (protecting workers from labor abuse), excluded the vast majority of Black workers—farm laborers and domestics—at the urging of southern white politicians."[17]

She continues by discussing housing discrimination.

Further tipping the scales, the Federal Housing Administration was created to make homeownership easier for white families by guaranteeing mortgages in white neighborhoods while specifically excluding African-Americans who wished to buy homes . . . Together, these and other government programs extended a safety net and a leg-up to the parents, grandparents, and great grandparents of white Americans today, while shutting out the foreparents of African-Americans from those same job protections and those same chances to earn or build wealth.[18]

Wilkerson links the issues of race and poverty in a way that is impossible to refute and painful to remember. She says, "The subordinate caste was shut out of 'the trillions of dollars of wealth accumulated through the appreciation of housing assets secured by federally insured loans between 1932 and 1962' according to sociologist George Lipsitz."[19]

In a summary statement, she says:

These government programs for the dominant caste were in force during the lifetimes of many current-day Americans. These programs did not open to African Americans until the late 1960s, and then only after the protests for civil rights. The more recent forms of state-sanctioned discrimination, along with denying pay to enslaved people over the course of generations, has led to a wealth gap in which white families currently have ten times the wealth of their Black counterparts.[20]

Here is a clear instance in which the intersection between Black theology and Latin American liberation theology can be seen as they deliver a double blow of oppression to millions of African Americans over a period of hundreds of years.

Martin Luther King Jr. on Race and Poverty

Du Bois was not the only major African American thought leader who saw that issues of poverty had to be addressed as seriously as issues of race. The same pattern of expanding focus from racism to poverty and economic injustice was equally true for Martin Luther King Jr. For most people, Dr. King is remembered as an advocate for racial justice. He is usually associated with the effort to dismantle the system of racial segregation that became legalized by the 1896 U.S. Supreme Court case, *Plessy v. Ferguson*, which established a dual society, Black and white, separate but equal, that was certainly separate but was never equal in any sense of the word.

What many people forget or never knew is that after the passage of the 1964 Civil Rights Bill that addressed issues of racial discrimination in public accommodations and the 1965 Voting Rights Act that greatly expanded voting rights for African Americans, King turned his attention to issues of poverty. It began in earnest in the summer of 1966, when King moved his family into an apartment in the Lawndale section of my hometown of Chicago. He initially came to Chicago to dramatize racial segregation in housing patterns in that city. What he found was racial segregation that resulted in generational economic disparity between Blacks and whites. It became clear that racial integration would have limited effect if it was not coupled with economic opportunity. The remainder of his public ministry was devoted to calling attention to the impoverished conditions under which many Black people lived. He wrote:

> You can't get a job because you are poorly educated, and you must depend on welfare to feed your children; but if you receive public aid in Chicago, you cannot own property, not even an automobile, so you are condemned to the jobs and shops which are closest to your home. Once confined to this isolated community, one no lon-

ger participates in a free economy, but is subject to price-fixing and wholesale robbery by many of the merchants of the area.[21]

King went on to refer to such neighborhoods as "a jungle of poverty and exploitation."[22]

In his 1963 "I Have a Dream" speech delivered at the March on Washington, King spoke about America's Black communities as "islands of poverty and despair surrounded by an ocean of material prosperity."[23] That visual image of prosperity and poverty co-existing within proximity to one another was reinforced by the central finding of the 1968 Kerner Commission report that sought to identify the root causes of the urban violence that broke out in cities across the country between 1965 and 1968. That report concluded that "our nation is moving toward two societies, one Black and one white—separate and unequal."[24] There is no doubting the fact that for a multiplicity of reasons ranging from failing public schools to urban violence, fragile families, mass incarceration, and discrimination in hiring and promotions that there is a great economic gap between Blacks and whites as a group in this country. Racism and poverty have formed an oppressive environment from which it is difficult for people to escape.

Three years later, in response to his experience in Chicago in 1966 where racism and poverty were destroying the health and the hopes of many of the people in my hometown, King began a programmatic effort to let the oppressed go free when he established a new program arm of the Southern Christian Leadership (SCLC) that was named Operation Breadbasket. The Rev. Jesse Jackson was named Director of that program, and he immediately focused on both employment opportunities for Black workers, inclusion of Black workers into labor unions, and venture capital and contracts from large companies for Minority Business Enterprises (MBE). Saturday morning meetings of Operation Breadbasket became one of the most popular gatherings in Chicago for many years to come. After the assassination of Dr. King in 1968, the fortunes of SCLC began to fade. However, the strength of Operation Breadbasket steadily increased with new chapters popping up across the country.

When I arrived in New York City in the fall of 1970, the first thing I did was seek out the New York City chapter of Operation Breadbasket, which met at Bethany Baptist Church in Brooklyn, where William A. Jones Jr. was both pastor of the church and president of the chapter. The focus was entirely on the intersection of race and economic development. Two of the targets of our attention were the Robert Hall Clothing Company and the A&P grocery chain. Both of those chains depended on Black people as shoppers in their stores, but neither of those stores had any Black people serving as managers of a store or sitting on their board of directors. The national office of Operation Breadbasket had initiated a citywide boycott in Chicago in 1967. Three years later, we immediately called for an economic boycott of all their stores in the metropolitan New York City region.

On one occasion, we decided to hold a picket-line protest in front of A&P headquarters in Manhattan followed by a sit-in that extended after their closing hour. All who refused to leave were arrested for trespassing and taken to a New York City jail. Much to my surprise and great honor, I was placed in the same cell as Ralph David Abernathy, who succeeded Dr. King as president of SCLC, and who had come to lend his support to our effort. Not long after our release from jail the next day, A&P consented to many of our demands involving the hiring of more Black employees and some newly named Black store managers.[25] I write about these boycotts and the efforts to break the link between race and poverty in the United States in a forthcoming book, *God in the Ghetto: A Prophetic Word Revisited*, that discusses the ministry of Dr. Jones and Operation Breadbasket.[26] This is but one of many instances when the civil rights community in the United States extended its focus from race relations and social integration to the much more difficult task of creating economic opportunity and the eradication of poverty in America's Black communities.

It is essential that people remember that this was the focus of Dr. King during the last year of his life. He discussed poverty as part of what he called a tri-partite system of evils: racism, poverty, and militarism. Three things come immediately to mind. First, a large reason for his opposition to the Vietnam War was because he believed that the money being spent on war and war production was draining money away from the War on Poverty that President Lyndon B. Johnson had declared in 1965. King addressed this in his famous speech, "A Time to Break Silence," delivered at Riverside Church in

New York City on April 4, 1967 (one year to the date and almost to the hour of when he was assassinated). He said:

> I knew that America would never invest the necessary funds or energies in rehabilitation of its poor so long as adventures like Vietnam continued to draw men and skills and money like some demonic destructive suction tube. So, I was increasingly compelled to see the war as an enemy of the poor and to attack it as such . . . We were taking the Black young men who had been crippled by our society and sending them eight thousand miles away to guarantee liberties in Southeast Asia which they had not found in southwest Georgia and East Harlem [27]

Here was the intersection of race and poverty in all of its horror and cruelty for the world to see.

The second thing King focused on was to call attention to the poverty that was gripping millions of people across the country through the planning in 1967 for would be called the Poor People's Campaign. The plan was to bring thousands of poor people from across the country to set up a tent city on the National Mall in Washington, DC, and remain there until the Congress passed and President Johnson signed new measures to address poverty among Blacks in the rural South and the urban ghettos of the North, among poor whites living in Appalachia, and among Native Americans living on reservations in the Southwest. In calling for this protest of economic conditions, King said, "The dispossessed of this nation—the poor, both white and Negro—live in a cruelly unjust society. They must organize a revolution against that injustice, not against the lives of the persons who are their fellow citizens, but against the structures through which the society is refusing to take means which have been called for [the War on Poverty], and which are at hand, to lift the load of poverty."[28]

It should be noted that the spirit of the Poor People's Campaign has been revived fifty years later by William Barber and others who are making the case that the issue of poverty in America remains as present and pressing as ever.[29] This group conducted its own Poor People's March on Washington (made largely virtual due to COVID-19) on June 20, 2020. A combination of civil rights groups convened by Al Sharpton and Martin Luther King III held an actual March on Washington on August 28, 2020.[30]

There was a third action taken by King that signaled his concern about poverty. It was King's decision to step away from the planning of the Poor People's Campaign to support sanitation workers in Memphis, Tennessee, who had gone out on strike to seek better wages and safer working conditions. The issue in Memphis was not integrating lunch counters or amusement parks or public-school classrooms. The issue was economic justice and the fight against poverty. In his second-most famous speech, delivered at Mason Temple in Memphis on the evening of April 3, 1968, he said, "I've been to the mountaintop and I've seen the promised land." However, before he said that, he took time to commend some of the clergy in Memphis who had joined him on the picket line and in the protest marches: "It's alright to talk about long white robes over yonder in all of its symbolism. But ultimately people want some suits and dresses and shoes to wear down here. It's alright to talk about streets flowing with milk and honey, but God commanded us to be concerned about the slums down here, and his children who can't eat three square meals a day . . . This is what we have to do."[31]

In that same speech, King called for boycotts of such notable companies as Coca-Cola, Seal Test Ice Cream and Milk, and Wonder Bread. He also encouraged the people of Memphis to withdraw their money from white-owned banks and deposit their money in the Black-owned Tri-State Bank.[32] This focus on issues of poverty and economic justice is not the image of Martin Luther King Jr. America has chosen to celebrate. There is an obvious preference for the King of racial integration over the King who calls for eliminating wealth disparity in the United States. In *The Radical King,* Cornel West reminds us of the fact that King's legacy included a commitment to the elimination of poverty through radical actions. On the matter of poverty, King said in 1966, "There must be a better distribution of wealth, and maybe America must move toward a democratic socialism."[33] King was advocating democratic socialism fifty years before Senator Bernie Sanders of Vermont introduced that term into American presidential politics.

These words from both Du Bois and King point to the systemic and systematic oppression grounded in racism that locked generations of African Americans into nearly inescapable poverty. The racism condemned by Black theology and the poverty condemned by Latin American liberation theology were simultaneously experienced by a great many African Americans beginning in the days of slavery in the seventeenth century, when Black bodies were worked without wages to increase the wealth of white slave owners.

It is essential that people committed to the work of setting the captives free should realize that racism is not the only captor with which people are struggling. Poverty in the forms earlier described by Leonardo Boff, Clodovis Boff, and Gustavo Gutiérrez in Latin America are equally urgent and destructive forces affecting African Americans in the United States. That is why our discussion here must move from James Cone and Black theology that emerged in 1969, and from the various theologians that began shifting the focus to what became more generally known as liberation theology with a clear focus on class, economics, poverty, and wealth disparity in this country and around the world. We must link those two theologies together as we talk about letting the oppressed go free.

Let me return to the point raised by Gates about the rise of a Black middle class and a Black upper middle class. There is a problem that needs to be addressed when economic security for some African Americans is being greatly improved, while for many others it is gotten consistently worse. Gates acknowledges this point as well when he asked this question in a 1998 PBS program called "The Two Nations of Black America": "How have we reached this point, where we have both the largest Black middle class and the largest Black underclass in our history?"[34] More than twenty years later things have not improved. Thus, Gates can say, "Usually when we're talking about equality we're talking about the Black community vs. the white community. But I'm very concerned about the inequality within the African community."[35]

In the foreword to *Preaching to the Black Middle Class*, Dr. Gardner C. Taylor wrote, "This internal chasm within Black life, with its potential for suspicion and mutual enmity, may compound the evil that the Kerner Commission pointed out in 1968 as two America's, one white, one Black, separate and unequal."[36] The need at this point in history is for people to care as much about poverty as they have cared about racism, whether they are directly impacted by poverty or not. For the sake of those who have not and cannot easily escape the grip of poverty with its power to stifle dreams and limit horizons, those of us who occupy a place of economic security must use every ounce of passion we invested in our struggle against racism to eliminate the systematic policies and the private conduct that results in poverty in this country and around the world. If Black theology has done its proper work in one's life, it encourages us to work to set all the captives free, including the ones held in the captivity that is poverty.

The Faces and Forms of Poverty in the United States

I want to continue my discussion on the intersection of race and poverty in the context of my own ministry, which is in multiple urban settings in the United States over the last fifty years. I have lived my life in Chicago, Illinois; Cleveland, Ohio; Rochester, New York; and in a suburb just five minutes from Newark, New Jersey. What I have discovered about poverty is that it should be described under three separate though interrelated headings. First, there is poverty as experienced by the working poor, which involves people who have part-time employment or even multiple jobs but do not earn enough to climb out of poverty and still need some sort of government assistance. Part of their dilemma is if they earn even one dollar more than the federal guidelines that define poverty, they lose all the federal benefits such as child-care subsidies and food stamps (otherwise known as SNAP, Supplemental Nutrition Assistance Program). Thus, there is a built-in disincentive for people who earn more than the federal guidelines allow but less than they need to be self-sufficient. The issue of poverty for the working poor involves any individual living in the United States whose annual income is $12,760 or less, or any family of four living on an annual income of $26,200 or less.[37]

The second way to think about people living in poverty involves the issue of extreme poverty, which means persons who subsist on one-half of the federal guidelines for what constitutes living in poverty in the United States. That means any person who is forced to live on $12,000 annually for a family of four, which equates to a daily income of $1.90 per person.[38] According to the National Poverty Center, 1.65 million American households are living in extreme poverty, and these households include 3.5 million children.[39]

Forty-six percent of all African American families living below the federal poverty level are living in extreme poverty.[40] According to a recently released report on poverty in the United States, Rochester, New York, where I lived from 2011 to 2019, has the highest rate of childhood poverty of all comparably sized cities (250,000) in the country with a rate of 50.1 percent. It also has the second highest rate of poverty among individuals and families in the country, with some neighborhoods that have 60 percent of the population living below the poverty level.[41] Yet, at the same time that in Rochester, as in every other urban center in the United States, there are African Americans who enjoy great financial security. These realities co-exist side by side.

The third issue involves concentrated poverty. This issue points to housing policies and to the refusal of certain towns and neighborhoods to allow for the construction of low-income housing within their communities. Often referred to as NIMBY or "not in my back yard," it is the notion that housing should be made available for low-income persons and families, but many persons do not want such housing to be constructed anywhere near where they live. This results in people who do live in poverty being clustered together in densely populated, demographically similar neighborhoods. Those neighborhoods are islands of despair cut off from quality public education, health care facilities, public transit connections for work and/ or shopping, restaurants, and places of entertainment except for fast food outlets and an abundance of liquor stores.

Living in poverty is hard enough. Being ghettoized in places that offer few if any visible opportunities or paths to escape that poverty or any role models or examples of persons who have managed to escape the grip of poverty is even worse. This was the experience for my family and thousands of others when I was growing up in Chicago in the 1950 and 1960s. Chicago was designed to limit the access that African American families could have to certain neighborhoods in the city. This was the premise of the popular play made into a movie, *A Raisin in the Sun*, by Lorraine Hansberry.

Even when a Black family reached a point where they could afford to buy a home in a largely white section of the city, that neighborhood would soon become an all-Black community as white families moved out in something that came to be known as "white flight." My own family was able to move to one of those largely white neighborhoods called Foster Park in 1966, during my first year in college. However, by the time I graduated from college in 1970, Foster Park was nearly an all-Black community. Chicago was and is one of the richest cities in the world in terms of its industrial base, its financial district, its corporate headquarters, its luxurious lakefront properties, and its sports and theater franchises. Yet, my hometown is home to great poverty, extreme poverty, and concentrated poverty.

The issue being addressed here is not simply that of poverty as a reality unto itself. Rather, it is poverty existing in proximity to great prosperity that makes the reality of poverty more glaring. Returning to the years of 2011 to 2019, when I lived in Rochester, New York, an issue of the *City* newspaper in Rochester carried two stories that set these two realities in sharp contrast. The first story focused on the public school system. It noted that "Rochester's child poverty rate is among the worst in the nation. And this is a highly segregated community, racially and economically. Growing research indicates that living in high-poverty neighborhoods has a debilitating effect on many residents. Poverty and isolation can snuff out hope and breed violence, and all this causes real documentable trauma in children."[42]

In that same issue, another story appeared that pointed directly to the wealth disparity that grips this and other regions of the country. The headline read, "High-Class Dog Hotel Planned for Penfield."[43] In a suburban community less than five miles from the poverty that grips Rochester there will soon be a "high-end" dog hotel. Each dog will get its own room, and every room will be equipped with flat panel televisions. The hotel will also be equipped with a pool, a playroom, a training area, and a grooming salon. These so-called lux canine accommodations already exist in Chicago and Los Angeles.[44] Thus, as with the nation as a whole, great poverty and great wealth that takes the form of conspicuous consumption reside within the shadow of one another. The dogs of the wealthy will be living at a level that cannot be approached by the children of the poor.

In truth, the problem of income inequality and the devastating effects of poverty on the human spirit and on our society are not new in the United States. On November 22, 1787, James Madison, one of the founders of this republic, wrote, "The most common and durable source of factions has been the various and unequal distribution of property. Those who hold and those who are without property have ever formed distinct interests in society."[45]

The irony in this statement from my perspective as a member of the African American community is that my ancestors were part of neither faction (those who own property and those who do not). Our ancestors were listed as among the property that generated wealth for others. That fact was made explicit in the United States Constitution, Article 1, section 1, clause 3, stating that "representatives and direct taxes shall be apportioned among the several states which may be included within this union, according to their respective numbers, which shall be determined by adding to the whole number of free persons, including those bound to service for a term of years, and excluding Indians not taxed, three fifths of all other persons."

It continues to be the case that the legacy of slavery that was enshrined in the Constitution and the offshoots of slavery, which were sharecropping, legalized segregation, the denial of voting rights, and the relentless exposure to terrorist attacks from the Ku Klux Klan and other white supremacist groups and individuals has had an incalculable impact on the persistent levels of poverty that affect African American communities to this day.

The reasons for poverty in America take many forms. Chief among them may be the increasing concentration of wealth and political influence in the hands of fewer and fewer people. The total compensation of CEOs in many US corporations is more than two hundred times the salary paid to their workers, and some corporations pay their CEOs at a rate of one thousand times their median worker's salary.[46] A recent study by the Harvard Business School revealed that it takes a typical worker at Starbucks or McDonald's more than six months to earn what each company's CEO earns in a single hour.[47]

Those persons and the banks and corporations they control decide what factories are closed, what jobs are outsourced, what wages will be paid to workers, what levels of health care, maternal leave, sick days, and working schedules will be provided, and at what cost to their workers. They decide what environmental regulations will be observed or circumvented. They decide what use or abuse of legal and illegal immigrant labor will be employed and at what wage level, usually offering wages and working conditions that lock many native-born American citizens out of many sectors of the labor market. As I wrote in *Just Preaching* in 2003:

> Poverty is a grinding and degrading way of life that drains the hopes and breaks the spirits of many of those within its grasp. Poverty takes the form of an inadequate diet that frequently results in sickness. That sickness is complicated by an absence of available and affordable health care. The best cure for poverty is a job. However, the poor find it difficult to secure employment, because so many employers are moving their operations out of the cities where the poor are clustered. They then open new factories or offices in outer-ring suburbs that are not served by public transportation. [48]

Contrast the plight of corporate CEOs with that of the so-called working poor. "This would include migrant workers, temporary employees, and non-unionized workers with no job security or collective bargaining strength. Sadly, many of the working poor are single females who are heads of households. Thus, the hardships of poverty affect not only them but their young children as well."[49] Having been raised in such a household after my father abandoned our family when I was ten years old, I know this face of poverty all too well. I described it in an article I wrote for *The African American Pulpit* in 2001:

> They lead the most anxious of lives of any persons in America. They work hard but never get ahead. They usually work more than one job just to make ends meet. They fear sickness, first because they have no medical insurance to cover the cost of prescription drugs and medical procedures, and secondly because if they miss too many days from work, they will lose one or more of their jobs. Why do people have to live under such conditions in the richest country in the history of the world?[50]

Marian Wright Edelman, president of the Children's Defense Fund in Washington, DC, wrote this about the facts of poverty in the United States:

> The United States ranks second out of 35 developed countries on the scale of what economists call relative child poverty, with 23% of its children living in poverty. Only Romania with an economy 1% the size of the US ranked higher in child poverty. It is a shameful reminder that, as economist Sheldon Danzinger put it, among rich countries the US is exceptional. We are exceptional in our tolerance for child poverty.[51]

Here is the dilemma involving poverty in the United States. There is an unconscionable concentration of wealth in the hands of a small number of persons relative to the national population. There is "exceptional tolerance" for poverty even as it affects the lives of children across the country. Add to these factors the role of America's original sin, which is racism, and the problem of poverty, extreme poverty, and concentrated poverty in the African American community comes more clearly into focus. The words of Gutiérrez are true and compelling: "Christians cannot forgo their responsibility to say a prophetic word about unjust economic conditions."[52] Gutiérrez further reminds us, "All theological inquiry is contextual. Our context today is characterized by a glaring disparity between the rich and the poor. No serious Christian can quietly ignore this situation. It is no longer possible for someone to say 'Well, I didn't know about the suffering of the poor.' Poverty has a visibility today that it did not have in the past. The faces of the poor must now be confronted."[53]

No amount of religiosity can ever be an acceptable alternative to working to end poverty in our world. On more than a few occasions, I have been reminded of the words of Amos, who said, "Alas for those who lie on beds of ivory, and lounge on their couches, and eat lambs from the flock, and calves from the stall; . . . but are not grieved over the ruin of Joseph!" (Amos 6:4,6). When I hear churches and pastors suggesting that the worship of God is their primary interest, with no interest being expressed or exhibited in the issues of poverty and human suffering that is apparent and visible all around them, another passage from Amos comes to mind that needs to be employed by churches on an ongoing basis:

> I hate, I despise your festivals,
>   and I take no delight in your solemn assemblies.
> Even though you offer me your burnt offerings and grain offerings,
>   I will not accept them;
> and the offerings of well-being of your fatted animals
>   I will not look upon.
> Take away from me the noise of your songs;
>   I will not listen to the melody of your harps.
> But let justice roll down like waters,
>   and righteousness like an ever-flowing stream. (Amos 5:21-24)

This is the work of liberation theology. This is what is required in order to let the oppressed go free.

NOTES

1. Aldon D. Morris, *The Origins of the Civil Rights Movement: Black Communities Organizing for Change* (New York: The Free Press, 1984).

2. Ibid.

3. Maggie Astor, "What to Know About the Tulsa Greenwood Massacre," TheNewYorkTimes.com, July 17, 2020.

4. Ibid.

5. Ibid.

6. Ibid.

7. Ibid.

8. Ibid.

9. Ibid.

10. Marvin A. McMickle, *Preaching to the Black Middle Class: Words of Challenge, Words of Hope* (Valley Forge, PA: Judson Press, 2000), 19.

11. Olivia B. Waxman, "Q+A with Henry Louis Gates Jr.," *Time*, March 2-9, 2020, 88.

12. Abby Goodnough, "Harvard Professor Jailed; Officer Is Accused of Bias," TheNewYorkTimes.com, July 20, 2009.

13. Glenn Kessler, Salvador Rizzo, and Meg Kelly, "President Trump Has Made More Than 20,000 False or Misleading Claims," Washington Post.com, July 13, 2020.

14. Eddie Glaude Jr., *Begin Again: James Baldwin's America and Its Urgent Lessons for Our Own* (New York: Crown Books, 2020), 202, 211.

15. W. E. B. Du Bois, *The Souls of Black Folk*, ed. David Blight and Robert Williams (Boston: Bedford Books, 1997), 45.

16. David Levering Lewis, *W. E. B. Du Bois: The Fight for Equality and the American Century, 1919–1963* (New York: Henry Holt, 2000), 203.

17. Isabel Wilkerson, *Caste: The Origins of Our Discontents* (New York: Random House, 2020), 184–85

18. Ibid., 185.

19. Ibid., 186.

20. Ibid., 185.

21. Martin Luther King Jr., *Where Do We Go from Here: Chaos or Community* (New York: Bantam, 1967), 137.

22. Ibid.

23. James M. Washington, ed., *Testament of Hope: The Essential Writings of Martin Luther King Jr.* (New York: Harper & Row, 1986), 217.

24. *Report of the National Advisory Commission on Civil Disorders* (New York: Bantam, 1968), 1.

25. Martin Deppe, *Operation Breadbasket: An Untold Story of Civil Rights in Chicago: 1968–1971* (Athens: University of Georgia Press, 1971), 108.

26. Marvin A. McMickle in *God in the Ghetto: A Prophetic Word Revisited* by William Augustus Jones Jr.; edited by Jennifer Jones Austin (Valley Forge, PA: Judson Press, 2021).

27. James Melvin Washington, ed., *A Testament of Hope: The Essential Writings of Martin Luther King Jr.* (San Francisco: Harper & Row, 1968), 232–33.

28. Martin Luther King Jr., *The Trumpet of Conscience* (New York: Harper & Row, 1967), 59–60.

29. Poorpeoplescampaign.org, June 20, 2020.

30. Ibid.

31. Washington, 282.

32. Ibid., 283.

33. Cornel West, *The Radical King* (Boston: Beacon Press, 2015), ix.

34. McMickle, *Preaching to the Black Middle Class*, xi.

35. Waxman, 88.

36. McMickle, *Preaching to the Black Middle Class*, vii.

37. Federal Poverty Level Guidelines, obamacarefacts.com.

38. Poverty Facts and Figures, www.globalincome.org.

39. "Extreme Poverty on the Rise in the United States," National Low-Income Housing Coalition Resource Library, nlihc.org, May 17, 2013, 1.

40. Ibid.

41. "Rochester-Monroe Anti-Poverty Initiative: Progress Report" (Rochester, NY: The United Way, 2015), 7.

42. Mary Anna Towler, "Forcing Urbanski Out Won't Help City Students," *City*, November 25-December 1, 2015, 3.

43. "High-Class Dog Hotel Planned for Penfield," *City*, November 25-December 1, 2015, 4.

44. Ibid.

45. James Madison, "The Federalist Papers #10," thefederalistpapers .org, 2.

46. Jenny Che, "Here's How Outrageous the Pay Gap between CEOs and Workers Is," TheHuffingtonPost.com, August 27, 2015, 1.

47. Robert Ferdman, "The Wage Gap between CEOs and Their Workers Is Much Worse Than You Think," WashingtonPost.com, September 25, 2014, 1.

48. Marvin McMickle, "Preaching in the Face of Economic Injustice," in *Just Preaching: Prophetic Voices for Economic Justice*, ed. Andre Resner (St. Louis, MO: Chalice Press, 2003), 4–5.

49. Ibid., 5.

50. Marvin A. McMickle, "The Prophet Amos as a Model for Preaching on Issues of Social Justice," *The African American Pulpit* (Spring 2001): 6–10.

51. Marian Wright Edelman, "Child Watch Column," Children's Defense Fund, childrensdefense.org, June 8, 2012.

52. Gustavo Gutiérrez, *A Theology of Liberation* (Maryknoll, NY: Orbis Books, 1971), 1.

53. Daniel Hartnett, "Remembering the Poor: An Interview with Gustavo Gutiérrez," *America: The Jesuit Review*, February 3, 2003.

CHAPTER 5

Feminist Theology and the Voices of Women in the Church

In 1984, my mother was selected to serve on the search committee for a new pastor for her local church in Chicago. Park Manor Christian Church of the Disciples of Christ denomination had always seemed to me to be an enlightened and progressive congregation with a long history of seminary-trained pastors. They had a Junior Church and a Teen Church, which was where I and dozens of my peers were nurtured in the Christian faith from the time my family joined there in 1958 until I went off to seminary in 1970.

At the first meeting of the search committee, a discussion was had about the criteria that would be used in selecting the next pastor. Someone raised the question of whether it was time for the church to at least consider a woman for the position. The feminist movement was well underway. Women were serving in various leadership positions in the local church and within the national headquarters as well. In 1972, Congresswoman Shirley Chisholm of New York had run as a candidate for the Democratic Party nomination to be president of the United States. In 1984, Congresswoman Geraldine Ferraro was nominated as the Democratic Party candidate to be vice president of the United States. Even closer to home, Jane Byrne had served as mayor of Chicago from 1979 to 1983. Surely it was not an outlandish notion that a woman would be invited to apply for the position of senior pastor in the church where I was raised and where my mother was on the search committee.

At some point in the process, I asked her how the search for the next pastor was going and whether any women were being considered. In a tone that was close to a biblical lament, she informed me of something that at least one member of the committee had said about women in the ministry: "I would rather have an unqualified man than the most qualified woman." I do not know the degree to which that comment reflected the views of others on that search committee, but it came as a shock to her ears—and later to mine as well.

As is the case in most African American congregations, women were the largest percentage of the membership of that church. Their investment of tithes, time, and talent was the essential glue that held that congregation together. Within that church were women who were schoolteachers and administrators. There were small business owners and city and federal government employees. Women with college and graduate degrees were common in that church. Women served on the governing boards of the church, and over the years many women in that church had served on national committees and boards of the denomination. Women were serving in leadership in that church in the 1960s, and yet there remained within that church a sentiment that was voiced on the search committee for a new pastor: "I would rather have an unqualified man than the most qualified woman."

The reason my mother and I were so surprised by this viewpoint was because before we joined that church in 1958 our family attended Cosmopolitan Community Church on Wabash Avenue in Chicago, where the pastor was the Rev. Mary G. Evans. For the first ten years of my life, the only preaching voice I heard was a woman's voice. Pastor Evans would later be included in an anthology on women preachers entitled *Daughters of Thunder*.[1] She received a bachelor of divinity degree from Payne Theological Seminary in 1911. By 1943 she had earned master of science degrees from Columbia University in psychology and sociology; and she did post-graduate work at the University of Chicago and Butler University. Betty Collier-Thomas notes:

> Between 1924 and 1966, she successfully pastored several churches, including the St. John AME Church in Indianapolis and the Cosmopolitan Community Church in Chicago which had a membership of eight hundred in 1966 . . . Evans served as pastor of the

Cosmopolitan Community Church for thirty-five years. Although Evans received no salary, by 1954 the church presented her with a "love offering" of $10,000 a year, more perhaps than any Black minister in Chicago.[2]

Having a woman as my pastor and hearing a woman preach every Sunday in my local church was the spiritual environment into which I was born. It was the faith community in which I was introduced to the name of Jesus. There has never been a day in my life from birth until this present moment at the age of seventy-one that I ever questioned whether a woman could or should be in the Christian ministry. How could I, when the first person I ever heard preach the gospel was a woman, Mary G. Evans, "a daughter of thunder"? It was with this life experience in mind that my mother and I were so shocked to hear someone say in the early 1980s, "I would rather have an unqualified man than the most qualified woman." That meant that he would not have wanted Mary G. Evans as his pastor, and to me that was incomprehensible.

The year 1984 was not the first time I heard of men suggesting that women should not be in the ministry. That debate was well underway in New York City when I arrived at Union Theological Seminary in the fall of 1970. While it was the rise of Black theology and the work of James Cone that led me to attend Union, it was impossible at that school not to be drawn into the rise of feminist theology as well. Beverly Wildung Harrison was also on that faculty, and she was an early voice in the formation of feminist theology and Christian feminist ethics.[3] As was true of the issue of racism and prejudice based upon ethnicity, both church and society were equally guilty of the practice of sexism and of prejudice based solely upon gender.

Setting Free the Captives of Sexism and Gender Bias

While terms like "Black theology," "Black power," and "Black is beautiful" were working their way into the American lexicon, there was a parallel struggle going on about inclusive language in the church. Women students were pushing hard to end references to God in male-only terms like "Father" or "him" or even the "kingdom of God." This call to pay attention to inclusive language called for a reconsideration of every aspect of Christian worship from church hymns, to public prayers, responsive readings, the ways in which classroom lectures were presented, to chapel service sermons that were being preached in James Chapel.

I clearly recall those instances when some female students walked out of chapel services when male students refused to use inclusive language. I recall with equal clarity the times when some male students walked out of chapel when God was referred to as "God our Mother and Father" or as "the heavenly parent." I remember male students wondering why female students were even allowed to enroll in classes at Union, and why male students had to consider such issues as inclusive language and feminist readings of Scripture. This may sound as old-fashioned in 2020 as an episode of *Lassie* or *Gunsmoke* or *I Love Lucy*. Rest assured, however, that in the early 1970s at the liberal or progressive bastion of Union Theological Seminary in New York City, the rise of feminist theology met with at least as much resistance and even rejection by some students as the rise of Black theology and Latin American liberation theology.

I cannot say, and I will not imply, that such resistance reached into the faculty and/or the administration of the school. I was never privy to any faculty discussions about feminist theology to the same degree that I heard Union faculty openly challenging and critiquing Black theology. To their credit, however, that faculty voted in 1972 to grant tenure to James Cone, who gave voice to Black theology, and in 1980 to Beverly Wildung Harrison. As Cone observed, "Union was a liberal school, well-known for supporting outrageous, independent-thinking professors."[4] That being said, disagreements within the student body over the legitimacy of both Black theology and feminist theology were undeniable.

There were times at Union when it seemed as if persons felt the need to identify which of those two forms of discrimination was the more urgent: the battle against racism in the United States or the battle against sexism in countries all around the world. Most Black male students were insistent that racism was the issue that demanded the nation's attention and the attention of the Union itself.

At the same time, a substantial number of female students felt strongly, in keeping with the rise of feminism under Gloria Steinem and Betty Friedan, that the time had come to assert equal rights for women in all aspects of American society. Beyond feminism as a social construct, the 1970s also saw the rise of feminist theology driven in large part by the work of Rosemary Radford Reuther, Letty Russell, Phyllis Trible, and others.[5] If Black theology emerged as a faith-based response to the nation's history of racism and the practices of white supremacy, feminist theology emerged as a faith-based response to the equally evil legacy of sexism and male domination in the church and in society.

Christine M. Smith offers this definition of the forms and functions of sexism when she says:

> Sexism involves the systematic denial, exploitation, and oppression of women. As the hierarchical gender structuring of personal and social reality, sexism assures and secures male domination . . . Male dominance is dependent on men exercising their control and power over women with whatever means necessary. Violence often becomes the means within which men create, maintain, and expand their male dominance.[6]

Smith contends that at the heart of sexism is misogyny, or "the hatred of women as manifested in various forms of violence by men against women." She notes, "Rape, incest, and woman battering are forms of sexual violence. All forms of violence against women, all forms of sexual violence, serve to reinforce male domination and gender hierarchy. Male supremacy demands control and fear for its maintenance."[7] Sexism takes many forms. It is the sexual violence referenced by Smith. It is the devaluing of the lives and worth of women in society. It is the monopolizing of power by men in church and society that allows male dominance to continue.

Christine A. Smith of Covenant Baptist Church in Wickliffe, Ohio, calls sexism in the ongoing life of the church "the stained glass ceiling."[8] She means by that the invisible but often impenetrable limits that are subtly and silently imposed upon female clergy pursuing careers in ministry. This stained-glass ceiling takes many forms. Among the most common are differences in salary between men and women performing the same functions. It shows up in invitations to women to serve as one of several staff ministers with responsibility limited to a single area of church life such as youth ministry, Bible study, or some outreach activities.

The stained-glass ceiling appears when women are offered pastoral assignments that many men may have already passed up because the men deemed those churches either to be too small, or where the church has undergone severe membership decline and is near financial death and a woman is seemingly called to preside over its final days.

The stained-glass ceiling is most often shattered in one of two ways. Option one is to change denominations and serve a largely white congregation or serve a Black congregation that belongs to a predominantly white national church body. Option two is to organize their own church and grow a congregation from the ground up. What has been and continues to be less available to women is the steady, upward mobility from a smaller to a larger congregation that is the normal career path for most male clergy.

Smith reflects on the limited opportunities for women in ministry when she states:

> Contrary to some reports, female clergy have not yet arrived. While a few denominations such as United Methodists, the Presbyterian Church (USA), United Church of Christ, Disciples of Christ, and American Baptist Churches USA have accepted and called women to serve as senior pastors, many qualified and well-equipped sisters still struggle to have their gifts of preaching and pastoring recognized. Among those who have become senior pastors, remnants of the stained-glass ceiling persist.[9]

What the Bible Says about Women

Differing Ways of Reading Scripture

One of the tools used by opponents of women in ministry has been the interpretation of selected biblical texts. One of the things women have discovered in their study of the Bible has been the number of texts in the Bible that seem to normalize or rationalize physical and even sexual abuse of women. Phyllis Trible, an Old Testament scholar, refers to such texts as "texts of terror." She uses that term to describe the experiences of various women found throughout the biblical narrative. Those texts are almost always used out of context and without regard for accurate interpretation and contemporary application.

Trible speaks about three approaches to the study of the Bible as a means of moving the church away for a sexist reading of Scripture. She describes those three approaches as follows:

> One approach documents the case against women. It cites and evaluates long neglected data that show the inferiority, subordination, and abuse of the female in ancient Israel and the early church. By contrast, a second approach discerns within the Bible critiques of patriarchy. It upholds forgotten texts and reinterprets familiar ones to shape a remnant theology that challenges the sexism of scripture. Yet a third approach incorporates the other two. It recounts tales of terror **in memoriam** to offer sympathetic readings of abused women.[10]

This issue of the use of Scripture as a way to define and limit the role and status of women in and outside the church is also discussed by Wilda Gafney in *Womanist Midrash*.[11] She credits the term "womanist midrash" to Mark Brummitt, my former colleague at Colgate Rochester Crozer Divinity School. According to Gafney:

> Womanist midrash is a set of interpretive practices, including translation, exegesis, and biblical interpretations, that attends to marginalized characters in biblical narratives in biblical narratives, especially women and girls, intentionally including and centering on non-Israelites people and enslaved persons. Womanist midrash listens to and for their voices in and through the Hebrew Bible, while acknowledging that often the text does not speak, or even intend to speak, to or for them, let alone hear them.[12]

Cultural Contexts

In the context in which Paul spoke and wrote in first-century Palestine, women were not considered independent citizens of the country. Their status was always in relation to some male member of their family, such as a husband, brother, father, son, or uncle. Consider the feeding of the five thousand in Matthew 14:13-21. The text says that Jesus fed "about five thousand men, besides women and children." Even the touching scene on the cross in John 19:26-27, where Jesus assigns care of his mother to the apostle John, was a reflection of the status of women in first-century Palestine. The text says, "From that time on, this disciple took her into his home." (NIV) All of this was a continuation of the principle of the kinsman redeemer at work in the Book of Ruth, where Boaz took Ruth into his house after the death of her husband (Ruth 4:8-12). Ruth had no standing on her own in that society.

One of the reasons the laws of the Old Testament made a point of condemning the abuse or exploitation of women, orphans, and strangers was because all such persons were without status, without protection, and without personal resources in the patriarchal world of ancient Israel (Deuteronomy 10:18; James 1:27). It was a patriarchal reading of Scripture that Jesus had to correct in John 8:3-5 when the teachers of the law brought to Jesus a woman who was caught in adultery. They wanted her to be stoned in accordance with Mosaic law. The problem was that Mosaic law required the man and the woman both to be stoned (Leviticus 20:10). I imagine that when Jesus knelt down to write something in the ground, what he wrote was a question to that self-righteous and bloodthirsty mob: "Where is the man who must have also been caught in that same act of adultery?"

Women had no role in any aspect of social, political, or religious life in ancient Israel. The Roman Catholic Church makes the argument that women cannot be priests in the twenty-first-century church because no woman served as one of the twelve apostles of Jesus. How could such a thing have been possible in Israel in the first century? This is an absurd argument based upon a faulty first premise. Women could not have been disciples of Jesus because women were not at liberty to leave their homes and travel around the countryside. More importantly, they would not have been taken seriously when they attempted to speak in the name of Jesus.

One cannot quote 1 Corinthians 14 and 1 Timothy 2 without considering the cultural differences that separate the first-century world from the twenty-first-century world. Today, women do not need a kinsman redeemer if their husband dies. In keeping with the story of Ruth, nobody hands over a shoe as a means of transferring property from one person to another. And with the use of the word "property" in Ruth 4:7, there is yet another indicator of the status of Ruth: she was property and not a person. By comparison, the US Constitution defined African American slaves as 3/5ths of a person for purposes of the taxation and representation of white men. That 3/5ths designation, along with the exclusion of all citizenship rights, made Black people in America into chattel or personal property. How is it that men who rebelled against being viewed as property in the eyes of white men can so easily seek to use biblical texts that relegate women to that same status? This is bad exegesis.

I recall with frightening clarity a meeting in 1984 of the New Jersey Baptist Convention meeting in Paterson, New Jersey, when the topic of women in ministry was introduced by the ordination committee of which I was a member. After the business session, during which a heated discussion was held about the ordination of women, we moved into the evening worship service. The preacher for that service was still stirred up about the idea of women in ministry, and he wanted to make it clear how he felt about the matter. So he turned to his wife, who was seated on the front row of the pews, and said to her that if she ever decided to say that God had called her to the ministry, their next stop would be divorce court. That comment was matched in its intolerance only by the words of a New Jersey pastor who said, "The only place for a homosexual in his church is on the mourner's bench" (the place for spiritual confession and conversion, for those unfamiliar with that term).

What the Bible Says about Women in Ministry

At the center of the church's resistance to women in leadership roles in ministry are two biblical passages from Paul that are employed in the twenty-first century as though time has stood still so far as the role and status of women in society is concerned. In 1 Corinthians 14:34-35, Paul states that "women should remain silent in the churches. They are not allowed to speak" (NIV). In 1 Timothy 2:11-12, Paul says, "A woman should learn in quietness and full submission.

I do not permit a woman to teach" (NIV) or to have authority over a man; she must be silent" (NRSV).

As Marilyn Parker Jeffries notes as a contributor to Christine A. Smith's book, the church today is handicapped and hindered by what can only be called bad exegesis from people who use Scripture to maintain and preserve their privilege. Jeffries says:

> Out of the pulpits we have had poor exegesis. That has been the major barrier that has prevented women from assuming their rightful place in the kingdom. I had to wrestle when I heard God call me, because I'd never been taught it was right for women to preach. I experienced a dual wrestling match between the call to preach (which was mind-boggling in itself) and what that meant for me as a woman, something that I'd never seen before. That struggle precipitated the development of a panic disorder within me. I was a wreck.[13]

I had the privilege of writing the foreword for Smith's book. In it, I sought to reinforce the point made by Smith and Jeffries:

> There is no doubt [. . . ,] given the patriarchal nature of the era in which the Bible was written, that women would be excluded from many, if not most leadership roles. However, we have already moved beyond many of the cultural practices that were in force thousands of years ago. We do not observe kosher diets or sacrifice animals in worship. We do not stone disrespectful children or exclude from worship persons with physical disabilities. Biblical interpretation done responsibly allows us to recognize that some parts of the Bible were the products of their own time, but were not necessarily meant to be enforced for all time.[14]

In the twenty-first century, when women are serving in every imaginable role and are exercising great responsibility in business, government, education, the armed forces, as first responders, and as physicians and surgeons, there is still debate about whether women can or should serve in pastoral ministry. Are we really prepared to say that women can protect our country as soldiers and sailors, take care of our bodies as doctors and nurses, safeguard our financial well-being as accountants and bankers, and legislate our national affairs as governors and members of Congress, but they cannot be allowed to minister to our souls through word and sacrament? Did all male clergy vote for Donald Trump in 2016? If not, did they cast a vote for Hillary Clinton to be president of the United States? If so, are those male clergy who lean so heavily on 1 Corinthians 14:34ff. and 1 Timothy 2:11ff. prepared to say that they can accept a woman as the leader of the free world, but they cannot accept a woman as the leader of a local Baptist or Methodist church? At what point does the insanity of this position become so self-evident that all that can be concluded is that it is gender bias and not Scripture that stands in the way of so many women being allowed to exercise their gifts and follow their call into ministry?

Selective Use of Biblical Texts

This selective use of Scripture should not be an unfamiliar practice for any African American with enough awareness of the slave era to know that slaveowners and the preachers they allowed to address their slaves made expert use of selected and preferred biblical texts that reinforced the notion that slavery was ordained by God and that slaves should be content in their bondage and obedient to their masters. Howard Thurman tells the story from his childhood of reading the Bible to his grandmother, who had been a slave. He recalls that he was never allowed to read anything from Paul. When he asked her about that in later years, she said:

> During the days of slavery, the master's ministers would occasionally hold services for the slaves. Old man McGhee was so mean that he would not let a Negro minister preach to his slaves. Always the white minister used as his text something from Paul. At least three or four times a year he used as a text: "Slaves be obedient to them that are your masters . . . as unto Christ." Then he would go on to show how it was God's will that we were slaves and how, if we were good and happy slaves, God would bless us.[15]

Do the men who cling to the eternal and unchanging status of women based upon two Pauline texts also cling to this Pauline text from Ephesians 6:5 or a similar text in Colossians 3:22 that says,

"Slaves, obey your earthly masters in everything; and do it, not only when their eye is on you and to curry their favor, but with sincerity of heart and reverence for the Lord" (NIV)? Do the Black male preachers who use Paul to prohibit women in ministry also embrace 1 Peter 2:18, "Slaves, in reverent fear of God submit yourselves to your masters, not only to those who are good and considerate, but also to those who are harsh" (NIV)? What about Romans 13:1-5, which says, "Let everyone be subject to the governing authorities, for there is no authority except that which God has established . . . Therefore, it is necessary to submit to the authorities, not only because of possible punishment but also as a matter of conscience" (NIV)?

It is unimaginable that any Black male preacher would want to defend the principle of slavery reinforced in these passages. They would undoubtedly argue that times have changed and those passages are no longer in force since slavery has been legally ended in this country. How can times change when it involves slavery but remain the same when it involves gender bias and sexism? How can the same Bible set free the captives from racism while maintaining others in the captivity of gender discrimination?

I say with both deep sadness and regret that when it came to setting the captives free from racism and segregation, the African American church and many of its clergy were all on board, that same desire for liberation all but vanished when the issue turned to women in ministry. It was as if they wanted to slice away a portion of the words of Paul in Galatians 3:26-29, where he says, "You are all sons of God through faith in Jesus Christ, for all of you who were baptized into Christ have now clothed yourselves with Christ. There is neither Jew nor Greek, slave nor free, male or female, for you are all one in Christ Jesus. And if you belong to Christ, then you are Abraham's seed and heirs according to the promise." (BSB)

One of the things I have found most disturbing about the use of this text is the way some readers try to ignore, overlook, minimize, or rationalize away the reference to "neither male nor female." In this passage, Paul took direct aim at the three major forms of social distinction in first-century Jewish culture: ethnicity, class, and gender. Paul argues that while those distinctions might still hold firm in secular society, they have no place within the church and among those who believe in Christ. However, as Demetrius Williams argued in *An End to This Strife*, the Bible cannot be used to condemn racism yet cited to justify or support sexism. He insists that "African American churches can no longer advocate racial equality on biblical grounds and at the same time support sexism in the churches using the same Bible."[16] Echoing the language of Martin Luther King Jr., Williams asserts, "African American churches must have the courage to judge a person by the content of their character and abilities, especially in the church."[17]

Courage is the missing ingredient in the discussion about women in ministry; courageous women willing to put themselves forward as persons called by God to be ministers and preachers, and courageous male pastors and congregations willing to break ranks with their more conservative male colleagues and open their pulpits and their payrolls to women who have obvious gifts for ministry. Writing in a pamphlet sponsored by American Baptist Women in Ministry 2001, I used the term "moral conviction." In that short essay I said, "All that remains in the fight against gender discrimination is moral conviction and personal courage to do what one believes to be right, whether or not other persons or other congregations do the same. It is undoubtedly true that discrimination in all its ugly forms continues to exist, because people who know better are still afraid to break away from the status quo and behave differently than their peers."[18]

Martin Luther King Jr. and Mary G. Evans

Returning to the debate I encountered when I arrived at Union in 1970, I was in a unique position. My commitment to Black theology and to the work to end racism was rooted in my experiences with Martin Luther King Jr. when he came to Chicago in 1966 to call attention to racism and segregation as national problems, and not something limited to life in the states of the former Confederacy and the Deep South. Between 1966 and 1970, I was a frequent attendee at Operation Breadbasket, which later evolved into Operation PUSH (People United to Save Humanity) hosted by Jesse Jackson every Saturday morning at various Chicago locations. When I could not attend, I could tune in on the radio. When I arrived in New York

City, I continued my involvement with Operation Breadbasket which met in Brooklyn, New York, at Bethany Baptist Church where William A. Jones Jr. was both pastor and chapter president.

However, while there were days when my soul simmered over the cruel and brutal forms of racism and segregation still at work in American society at that time (and to this present day), that did not prevent me from being open to hear the voices of those who felt captive to issue of sexism and gender discrimination. I was still treasuring in my heart the memory of Pastor Mary G. Evans, who lived until 1966. Even though my immediate family had moved away from the neighborhood where Cosmopolitan Community Church was located, we were regularly drawn back there for one program or another.

While I arrived at Union as a veteran of the civil rights movement, I came with a twenty-year history of exposure to a woman as a pastor and a spiritual force in Chicago. Thus, when Black theology and feminist theology were presented as part of my seminary curriculum and as topics of evening discussion groups in student lounges, I did not feel the need to take a side. I was all-in on both counts as a matter of life experience. I quickly discovered that not all my male classmates and very few New York City pastors were equally sympathetic to both Black theology and feminist theology. For many of them, race seemed to be a more urgent issue than gender, and Black theology and Black liberation seemed more important that gender equality and feminist theology.

Frederick Douglass and Susan B. Anthony

This tug of war between race and gender or between the liberation of Black people versus the liberation of women did not begin with Union Theological Seminary in the 1970s or with the search committee at my mother's church in the 1980s. It dates back at least one hundred years earlier with the tense exchanges between Frederick Douglass and Susan B. Anthony over the right to vote in the United States, and which group ought to be the first to enjoy that most basic form of American freedoms. As early as 1866, Douglass was arguing that when it came to voting, "Women should realize the dire urgency faced by Blacks—and wait."[19] This must have been a challenging time for suffragists in their relationship with Douglass, because many of them were also active in the abolitionist movement. That being the case, after an exchange of correspondence involving Douglass, Elizabeth Cady Stanton, and Susan B. Anthony, "an ugly and prolonged breach developed over whether women's suffrage and Black male suffrage coexisted on the same agenda."[20] Things only got worse after the Fifteenth Amendment to the Constitution of the United States was adopted in 1870.

It is one of the great ironies of US history that Black males who had formerly been enslaved were given the right to vote fifty years before that right was given to the white women who may formerly have owned those Black males. That irony was not allowed to stand for very long. Suppression of the Black vote was immediate, intense, and intimidating. Within a decade of gaining the right to vote by federal law, that right was taken away by state legislatures and by the terror and brutality of white supremacist groups like the Ku Klux Klan. By the time women were granted the right to vote through the Nineteenth Amendment in 1920, Black voting rights in most of the country had been obliterated. Since the Nineteenth Amendment was allowed to apply only to white women, the roots of the womanist movement were already being spread.

It seems that issues of race and gender have long been points of contention in this country where white males decided, based upon their desire to wield power have sought to keep both groups on the margins of society. If one's desire is to set the captives free, then one must be equally committed to setting free all the captives, whatever form their captivity takes, be it race, class, or gender. What is sad to see is how people who have long been held in the captivity of racism seem quite content to enjoy their newfound liberties while leaving gender firmly in place as a reason to keep women in a marginal if not subordinate position.

I have heard it said by both men and women that the Black church was the only place where Black men could exercise a leadership position in American society because of the restrictions imposed upon them by the Jim Crow culture that surrounded them. Forgetting the fact that Jim Crow laws affected Black women as well as Black men, that argument holds no merit today. Black men have served as admirals and generals in the armed forces. They have served as CEOs of major corporations. They hold endowed chairs at elite universities. They have been launched into space as astronauts. They have been mayors of great cities, governors of states, and members of both the House of Representatives and the United States Senate. A Black male has already served two terms as president of the United States. It can no longer be argued that leadership in the church must be preserved as a male-only enclave. Women are not preventing men from holding leadership outside the church, and men should not use that excuse to prevent women from holding leadership positions inside the church.

I want to close this chapter by referring to a 1933 statement from the National Board of the NAACP on the issue of racial segregation. In expressing their opposition to, and their outrage over, the intensity with which the principle of "separate but equal" status was being enforced in the United States they wrote, "Enforced segregation by its very existence carries with it the implication of a superior and inferior group and invariably results in the imposition of a lower status on the group deemed inferior. Thus, both principle and practice necessitate unyielding opposition to any and every form of enforced segregation."[21]

Going back to my earlier references to Galatians 3:26-29, there is not a Black male in this country that would stand opposed to this statement by the NAACP in 1933 or stand for the racial segregation denounced in this statement. Yet almost ninety years later, there are Black men and women who defend and justify another kind of enforced segregation, which is the exclusion of women from the ministry and the maintenance of and preference for a male-only domain. What makes this worse is that they do so based upon antiquated and indefensible uses of selected texts of Scripture.

There is no way to be against racism and ethnic discrimination but remain in support of sexism and gender discrimination. How can you oppose racism using a biblical text, and uphold sexism using that same text? "There is neither Jew nor Greek, slave nor free, male nor female, for you are all one in Christ Jesus" (Galatians 3:28 BSB). The captivity from which women and men both need to be set free requires a liberating theology that affirms freedom and opportunity for men that is equally available to women. "So if the Son makes you free, you will be free indeed" (John 8:36).

NOTES

1. Betty Collier-Thomas, "Mary G. Evans and The Wages of Sin is Death," *Daughters of Thunder: Black Women Preachers and Their Sermons: 1850–1979* (San Francisco: Jossey-Bass, 1998), 148–52.

2. Ibid., 150.

3. Rebecca Todd Peters, "Beverly Wildung Harrison: Forefronting Women's Moral Agency," *Journal of Feminist Studies in Religion* 30, no. 1 (Spring 2014): 121–22.

4. James H. Cone, *Said I Wasn't Gonna Tell Nobody* (Maryknoll, NY: Orbis Books, 2018), 73.

5. Rosemary Radford Reuther, *Liberation Theology: Human Hope Confronts Christian History and American Power* (New York: Paulist Press, 1972); Phyllis Trible, *Texts of Terror: Literary Feminist Readings of Biblical Narratives* (Philadelphia: Fortress, 1984); B. Diane Lipsett and Phyllis Trible, eds., *Faith and Feminism: Ecumenical Essays* (Louisville, KY: Westminster/John Knox, 2014); Letty Russell, ed., *Feminist Interpretation of the Bible* (Louisville, KY: Westminster/John Knox, 1985).

6. Christine M. Smith, *Preaching as Weeping, Confession, and Resistance: Radical Responses to Radical Evil* (Louisville, KY: Westminster/John Knox, 1992), 67–72.

7. Ibid., 70.

8. Christine A. Smith, *Beyond the Stained-Glass Ceiling* (Valley Forge, PA: Judson Press, 2013).

9. Ibid., ix–x.

10. Trible, 3.

11. Wilda C. Gafney, *Womanist Midrash: A Reintroduction to the Women of the Torah and the Throne* (Louisville, KY: Westminster/John Knox, 2017).

12. Ibid., 3.

13. Smith, *Beyond the Stained Glass Ceiling*, 43.

14. Ibid., viii.

15. Ibid.

16. Demetrius Williams, *An End to This Strife* (Minneapolis: Fortress, 2004), 71.

17. Ibid.

18. Marvin A. McMickle, *Challenging Gender Discrimination in the Church* (American Baptist Women in Ministry, 2001).

19. David W. Blight, *Frederick Douglass: Prophet of Freedom* (New York: Simon & Schuster, 2018), 488.

20. Ibid., 489.

21. David Levering Lewis, *W. E. B. Du Bois: The Fight for Equality and the American Century, 1919–1963* (New York: Henry Holt, 2000), 342.

CHAPTER 6

Listen to These Women!

The challenges facing female clergy are not limited to matters of semantics and inclusive language. The far more intense struggle for women has always been about a different kind of inclusion, namely, inclusion within the ranks of the clergy in the denominations in which they had been raised. Nothing gained more attention during my years at Union and later at Columbia University than what was called "the irregular ordination" of the Philadelphia Eleven, who were eleven women ordained as Episcopal priests without the permission of the Episcopal Church on July 29, 1974.[1]

One of those who was ordained that day was my Union classmate, Carter Heyward. In 1975, four more women were ordained In Washington, DC, as Episcopal priests. Their ordination was also deemed to be "irregular" and "invalid." That changed in 1976, when the national governing body of the Episcopal Church changed the rules and allowed for the ordination of women as priests.[2] Things evolved quickly concerning the role of women in the Episcopal Church. In 1988, Barbara Harris was elected a Suffragan Bishop in the Diocese of Massachusetts; and in 2006, Katharine Jefferts Schori was elected Presiding Bishop of the Episcopal Church.

I leave it to other voices with more experience with and inside largely white denominations to discuss the experiences of white women within those settings. While my years as a seminary professor and president have given me some familiarity with how white women have been welcomed, marginalized, or blatantly dismissed when they applied for opportunities with local churches or denominational offices, I by no means possess enough knowledge or exposure to those communities of faith to do anything more than be a constant and vocal advocate for white women who have declared their call to ministry and who have career aspirations to serve God as members of the ordained clergy.

Women in Ministry in the African American Church

While things are evolving within those white church bodies and with white women, I can speak with more authority and experience regarding the way in which women have been received within Black churches across the country. With only two exceptions, I will not be the voice discussing this issue. Rather, I have engaged a cross-section of African American clergywoman to speak for themselves. Far more can be learned about women in ministry in African American churches and denominations when one can hear the unfiltered comments and concerns of these women who have agreed to tell their own story. I acknowledge that most of these women have sought a ministry home within the context of the Black Baptist world. However, women from other faith bodies are also present to bring depth and balance to this discussion.

I should state that this list of women in ministry is limited to those whose primary focus is within the life of the local church and pastoral ministry. Womanist theologians whose focus is within academia and theological education will be the focus of a subsequent chapter in this study.

Carolyn Ann Knight

I studied for and served in ministry in the Greater New York City region and in New Jersey as well from 1970 to 1986. During all that time, one would have to look long and hard to find churches where women were being welcomed into the ordained ministry, much less being called to serve as pastors of churches of any size. The metropolitan New York City area was home to some of the most notable

Black churches and some of the most vocal proponents for racial justice to be found anywhere in the United States. Whether they were affiliated with the National Baptist Convention, USA, Inc., or the Progressive National Baptist Convention, New York City and northern New Jersey were home to a stunning array of Black preachers who operated at the national and international level.

That being said, there was no Black Baptist church in New York City in the 1970s that had a woman as part of its ministerial staff until Carolyn Ann Knight was invited by Wyatt Tee Walker to join the staff of Canaan Baptist Church as its youth pastor in 1978. She is a graduate of Bishop College in Texas, with a master of divinity degree from Union Theological Seminary in New York City and a doctor of ministry degree from United Theological Seminary in Dayton, Ohio.

Knight reflected on that experience:

Sandwiched between the civil rights and Black Power movements, the church was beginning to wrestle with the issue of sexism as well as racism . . . Dr. Walker's sense of justice was greater than any prohibition against women in the ministry . . . I still remember when Canaan was invited to share with a sister church in Brooklyn. This church did not allow women in the pulpit or acknowledge women in ministry. Upon learning this, Dr. Walker informed the pastor that he would be unable to fellowship with them as his assistant was female. On the Sunday when Walker announced this to Canaan Baptist Church, there was overwhelming support for the decision. That day I gained a measure of affirmation and confidence in my place as a woman in ministry.[3]

However, despite Knight's acceptance within Canaan Baptist Church, her acceptance within the broader community of Black Baptist pastors and churches was another matter. Walker was the former executive assistant to Martin Luther King Jr. and the planner of the demonstrations in Birmingham, Alabama. He was the person who smuggled out King's "Letter from Birmingham Jail" on scraps of newspaper. King himself preached Walker's installation as pastor at Canaan Baptist Church only weeks before he was assassinated in 1968. Walker was one of the most celebrated Black religious leaders of the twentieth century. Yet, when he sought to have Carolyn Knight admitted as a member of the Baptist Ministers Council of New York and vicinity he was refused, and her membership was denied.

No one who has heard Carolyn Ann Knight preach can doubt that God has called her to the ministry. She has declared the gospel of Jesus Christ at churches and conferences across the country. She has taught preaching at the Interdenominational Theological Center. Yet, despite her gifts, her academic training, and her professional involvements, she has had to press her way in a church culture that remains resistant to the very thing she embodies: women in ministry who are preaching in the pulpit.

I invited Carolyn Ann Knight to preach revival services at Antioch Baptist Church when I served there as senior pastor. During my twenty-four years at that church we invited the best preachers we could find. That included Gardner Taylor, William A. Jones Jr., Samuel Proctor, Charles Both, Harold Carter Sr., Prathia Hall, James Perkins, William Shaw, Calvin O. Butts III, Jesse Jackson, Suzan Johnson Cook, Otis Moss Jr., Henry Mitchell and Ella Mitchell, Benjamin Hooks, and many more. We were honored to include Carolyn Ann Knight in that succession of pulpit giants.

Sharon Williams

While Carolyn Knight was serving in a paid staff position at Canaan Baptist Church in Harlem, Sharon Williams was accepted as an unpaid student intern at nearby Abyssinian Baptist Church between 1977 and 1980. Because she was a graduate of Hunter College and Union Theological Seminary, both in New York City, I took special interest in her story because I had been a paid staff member at that same church from 1972 to 1976. William S. Epps and Calvin O. Butts III were also paid members of that staff working with Samuel Proctor, who was the senior pastor. He was essentially serving as a part-time pastor since he maintained his faculty appointment at Rutgers University as the Martin Luther King Jr. Distinguished Professor of Education. His plan was to receive one-half of the senior pastor salary and use the other half to help in the compensation of his three associates. In reflecting on her three-year relationship with the church, Williams offered the following comments:

> I was never offered a paid position, never allowed in the pulpit. I was allowed to minister in the basement to children and carry out a project with teenagers for my MDiv thesis. I was licensed but [was] always called by my first name, unlike the male ministers. The pastor at that time called me "Sister Girl." I was ordained at Abyssinian in 1980 after the state board of chaplains requested that it be done for a prospective job, but I was never hired [at Abyssinian]. The same Friday afternoon that I (woefully prepared) passed my ordination exam, I was ushered through a hallway into the sanctuary for my ordination ceremony. As I walked that hallway, I was greeted by a smiling, teary-eyed group of sisters who had prepared a collation and set it up to celebrate me. I still cry when I remember their love and pride.
>
> Unlike the male interns, I was never offered a position at Abyssinian beyond my student internship nor was a pulpit "found" for me. Instead of going into prison chaplaincy, I was hired (by the grace of God) by Ollie B. Wells to serve as minister of Christian education at Union Baptist Church in Harlem. I was there three years. In 1984 I was called to pastor Baptist Church of the Redeemer in Brooklyn through the traditional search process [unusual for women in those years]. I plan to retire from there in February 2021 upon completion of a new, replacement building housing the church and seventy-six units of affordable housing. God is SO GREAT![4]

Sharon Williams is an inspiration to this present generation of female clergy since she was among the pioneering Black women who faced the first wave of resistance to female clergy and especially female pastors. There are few male pastors in New York City who have had a longer and more productive ministry within the church and in the surrounding community than Sharon Williams.

Suzan Johnson Cook

In light of the experiences of Carolyn Knight and Sharon Williams in New York City, it was a *cause célébre* when Suzan Johnson Cook was called to be senior pastor of Mariners Temple Baptist Church in New York City (Manhattan) in 1983. She was the first women to serve in that position at Mariners Temple since the church was founded in 1845.

She earned a bachelor of arts degree at Emerson College, a master of arts degree from Columbia University, a master of divinity degree from Union Theological Seminary in New York City, and a doctor of ministry degree from United Theological Seminary. Greatly influenced by the liberation theology of Gustavo Gutiérrez and the womanist theology of Katie Cannon, whom Johnson Cook called "her big sister" for fifty years, she learned two lessons. First was that "females could not only accept the call to preach the gospel but realize that call as well." Second was that "that shackles of any type would not be in my life nor upon my spirit."[5]

She left Mariners Temple in Manhattan after thirteen years to plant a new church in the Bronx neighborhood of New York City where she had been born and raised. She named the new church Bronx Christian Fellowship Church. Johnson Cook reflects on her transition to the church in the Bronx and on other aspects of being a woman in ministry in *The Sister's Guide to Survive and Thrive in Ministry*.[6] In explaining her move to those who thought she should stay at what was at that time a one-thousand-member congregation, Johnson Cook said:

> Many people told me not to leave the thousand-member historic congregation in downtown Manhattan and go to a start-up, storefront church in the Bronx. You're making great money, you're highly visible, why leave? But God had called me; God said, "Go." . . . Because we live in a megachurch, megamedia ministry age, many of us think we've failed when we're not operating at that level . . . The church that I went on to pastor in my community was not on a main street, but people found it. God led them there. It was on a street known as the Grand Concourse, so I said, "OK, God, let's build this grand ministry for your great glory."[7]

Johnson Cook rose to the ranks of national recognition through her selection as a White House Fellow in 1993 and as a member of President Bill Clinton's seven-member Initiative on Race and Reconciliation that was chaired by John Hope Franklin. She would go on to serve as president of the Hampton Ministers Conference, an annual gathering of thousands of Black preachers from across the country. She commented on that experience as she reflected on the moments in her life that served to confirm her call to ministry:

> The ultimate moment was the election as the first female president of the historic Hampton Ministers Conference. It took twenty-three years of attending, serving, and learning to navigate the male-dominated waters. But God rewards faithfulness, and God intervenes against all odds. Despite the rumors of a "standoff" and stay away from the conference my first year, it was standing room only, flooded by civil rights icons and celebrities, and transformed into a new era of leadership.

Johnson Cook offered some painful concluding observations concerning women who are pursuing careers in ministry. First, she said, "Many of the trailblazing women who began with me are no longer here. Most died much too soon, but they were burnt out." She concluded, "Some advances have happened in my forty years of ministry, but not nearly enough. Just as many are intentional about keeping us out. I must be fiercely intentional about bringing our chair—even if it is a 'folding chair' as Shirley Chisholm once said—to the table."[8]

I can only imagine how much the pressure of gender bias and sexism resulted in the demise of women who "died too soon" and who were "burnt out."

Prathia Hall

I want to include Prathia Hall in this chapter, even though she is no longer alive to tell her own story. Prathia Hall of Philadelphia was called in 1978 to be the pastor of Mt. Sharon Baptist Church, where her father had been a founding pastor. At that point in her life, she was already a preacher of national reputation. In the early 1960s, she was part of the Student Non-Violent Coordinating Committee (SNCC) serving in Albany, Georgia. She was also one of the Freedom Riders who challenged segregation in interstate transportation in the Deep South. It was confirmed by James Bevel and John Lewis, two of the leaders of the civil rights movement, that Martin Luther King Jr. borrowed the phrase "I have a dream" from Prathia Hall when he heard her preach at Mt. Olive Baptist Church in Terrell County, Georgia, in September 1962.[9]

She was the first woman to be admitted to the Baptist Ministers Conference of Philadelphia in 1982. With an undergraduate degree from Temple University, Hall earned her master of divinity degree at Princeton Theological Seminary, where she was a student of mine in a preaching course. In that course, which included several Black female students, she lamented about the resistance that women were experiencing in their pursuit of a position in pastoral ministry. Hall went on to earn a PhD from Princeton Seminary. Given her gifts, talents, credentials, and experiences, Hall should have been invited to be pastor of one of the larger churches in the Progressive National Baptist Convention (PNBC), where she served for several years as chair of the program committee. However, that progressive convention has still not elected a woman as its national president, and Hall died without being called to one of the major PNBC churches.

Commenting on her experience as a woman in ministry and on her determination to remain within the Black Baptist church, Hall said, "The Baptist church is going to have to deal with me. Some of us have to remain in the recalcitrant church. Everything we know about God is that the living God is not a bigot."[10] Commenting on how difficult it was for her to be a woman in ministry in that setting, she said, "As a Black Baptist woman preacher I am therefore painfully aware of powerlessness."[11] Having had her as a student and having heard her preach in multiple locations across the country, including twice at my own church in Cleveland, I regret that no congregation beyond Mt. Sharon In Philadelphia had the experience of sitting under her preaching as their pastor over the course of many years. If they had, the power of her preaching could have seeped deep into their souls.

Leslie Callahan

Another milestone involving women in ministry occurred in Philadelphia in 2009, when Leslie Callahan was installed as senior pastor at St. Paul's Baptist Church in that city. Prior to that, she served on the faculty of the University of Pennsylvania teaching church history. With a bachelor of arts degree from Harvard, a master of divinity degree from Union Theological Seminary in New York City, and a PhD from Princeton University, it is notable that she felt drawn to invest her talent and training in the preaching ministry. Along with Carolyn Ann Knight, Leslie Callahan is a contributor to a collection of essays I edited for the Progressive National Baptist Convention entitled *Let Justice Roll*. She embodies what William Augustus Jones Jr. of Bethany Baptist Church in Brooklyn, New York, once said to me: "The Black church pulpit needs all the education we can give to it."

This is how Callahan describes her journey in ministry:

> I sensed that my principal call was not to the academy but to pastoral ministry, but I wondered whether I would ever get an opportunity especially in view of my gender. When I moved to Philadelphia, Pennsylvania, I affiliated with the Philadelphia Baptist Association [this is an American Baptist regional body] and served on a regional committee. There I got to know the regional executive, and he recommended me for an interim pastorate. That pastoral experience solidified my sense of call and gave me exposure so that I became known to other churches. That same regional executive placed my resume in the hands of the search committee at St. Paul's Baptist Church.

Callahan continues:

> The search took more than a year, but the committee consistently communicated their progress, from the initial resume through the vetting to election. Although there was some dissent, the congregation resolved to give women full consideration early in the search. They presented two finalists to preach and teach Bible study. On May 17, 2009, the 119-year old St. Paul's Baptist Church elected me their fifth pastor, the first woman to hold the position. Eleven years later, I am still rejoicing.[12]

One sign of effectiveness in ministry, at least within the Baptist church tradition, is longevity in the position. It is one thing to be called to an assignment. It is something else to be able to say that one is still rejoicing after more than a decade on the job. That implies that Callahan has confronted the gender bias she has faced and has persevered. That is something that should encourage other women who are contemplating their future in ministry, and it should confound those men who still believe that women cannot be successful in ministry.

Gina Stewart

To be the senior pastor of a Baptist church in a southern city like Memphis, Tennessee, is no small thing. That is the context in which Gina Stewart has had to operate. She earned a bachelor of arts degree from the University of Memphis, a master of divinity degree from Interdenominational Theological Center in Atlanta, and a doctor of ministry degree from United Theological Seminary in Dayton, Ohio. She is now part of the inaugural class of PhD students in African American Preaching and Sacred Rhetoric at Christian Theological Seminary in Indianapolis, Indiana, under the direction of Dr. Frank Thomas.

Stewart is senior pastor of Christ Missionary Baptist Church in Memphis. This is how she reflects on her experiences as a woman in ministry:

> Although the members of Christ Missionary Baptist Church courageously made the historic decision to elect a woman pastor, this decision was not without opposition. Patriarchy was one of the persistent challenges I encountered as I was considered for the position. Deeply embedded sexism coupled with the use of problematic interpretations of texts were used to justify the elimination of my candidacy. Many well-intentioned people tried to counsel our congregation against electing a woman.

She continues, "The same is true for male colleagues. While some were unequivocal in their support and endorsement, others were less supportive, and vocal in their opposition. Nevertheless, God provided the strength and grace to persevere. I encourage sisters who have answered the call to rely on God to fulfill your ministry regardless."[13]

I had the privilege of being the preacher for the ceremony when she was inducted into the Martin Luther King Jr. Board of Preachers at Morehouse College in Atlanta. I have heard her preach on numerous occasions at conferences and conventions across the country. She is a genuine gift to the body of Christ despite, and perhaps because of, the gender bias she has encountered during her ministry.

Zina Jacques

Zina Jacques holds a bachelor of arts degree from Northwestern University, a master of arts degree from Columbia University, a master of divinity degree and a PhD from Boston University. While all the other women who tell their story in this chapter operate or operated within a largely African American urban church context, Zina Jacques offers her comments coming from what she describes as "an upper-middle-class, 85 percent white, suburban community." This is her story:

> The intersectionality of race, gender, and orientation is a blessing and a weight. I am not me if I am not equal parts African American, female, and cisgender. Yet, when I move in communities particularly unfamiliar with that combination as a leader, it is hard to untangle which part of me is bothersome. In particular, my gender has proven to be an obstacle as I hold authority in the presence of older, retired men who have not known the experience of reporting to women.
>
> But life has offered me an ascending set of experiences dealing with those ignorant of the expanded worldview my intersectionality brings. These experiences have taught me if I know who I am, if I find allies who are different than I, if I stay focused on my ultimate boss, if I seek to minister in love/with grace, if I pray for (not about) folk, and if I stand authentically in the authority granted by the contract God led the church and me to sign, then I can do just that, stand in all my intersectionality. God help us to stand.[14]

I have known and interacted with Zina Jacques across the years at various American Baptist Church events where she has been the featured speaker or a panelist. There is a grace about her that charms an audience, but there is also a fire within her that commands attention and respect. What a shame that any part of her would be considered "bothersome" to anyone.

Sabrina Ellis

Dr. Sabrina Ellis represents women who are pursuing careers in ministry within the Black Pentecostal tradition, a tradition well known for placing limits on the aspirations of women pursuing careers in ministry. With a bachelor of arts degree from Notre Dame College in University Heights, Ohio, and master of divinity and doctor of ministry degrees from Ashland Theological Seminary in Ashland, Ohio, she is in her second year as the senior pastor of Pentecostal Church of Christ in Cleveland, Ohio. She succeeded her husband, Bishop J. Delano Ellis, in that position.

Her church is the headquarters of a network of Black Pentecostal churches across the country called Pentecostal Churches of Christ (PCC), many of which had previously been part of the Church of God in Christ (COGIC), which is the largest Black Pentecostal body in the country, and possibly the largest of any Black denomination. The fact that her church is not a part of COGIC is a major factor in why she is able to serve as a senior pastor. She notes:

> My experience as a woman in ministry in the Pentecostal Church has been without much of the struggle that many of my colleagues have experienced. Under the leadership of Bishop J. Delano Ellis, women in ministry have been affirmed. However, as we considered returning to the church of our nativity [COGIC], the largest Pentecostal denomination in the world, we knew that my ordination and position as a pastor would not be readily accepted. To date, the highest position for a woman in that organization is an evangelist. One leader asked, "If we welcome them back, what will we do with Sabrina?"[15]

To date, there is no prospect of a restoring of ties between PCC and COGIC. Difference over the issue of women in ministry is one of the things that still divides these two Black Pentecostal bodies. She states, "Merging with COGIC will not happen. My husband had been in discussions with Bishop Blake [the presiding bishop of COGIC]; I was serving on the Publishing Board of the church by Bishop Blake's appointment. But in the end, it was clear there will be no merger."

It remains clear that COGIC does not yet know "what it will do with Sabrina." But God knows just what to do with Sabrina. In the words of T. D. Jakes, "Loose her and let her go."

Traci Blackmon

The Rev. Traci Blackmon is the first woman senior pastor in the 162-year history of Christ the King United Church of Christ (UCC) in Florissant, Missouri, near St. Louis. She is also the associate general minister of Justice and Local Church Ministries for the UCC. She earned a Bachelor of Science degree from Birmingham–Southern College and a Master of Divinity degree from Eden Theological Seminary in St. Louis, Missouri. She is a registered nurse, and before entering the ministry she spent twenty-five years in the health care field.

Her congregation is largely African. I was saddened and deeply disappointed when she reported to me for inclusion in this study a recent case of gender bias. Apparently, resistance to women in ministry and tolerance for sexism on the part of Black male clergy involving women in ministry is not limited to older men who might be living with the values of an earlier time in history. She shared a recent experience she had with younger preachers who exhibited the same pattern of being aggressive in opposition to racism but passive if not complicit when it came to sexism and gender bias.

Blackmon was frequently seen and even interviewed on national television when she took to the streets in Ferguson, Missouri, after the shooting death of Michael Brown by a white police officer. This tall, stately Black woman wearing a clergy collar stood in the face of riot police who were dressed in military-style body armor while unarmed Black people protested the shooting death of Brown and the further disregard for his humanity when his body was left lying in the street long after he was dead. It should be noted that few if any of the Black male clergy leaders from St. Louis joined in on those protests until many days later—and then did so more to attempt a takeover of the protests rather than to support the young people who had established the chant "Black Lives Matter."

Here is her report about how the pursuit of racial justice did not prevent blatant gender bias among some of the clergy in St. Louis and vicinity.

> It was November 2014, the year of Michael Brown's death. Toni, a regular caller on my weekly pastor's call, died. As the cancer progressed, our prayers became more frequent, and upon her death I was asked to pray at the funeral. I did not know her pastor, so when I arrived, I was heartened to see several of the young male pastors who sought my leadership in the streets of Ferguson. When Toni's pastor publicly declared I was not allowed in the pulpit, these same young men who protested racial injustice with me in the streets ignored me in the sanctuary on their way to the pulpit. Only one refused to collude. It was then I knew misogyny would not die out. We would have to kill it.[16]

This woman named among the *Ebony* Power 100 Black Americans in the country, with an honorary doctorate from Eden Theological Seminary in St. Louis, was not allowed to sit in the pulpit of a Black church in that same city. She was given the Stella Award by the *St. Louis American*, the African American community newspaper in that city. St. Louis University named her Community Leader of the Year. Along with Bishop William Barber, Sister Simone, and Dr. James Forbes, she has traveled the country promoting a moral revival that would include racial justice and an end to poverty.

I wonder if the pastor or any of the male clergy who denied her access to the pulpit of a local church have any such credentials or enjoy anywhere near such public acclaim and accomplishment. Given the fact that younger Black male clergy were complicit in this event, it makes me worry about the future of the Black church. In the Old Testament, most of an entire generation of Hebrews who had come out of slavery in Egypt had to die in the desert because of their sins before God would allow the people to enter the Promised Land. In this instance, it is bad enough that an older generation of Black male clergy may take their sexism and gender bias with them to their graves. It is heartbreaking to discover that a younger generation of Black male clergy may be carrying on this distortion of Galatians

3:26-29 when they are all in for the end of racism and ethnic discrimination but are either silent or accepting when it comes to gender bias and sexism.

Tonya Fields

In addition to Prathia Hall, another student in that preaching class at Princeton Theological Seminary in the 1980s was Tonya Fields. She had earlier earned her bachelor of arts degree at Bishop College in Dallas, Texas. I offered her a staff position at St. Paul Baptist Church in Montclair, New Jersey, upon her graduation from seminary in 1984. At that time, there had never been a woman on the staff of that church. Only one woman was serving as a pastor of a church anywhere in northern New Jersey, and that was Myrtle Jackson, who succeeded her husband as pastor of Rising Mt. Zion Baptist Church, also in Montclair. Today, the pastor of St. Paul Baptist Church is Dr. Bernadette Glover.

I was unable to hire Tonya Fields at that time, because she is also a world-class singer, and she opted to move to Los Angeles, California, to pursue a career as a recording artist. Having lost track of her after that, I was surprised when she was seated in the sanctuary of Antioch Baptist Church in Cleveland, Ohio, on that night in 1987 when I was installed there as senior pastor. We got together the following week, she said that she was looking for a job, and I offered her the same position but at a different church.

Tonya Fields met all our church's guidelines for ordination to Christian ministry. In addition to her bachelor of arts degree, she had a master of divinity degree from Princeton Theological Seminary in Princeton, New Jersey. She could sing like an angel, preach like a prophet, and pray like an old saint. She became the first woman ever ordained at Antioch Baptist Church in Cleveland. Once that was accomplished, she became my colleague in ministry in every sense of the word.

Not everybody in the church was willing to embrace this idea of women in the ordained ministry once it went into effect. The first time Rev. Fields presided at the Communion table, word came back to me that several members of the church refused to receive the elements when they were passed their way. They also sent word to me that unless I stopped letting her "put her hands on that Communion table," they would be changing their membership to a "biblical church." The next time Communion was served, I said that anyone wishing to leave Antioch because of their objection to the ministry of Tonya Fields would certainly be missed. However, she was going to remain as my associate for as long as she and I chose to serve in ministry together. To my knowledge, no one ever left Antioch over having a woman in ministry, and no one ever again complained about her serving Communion.

After ten years on staff at Antioch, she was eager to pursue a position as pastor of her own congregation. Despite her education and ten years of experience involving all aspects of pastoral work at a twelve-hundred-member congregation, we were unable to secure a pastoral assignment for her at a Black Baptist church anywhere in Greater Cleveland. Like so many women who find the doors of Black Baptist churches closed to them, she became a United Methodist and was quickly assigned to St. Paul United Methodist Church in Cleveland, where she launched a tremendously successful ministry.

Jacqueline Thompson

In 2019, Jacqueline Thompson was called as senior pastor of Allen Temple Baptist Church in Oakland, California. She holds a bachelor of arts degree from University of California Berkeley, a master of divinity degree from Howard University School of Divinity, and a doctor of ministry degree from Fuller Theological Seminary in Pasadena, California. In reflecting on her journey as a woman in ministry, Dr. Thompson stated that this momentous event at which I served as the morning preacher occurred largely due to the advocacy of Dr. J. Alfred Smith Sr., who had long been an advocate for women in ministry. Thompson said:

> Compared with many of my colleagues, my path to leadership may seem charmed. I grew up in a church where women were visible and active in every aspect of ministry from the pulpit to the pew.

Women called to ministry were affirmed publicly, encouraged to pursue higher education, and provided clear paths to ordination . . . In this church I was licensed, ordained, and installed as assistant pastor and ten years later as senior pastor. I am the first woman to be called as pastor in the hundred-year history of the church.[17]

Thompson reflects on the fact that there are limits to the level of leadership available to women in ministry:

Even in the most progressive and egalitarian churches, the face and voice of senior leadership has historically been male. As such, women in ministry find great acceptance, opportunity, even celebration in supporting roles. But the quest and call to senior pastoral leadership can reveal some of the same closely held gender-biased beliefs found and promoted in more conservative contexts. For some, these beliefs are rooted in faulty biblical interpretation, but most often are centered squarely in culture and fear.[18]

Jacqueline Thompson also observed that as a result of Dr. Smith's embrace of the idea of women in ministry, Smith "was often the object of contempt and scorn from other theologically conservative churches and pastors."[19] In an interview I had with Smith, he told me that in 1978 he had ordained Dr. Ella Mitchell, wife of Dr. Henry Mitchell, along with two other women, Melvina Stephens and Josie Lee Kuhlmann. It was because he had taken that action that he was voted out of the Baptist Ministers Conference of the Bay Area in California. Also voted out of that conference was Dr. Gillette O. James, who had ordained women at Beth Eden Baptist Church in Oakland.

Smith informed me that he agreed to ordain Dr. Ella Mitchell after a nationally esteemed pastor in Los Angeles who was outspoken on matters of racism in church and society refused to do so because he did not believe in women preachers. He noted that there was great resistance to his becoming the twelfth president of the Progressive National Baptist Convention in 1982, because many leading pastors in PNBC were afraid he would try to "move the skirts into leadership positions." It seems that in most settings, the idea of women in ministry not only results in limitations on the aspirations of women but can also result in condemnation of those male preachers who proceed with the ordination of women with or without the approval of their more conservative male colleagues.

Thompson offers a final word to all churches that claim to be progressive but cling to conservative values when it comes to women in ministry. She says, "The temptation in more progressive churches is to remain silent, given that these beliefs are not the prevailing position of the church." Then, with a final biblical flourish, she draws an analogy from the Song of Solomon 2:15, "Catch us the foxes, the little foxes, that ruin the vineyards—for our vineyards are in blossom." Jacqueline Thompson is flourishing in her ministry. What a shame that she or any of her sisters in ministry have faced opposition based upon bad biblical interpretation. To all the woman listed in this chapter, I dedicate this chapter and this book.

Why Have These Women Faced Obstacles in Their Ministry?

What can be observed in this review of Black women in ministry is the impressive level of academic and theological training each of them achieved as they sought to equip themselves for the ministry work to which God called them. All of them were seminary-trained women, and most of them earned doctoral degrees as well from the leading divinity schools and universities in the country. It must therefore be concluded that any limitations or obstacles they have faced in terms of honoring their call to ministry could not be the result of not being fully qualified by formal theological training.

When one considers the trajectory of their careers, it also seems that they were not lacking in the practical experience needed to be an effective senior pastor or denominational leader. All of them went through the normal process of starting out in smaller churches or in staff positions that should lead to larger and larger ministry assignments. This is the career path their male colleagues normally follow, including those male colleagues with far less academic and theological training and practical experience.

This is the career path I followed: two years at Bethany Baptist Church in Brooklyn, New York, with William A. Jones Jr., and four years at Abyssinian Baptist Church in Harlem, New York, with Samuel D. Proctor. Those two assignments immediately resulted in my thirty-four years of service: ten years at the five-hundred-member St. Paul Baptist Church in Montclair, New Jersey, followed by a twenty-four-year ministry at the fifteen-hundred-member Antioch Baptist Church in Cleveland, Ohio, where I am now pastor emeritus.

Why does this path not open for those women who were my students at Princeton, Ashland, or Colgate Rochester Crozer Divinity School? They were just as capable in their academic work and just as capable in their preaching skills. Why does this path not open for so many of my female colleagues in ministry who are not lacking in training or practical experience? There is no good reason why they are not moving into the pulpits of the largest and most prestigious churches in the country. There is no good reason why their career paths should be limited to smaller churches with lower salaries and insufficient budget and staff support. There is no good reason why a woman has yet to be elected president of any Black Baptist convention in the United States. There is no good reason for these things, but there is a reason. Who can deny that the only possible answer that can be reached is gender bias and sexism?

NOTES

1. Bill Tammeus, "Episcopal Church Celebrates Forty Years of Women in the Priesthood," NationalCatholicReporter.com, July 28, 2014.

2. Ibid.

3. Marvin McMickle, interview of Carolyn Ann Knight, April 22, 2020.

4. Marvin McMickle, interview of Sharon Williams, April 15, 2020.

5. Suzan Johnson Cook, comments sent to Marvin McMickle, May 25, 2020, for use in this book.

6. Suzan D. Johnson Cook, *The Sister's Guide to Survive and Thrive in Ministry* (Valley Forge, PA: Judson Press, 2019).

7. Ibid., 4–5.

8. Johnson Cook, comments.

9. Courtney Pace, *Freedom Faith: The Womanist Vision of Prathia Hall* (Athens: University of Georgia Press, 2019), 228–29.

10. Ibid., 185–86.

11. Ibid., 186.

12. Leslie Callahan, comments sent to Marvin McMickle, June 1, 2020, for use in this book.

13. Gina Stewart, comments sent to Marvin McMickle, June 4, 2020, for use in this book.

14. Zina Jacques, comments sent to Marvin McMickle, May 29, 2020, for use in this book.

15, Sabrina Ellis, comments sent to Marvin McMickle, May 18, 2020, for use in this book.

16. Traci Blackmon, comments sent to Marvin McMickle, May 5, 2020, for use in this book.

17. Jacqueline Thompson, written interview conducted by Marvin McMickle, completed May 4, 2020.

18. Ibid.

19. Ibid.

CHAPTER 7

What Does It Mean to Be a Progressive Black Baptist?

The issue faced by J. Alfred Smith Sr, inside the Progressive National Baptist Convention (PNBC) in a previous chapter points to the willingness of so many Black male clergy to be outspoken on matters of race but to be silent or openly resistant on matters of gender equality and women in ministry.

PNBC was formed in 1960–1961 for two reasons. The first was to provide a denominational home for Martin Luther King Jr., who was not being supported by Joseph H. Jackson, the long-standing president of the National Baptist Convention USA, Inc. The other reason was that earlier attempts had been made, without success, to remove Jackson from office so that a more progressive leader could steer the National Baptist Convention in a new direction so far as the civil rights movement was concerned.

Jackson was not disinterested in matters of race relations, but he was concerned about the aggressive methods used by King to address the issue of racial injustice.[1] When attempts failed in 1960 to replace Jackson with Gardner Taylor as president of the National Baptist Convention, some members moved to the PNBC, whose first session was convened in 1961. PNBC would be defined by two distinctives. The first was a limit on the number of years any one person could serves as president of the convention. The second was a strong endorsement of King and the fight for racial and economic justice.

The convention has remained more or less focused on matters of racial justice ever since.

What had not been made an initial priority for PNBC was to embrace those women in the convention who had been called to the ministry. The first major step toward the inclusion of women in the leadership of PNBC began with the presidency of Charles G. Adams, who invited Prathia Hall to preach before the full convention. He also appointed her to serve as chair of the program committee, which she did for much of the 1990s.[2] That was a significant step forward, because it was the first time a clergywoman was involved in planning the annual and mid-winter meetings of PNBC. Subsequent presidents of PNBC have tried to keep the convention moving in that direction.

There have been some significant signs of progress for PNBC in recent years. At the 2019 session, Dr. Jacqueline Thompson of Allen Temple Baptist Church of Oakland, California. served along with Dr. Gary Simpson of Concord Baptist Church in Brooklyn, New York, as the co-conveners of the Ministers Division. Women were given prominent roles in that bastion of male participation and leadership. Jewel London from Church Without Walls in Houston preached at one of the morning sessions. An afternoon session was devoted to the new book about Prathia Hall entitled *Freedom Faith*. That discussion was led by the author, Courtney Pace. In addition, Cynthia Hale of Atlanta, Georgia, was a preacher at one of the evening sessions. The 2019 annual session was a positive step in the right direction.

Gina Stewart of Memphis, Tennessee, was one of the preachers for the virtual gathering of PNBC in 2020. It should also be noted that Leslie Callahan, Millicent Hunter, Dee Dee Coleman, Prathia Hall, Martha Simmons, Jasmin Schulark, and Suzan Johnson-Cook all preached at recent sessions of PNBC.

However, while preaching at a national convention is a great honor, it does not have the same long-term institutional effect as if a woman were to be elected to be president of PNBC. No woman has ever been elected to the top three leadership positions of the convention. It takes eight years to rise from second vice president, to first vice president, to possibly being elected as president of PNBC. Since no woman is currently in that chain of succession, it is likely that no woman will be elected as president in this decade.

What makes this fact troublesome is that according to Dr. James Perkins of Detroit, Michigan and Dr. Timothy Stewart of Nassau, Bahamas, both former presidents of PNBC, the constitution of PNBC declares women to be eligible for election to any office. The actual language is, "Any member of the convention, clergy or lay, male or female, shall be eligible to hold any office in the convention."[3] It was that provision in the constitution that Perkins said he used to widen the involvement of women in PNBC while he was serving as president.

Perkins established a Women in Ministry Division that served two purposes. The first was to provide women already engaged in ministry roles the time and space to meet and support one another. The second was to provide mentorship and encouragement to younger women beginning their careers. Dr. Delores Cain of Tampa, Florida, the Rev. Emma Simpson of Brooklyn, New York, and the Rev. Jewel London of Houston, Texas, were among the women who provided leadership for that division.

While the language of the constitution may have been aspirational at the founding of the convention, and while it may have been true for the years when Perkins served as president, it has not proven to be true on a consistent basis over the sixty years of PNBC's existence. PNBC has never seriously considered nominating a lay person for a position that could lead to the national presidency. As of the 2018 election cycle, there has not been a woman that has successfully been elected to one of the offices leading to the national presidency.

Even more revealing in terms of the prospects of a woman being elected national president of PNBC is the fact that very few women have served at the state and regional levels. I asked several people with deep roots in PNBC to answer two questions:

1. Has a woman ever been elected as president of any state or regional PNBC affiliate?

2. Do you think a woman will be elected president of PNBC in the next ten years?

The respondents to these questions included three presidents of PNBC: Timothy Stewart, who is the current national president of PNBC, James Perkins of Michigan, who is the immediate past president of PNBC, and J. Alfred Smith Sr. of California, who is also a past president of PNBC. In addition, responses came from Tyrone Pitts, who is the former general secretary of PNBC, Otis Moss Jr. of Ohio, Clarence Wright and Leslie Callahan of Pennsylvania, Gary Simpson of New York, and Jacqueline Thompson of California. Here were their collective responses concerning how many women have served as state or regional presidents in the sixty-year history of PNBC.

1. Delores Cain was the state president in Florida.

2. Vickie Brinkley of California currently serves as second vice president of the Southwest region.

3. Deborah Wolfe served as president of the New Jersey State Convention.

4. The Michigan state convention has had three female presidents: Victoria Banks (1976–1978), Helen Hodges (1998–2000), and Sandra Fox (2006–2010).

5. Jacqueline Thompson ran unsuccessfully in 2018 to become second vice president of PNBC.

According to Clarence Wright, she was at a disadvantage since she was running against two men both of whom were regional vice presidents. Wright, who is the state president in Pennsylvania, points out how long it often takes to become national president of PNBC. He says, "The elongated (unofficial) line of succession can be problematic for anyone with eyes on national leadership, particularly women, since the path from regional second vice to national president would take twenty years if everyone completed four-year terms."

If this pattern remains in force, then it may take until 2040 for a woman to become president of PNBC. This is not to say that a woman could not jump to the head of the line and become a candidate for the national presidency without moving through the state, regional, and national offices that have historically been the path to that office. However, the heart of any institution is revealed by the persons it chooses for its leaders and the policies that govern access to those leadership positions. After more than sixty years as the Progressive National Baptist Convention, and after fifty years since the emergence of feminist theology and womanist theology and the spoken aspiration of women to be treated equally in pursuit of leadership opportunities in the local church and in national church bodies, the facts speak for themselves. PNBC, like other Black religious bodies, seems to be progressive on matters of racial justice and inclusion but less committed to embracing women as partners and colleagues in ministry at the local, state, regional, and national levels.

As PNBC looks to the future of women as leaders in the convention, it is important to consider more fully the responses of Dr. Timothy Stewart of Nassau, the Bahamas, who is the current president of PNBC, and has been a member since 1991. He was candid in his assessment that a patriarchal attitude has served to keep women from holding leadership positions in the convention. He also pointed to a dogmatic attitude when it comes to the Pauline passages that have been used over the years to prohibit women from serving in any kind of ordained ministry. His words were, "We have a way to go and some improvements to make until our sisters can receive genuine respect for their gifts, and for the balance they can bring to the work of PNBC."

However, he was certain that things are going to change. He said, "I am certain that this current cohort of convention leaders elected in 2018 is the last cohort without a woman in one of the top three national offices. Things will change with the 2022 election."

He offered his own view about how he has attempted to include women in the life of PNBC during his presidency. He differentiated between what he calls "political roles" (holding an elected office), and "benefitting from the gifts and abilities" of women as preachers, department heads, and other appointed positions. Knowing how difficult it has been for women to advance to elected positions at any level of PNBC, he has tried to compensate for that by using presidential discretion to offer prominent roles to many women. In doing so, he is certain that he is allowing women to gain a prominence that may eventually enhance their chances of being elected to the top levels of leadership in the convention.[4]

James Perkins, another former PNBC president, also believes that a woman will be elected president. His advice is that "she and her supporters must take the initiative and pursue it aggressively."[5] Perkins has done as much as any former president to support and encourage women in PNBC. It is important that this level of support exist within the convention so that women will have strong advocates for their aspirations for participation and leadership. Tyrone Pitts noted that the election of a woman to a national office in PNBC will likely happen in 2022 "if people start identifying the candidate and organizing right away, rather than just waiting until the 2022 session to nominate someone from the floor."

If women cannot be fully embraced within the Progressive National Baptist Convention, one is left to wonder what their experiences will be like in the other Black Baptist conventions. Is it likely that a woman will be elected president of the National Baptist Convention USA, Inc.? The same can be asked of the National Baptist Convention of America or the Full Gospel Baptist Church Fellowship. Even though the Southern Baptist Convention has elected a Black male as its national president,[6] it remains highly unlikely that a woman will reach that level in the near future.[7]

History has proven that progress involving women in ministry will happen most quickly and effectively when women themselves are involved in leadership positions. It has been demonstrated that having African Americans working inside government, corporate America, the US military, and higher education can speed up matters of racial inclusion within those environments. Similarly, having women in a leadership position inside PNBC or any other national, religious body can open the door to other women for wider participation in all areas of national convention life.

The absence of women from leadership roles in the local, regional, or national structures of the Black Baptist church has nothing to do with women having any lack of ability, preparation, or experience when measured against the male clergy who have held any of those offices. The issue here is gender bias rooted in bad biblical theology and scriptural interpretation. Nineteenth-century whites used the story of God's curse on the children of Ham to justify the slavery of African Americans, and they quoted from Pauline passages in an attempt to convince the slaves to accept their position as God's will. How tragic that Black male clergy are following this same pattern of using selected and badly interpreted biblical passages to justify their objections to women in ministry.

An Issue as Old as Richard Allen
and Jarena Lee

Courage in the face of gender discrimination has always been in short supply among African American male clergy and their churches, which oddly enough almost always have a membership that is primarily comprised of women. Dating as far back as Richard Allen and the formation of the African Methodist Episcopal Church there was an intolerance of white racist behavior as evidenced by the walkout from St. George Methodist Episcopal Church in Philadelphia in 1787 (some place the date at 1793). Richard Allen, Absalom Jones, and others left that church not only because they were forced to sit in a segregated section of the sanctuary. They were equally outraged by the fact that they were publicly humiliated when an attempt was made to forcibly remove them from the whites-only section of the sanctuary when the call to prayer was announced and they knelt in reverence in that whites-only section so as not to disturb the service by walking during the prayer.[8]

By his own confession, Richard Allen was determined to build "a Black church" so that racism could no longer intrude in where or how his followers chose to worship God. "Allen's belief in Black uplift may have added fuel to the church-building fire, for he realized that white Methodists would never let Black preachers rise in the church hierarchy. Trapped in a middling position, he decided that building an African Methodist church was his only true option."[9]

Allen was determined to set the captives free when the captives were defined by their race and their captivity was maintained by the whites in the Methodist Episcopal Church system.

However, when it came to the issue of women in ministry, Allen did not have a similar tolerance. In fact, he reflected in his own life the sexism that defined the status of women in the United States in the eighteenth and nineteenth centuries. When Jarena Lee approached Allen in 1809 with the announcement that God had called her to be a preacher of the gospel, it was clear that neither Allen nor anyone else in the African Methodist Episcopal Church was prepared to end the captivity and limitations imposed upon some persons on the basis of gender. Allen refused her request to be ordained in the AME Church on the grounds that "our discipline knew nothing at all about it—that it did not call for women preachers."[10]

Lee's response to Allen is worth noting because it is as relevant in 2020 as it was more than two hundred years ago:

> O how careful ought we to be, lest through our bylaws of church government and discipline, we bring into disrepute even the word of life. For as unseemly as it may appear nowadays for a woman to preach, it should be remembered that nothing is impossible with God. And why should it be thought impossible, heterodox or improper for a woman to preach, seeing the Savior died for the woman as well as the man. Seeing he died for her also. Is he not a whole Savior instead of half one? As those who hold it wrong for a woman to preach would seem to make it appear.[11]

All three major Black Methodist bodies have long since abandoned their opposition to women in ministry. The absence of Black women in leadership in Black Baptist churches and church bodies becomes all the more obvious and difficult to understand when the African Methodist Episcopal Church, the African Methodist Episcopal Zion Church, and The Christian Methodist Episcopal Church have all consecrated women as bishops, which is the highest office that can be attained in those church bodies. We are members of the same racial group. We read from the same Bible. Yet so many Black Baptists cannot bring themselves to embrace what their Black Methodist brothers and sisters chose to resolve over twenty-years ago. Vashti McKenzie of Maryland was consecrated as an AME bishop in 2000. Once that stained-glass ceiling had been broken in the AME Church, she was followed in quick succession by Carolyn Tyler Guidry and Sarah Francis Davis in 2004, and Anne Henning-Byfield in 2016. The African Methodist Episcopal Zion Church elected Mildred Hines as bishop in 2008. The Christian Methodist Episcopal Church elected Teresa E. Snorton as a bishop in 2010.

The Invisible Black Woman

It seems that African American men who worked tirelessly to reverse the status of "the invisible man" (a term coined by Ralph Ellison) have found ways to keep women as invisible as possible in the leadership ranks of the church. Nothing better illustrates this than the list of speakers at the 1963 March on Washington where Martin Luther King Jr. delivered his now famous "I Have a Dream" speech; the phrase may have been borrowed from Prathia Hall. The march was sponsored by the so-called big six civil rights groups, which included

1. The Southern Christian Leadership Conference headed by Martin Luther King Jr.
2. The Student Non-Violent Coordinating Committee headed by John Lewis
3. The National Association for the Advancement of Colored People headed by Roy Wilkins
4. The National Urban League headed by Whitney Young
5. The Congress of Racial Equality headed by James Farmer
6. The National Council of Negro Women headed by Dorothy Height

All the male leaders were given a speaking role at the March on Washington, but Dorothy Height was not allowed to speak that day. She stood next to King during parts of the program on August 27, 1963. However, while all the men were allowed to speak in the name of their respective sponsoring organizations, Height was the only leader who was denied that opportunity and visibility. She later said "her male counterparts were happy to include women in the human family, but there was no question as to who headed the household."[12]

In 2011, Clarence Jones, who was speechwriter and counsel to King, reflected on the role of women at the March on Washington. He observed:

Women were virtually exiled from the podium . . . Not Daisy Bates, president of the Little Rock chapter of the NAACP, not even Rosa Parks, though both were in attendance . . . Most of the women in The Movement at that time had to contend with a kind of religious glass ceiling—a glass steeple, you could call it . . . The Movement was male dominated, and those males were ego-driven. There were certainly no female clergy members in Martin's Southern Christian Leadership Conference . . . There would have been interest in what they had to say, and I wish we'd given them that opportunity.[13]

"I wish we'd given them that opportunity." That phrase sums up the essence of sexism and all the other forms of oppression and marginalization that are the focus of liberation theology. There is a group with the power to include or exclude other persons based upon race, class, or gender. In denying persons a chance to make their contribution to the movement and to let their voices be heard from their unique position in society, the world will never know what talent was sidelined and silenced because male leaders were determined to keep the spotlight on themselves. Male leaders in the civil rights movement not only had the power but also the best of all reasons to include women in the March on Washington. Without women, there would have been no civil rights movement. "I wish we'd given them that opportunity." That is how people with privilege speak about those whose lives they view as less valuable than their own.

Jamie Eaddy is a 2020 doctor of ministry graduate from Colgate Rochester Crozer Divinity School. She wrote her thesis on the micro-aggressions experienced by women in their pursuit of equality in society in general and in the Black church in particular. In that thesis, Eaddy states that "if your fight for liberation stops once you are free, it wasn't liberation you wanted, it was privilege."[14] In her thesis, Eaddy refers to Johnetta Cole, who was the first female president of Spelman College in Atlanta, Georgia. Cole captures the irony of people who fight against racism but openly engage in sexism. She says:

> In the name of white supremacy, every imaginable act of human atrocity was perpetrated against Blacks. Now, in an all-Black situation, we witness a chillingly similar type of oppression, we see sundry acts of inhumanity leveled against Black females . . . the centuries of slavery and racism, and the struggle to overcome them, have not informed the humanity of Black men when it comes to Black women . . . the oppressive experiences of Black men have not deterred them from being oppressors themselves.[15]

Clearly, the exclusion of women from any role in the March on Washington was a case of male privilege. The fight against racism was going on while sexism was in clear view. "I wish we'd given them that opportunity."

"Them." To whom was Clarence Jones referring? Who were the persons whose voices were intentionally and unanimously silenced? "Them" included Rosa Parks, who sat down on a bus in Montgomery, Alabama. on December 1, 1955. Her independent action set in motion the Montgomery bus boycott. It was that boycott that launched King into national leadership.

"Them" included Daisy Bates, who was president of the Little Rock chapter of the NAACP and the leader in the effort to integrate Central High School in that city in 1957. "Them" included Fannie Lou Hamer, a Mississippi sharecropper who in 1963, while King and the other civil rights leaders were planning the March on Washington, was brutally beaten in a jail cell by another Black prisoner under orders from white police officers because she was seeking the right to vote. In 1964 she was the leader of the Mississippi Freedom Democratic Party that sought recognition at the 1964 Democratic convention, challenging the all-white Mississippi delegation.

"Them" included Ella Baker, who not only worked for King at SCLC in the 1950s but also helped to organize the Student Non-Violent Coordinating Committee (SNCC) in 1960 and helped orchestrate the Freedom Rides in 1960–1961.

"Them" included Diane Nash, who, while a student at Fisk University in Nashville, Tennessee, in 1960 was one of the leaders of the sit-ins at the downtown Woolworth's Department Store that made national news.

"Them" included Septima Clark, who was removed from her position in the South Carolina public school system because she would not renounce her membership in the NAACP. She put her teaching skills and civil rights passion to work in the Citizenship Schools, eventually sponsored by SCLC, which taught Black people the literacy skills they needed to become registered voters.

"Them" also included Dorothy Cotton, who was the educational director of SCLC, and as much a part of the inner circle of SCLC as Andrew Young or Wyatt Tee Walker. She later founded the Atlanta-based Citizen Education Program that trained disenfranchised people to become civically and politically involved.

"Them" included Prathia Hall—who, as mentioned earlier, coined the phrase "I have a dream" that King popularized at that march.

The Bible Is Not the Obstacle

During my twenty-four-year tenure as senior pastor at Antioch Baptist Church in Cleveland, the church ordained four women to the ministry and seven others to the office of deacon. More women have been added to both categories during the tenure of Dr. Todd Davidson, who succeeded me at that church. When we started down this path, we were inundated with people inside and outside the church whose only opposition to what we were doing was their understanding of 1 Corinthians 14:34ff. and 1 Timothy 2:11ff. First with the deacon board and later with the congregation, I led the church through the analysis of all the passage that I have reviewed throughout the last two chapters. Only then did we vote as a congregation to move in this direction. We were able to resolve those issues, and with a near-unanimous vote we proceeded with the ordination services.

In addition to Tonya Fields, the church ordained and hired Mylion Waite in 1995. She was working with the Inter-Church Council of Greater Cleveland and was active in various social justice initiatives throughout the community. She continues to oversee the church's prison ministry which is called The Open-Door Prison Ministry Fellowship. That ministry hosts monthly gatherings at the church for the families of persons that are currently incarcerated. She also schedules trips to various prisons and jails throughout Northeast Ohio that involve preachers and choirs from Antioch that lead worship services with inmates and prison staff. In addition, she is ending her term as President of the Cleveland Baptist Association of the American Baptist Churches.

Gloria Chaney was ordained in 2007. She has served as pastor of two congregations. First, she was senior pastor of Shiloh Baptist Church in Scranton, Pennsylvania. Today she is senior pastor of Church of the Master in Cleveland Heights, Ohio. She has also served as an adjunct instructor in Black Church Studies and Religious Studies at Cleveland State University and Cuyahoga Community College, and as dean of the Ohio Leadership Academy and as chairperson of the ministry committee of the Cleveland Baptist Association.

We also ordained Monica Harmon in 2010, who now works as a recruiter and enrollment coordinator for Ashland Theological Seminary in Ashland, Ohio. She was also a chaplain for Crossroads Hospice from 2010 to 2016.

In addition to that, the church has also ordained more than ten women to be deacons in the church. Currently, both the chairperson and the vice chairperson of the deacon board are women.

More than twenty years after we ordained the first woman to the ministry, I am more convinced than ever that Scripture is not the real obstacle. As I wrote in *Deacons in Today's Black Baptist Church*, the real obstacle is gender bias:

> Women are not excluded from the offices of deacon or preacher in most Black Baptist churches because of our accurate adherence to biblical teaching. The primary reason for excluding women is gender discrimination—something that can no more be supported or defended through the use of Scripture than the racial discrimination so long directed against Black people in the United States.[16]

Let the oppressed go free! As someone who came to faith under the Rev. Mary G. Evans, I wholeheartedly support those women who seek to follow their call from God and serve as preachers in pastoral ministry. I do not embrace the notion that an unqualified or a less qualified male is a better choice than the best qualified woman. I do not accept the uninformed, noncritical, patriarchal-centered biblical analysis that seeks to lock women into a first-century Palestinian cultural context. If Judaism has evolved over the intervening years and now allows for female cantors and rabbis, can someone explain why Christianity cannot have female clergy?

Learning a Lesson from Samuel in the Old Testament

When it comes to men refusing to acknowledge the call that women have received from God, I want to offer a biblical perspective that might change the hearts and minds of some of my male colleagues. In 1 Samuel 8:1-7, the people of Israel asked the prophet Samuel to appoint a king who would lead the nation after he was dead. Samuel did not want to comply with that request, because he believed that Israel was meant to be a theocracy in which God would be the king, the ruler of the nation, no matter who the prophet was at any time. However, when Samuel prayed to God about this request from the people, God said, "Listen to all that the people are saying to you; it is not you they have rejected, but they have rejected me as their king."

I assert that when male clergy resist, deny, or obstruct the ordination and advancement of women in Christian ministry, it is not the male advocates of women in ministry like me and many others who are being rejected. When male clergy refuse to embrace those women who announce their call to ministry solely based on their gender, those male clergy are rejecting God—because it is God who is summoning these women into service. How strange that those who oppose women in ministry always quote 1 Corinthians 14:34-35 and 1 Timothy 2:11, but they never want to account for Joel 2:28-29, in which God speaks of a coming day when "I will pour out my Spirit on all people. Your sons and your daughters will prophesy, your old men will dream dreams, your young men will see visions. Even on my servants, both men and women, I will pour out my Spirit in those days." (NIV)

It is important that I pay tribute to my friend and colleague, Cleophus Larue of Princeton Theological Seminary, who made this same point fifteen years ago when he wrote *This Is My Story: Testimonies and Sermons of Black Women in Ministry*.[17] He talked about "women in ministry and the progressive males who welcomed their presence."[18] As one of those "progressive males," he boldly asserted in 2005:

> The twenty-first century will be the century for Black women in ministry. In ever-increasing numbers they are announcing their calls to the gospel ministry and making haste to establish themselves in viable ministries throughout this country. Their presence in all levels of ordained Christian service—including preaching and pastoral ministries—promises to reshape our understanding of traditional clergy leadership roles, tilts us even more toward a neo-Pentecostal fervor in the way we have church, and provides us with new and creative ways of addressing problems within the community.[19]

However, no sooner had he made that declaration than he went on to observe that the changes he believes will happen in the twenty-first century have not happened yet. Larue says:

Despite the promises inherent in this new century, ordained ministry for Black women continues to be an uphill battle. As one who grew up in a conservative Black Baptist church in south Texas, I know how wrenching decisions pertaining to women in ordained ministry can be. Many of us came to faith in church environments that simply did not accept women as preachers and pastors. Not only did the ordination of women violate our sociocultural mores, it was also, we believed, clearly forbidden in Scripture.[20]

What Larue goes on to do in his book is tell the story about how his mind and heart changed concerning women in ministry. The triggering event was an encounter with a young woman whom Larue refused to endorse for scholarship support to pursue her theological training. She said to him, "Who are you to get in the way of what God has called me to do?"[21] This was 1 Samuel 8 all over again, as a woman determined to pursue a call to ministry told a male preacher that he was rejecting what God was doing. Larue stated that like Saul on the Damascus Road, "She opened my blinded eyes that I might see . . . She succeeded in showing me a more excellent way."[22]

The experience of Cleophus Larue is instructive for other Black male clergy who remain resistant to the idea of women in ministry. Once he changed his mind on the subject and shared that change with his south Texas congregation, they celebrated his conversion on the issue and wondered when he was going to finally come around. His opposition and that of other Black male clergy have done nothing to stem the tide of women answering their call to ministry. As he observed, "Many Black women who have their heart set on ministry and who are determined to heed God's call continue to encounter stiff resistance from both men and women, yet they give no indication of backing away from what they believe to be their God-given right and undeniable destiny."[23]

As important as it is that women continue to advocate for themselves on the matter of answering their call to ministry, it is equally important that male clergy stand with their sisters in ministry and demonstrate in both word and deed that they fully support the fact that God calls women into Christian ministry, and that those who reject or resist that move of the Spirit are, in fact, rejecting God. As the young woman said to Larue, "Who are you to get in the way of what God has called me to do?"

During a Zoom conference with female clergy from across the country arranged by Jewel London, I gained a clearer sense of what male clergy can do to support and advocate for women in ministry. Over and over again, I heard those women saying how much they missed having a father or a parent in ministry who was willing to take them under their wing and mentor them as they sought opportunities. Those women were fully aware of how this works for their male colleagues. They saw males being employed, encouraged, endorsed, recommended, and installed into pastoral roles by their "father in the ministry." They also noticed how rarely if ever such a relationship had ever been extended to them.

This is what occurred with almost every male preacher I know; we were mentored, groomed, and occasionally chastised, but we were always supported as we shared with our "father in ministry" what our hopes were for our own ministry. There is no doubt in my mind that my journey was made easier by the support I received from Charles H. Webb Sr., William A. Jones Jr., Gardner C. Taylor, and Samuel D. Proctor.

There is also no doubt in my mind that I was greatly aided in my ministry by several of my male contemporaries with whom I worked, studied, and dreamed about the future. Men like William S. Epps of California, Calvin O. Butts III of New York City, Marion Franklin of New Jersey, Rickey Harvey of Rochester, New York, Ricky Woods of North Carolina, Wayne Croft of Pennsylvania, Charles Webb Jr. of Illinois, James Perkins of Michigan, Marcus Cosby and Ralph Douglas West of Texas, Forrest Harris of Tennessee, Otis Moss Jr., Larry Macon Sr., C. J. Matthews, William Myers, Rodney Maiden, Larry Harris Sr., and Charles Booth, all of Ohio, and so many others were all a part of my circle of colleagues and friends over a forty-five-year period. In short, I never lacked for either fathers or brothers in the ministry.

The cry of the women I met with in that Zoom conference was for equal access to that network of relationships that can gain one entry into ministry positions and can provide support and added opportunities along the way. Obviously, those women who have already gained a foothold in the ministry can provide this kind of mentoring and modeling for the women who are coming behind them. This is what Suzan Johnson Cook said she was committed to doing. However, there are not enough women currently in a position to fill this role for all the women who are coming forward to answer their call to ministry.

I find myself overwhelmed by the number of men and women who are inviting me to play that role for them, and I try to extend myself as far as I can to meet that need. I have mentored, ordained, hired, or recommended for pastoral ministry positions Tonya Fields, Mylion Waite, Gloria Chaney, and Monica Harmon. I also appointed Minister Audrey Fountain to a leadership role on our ministry team at Antioch. I have regularly shared in ministry with female pastors in Cleveland and in Rochester, New York. My book *Deacons in Today's Black Baptist Church* has been widely used in some churches, but passed over by others because of the chapter in which I expressed support for women as deacons in Black Baptist churches.[24] I participated in the ordination services for Christine A. Smith and Courtney Clayton Jenkins, both of Cleveland, a city that remains fiercely resistant to women in ministry.

The clear fact is, however, that many more male clergy are needed to meet the demand for mentoring and partnering coming from women seeking to engage in pastoral ministry. Just as racism cannot be resolved solely by the best efforts of Black people without the continued involvement of white people in this country, so too, sexism cannot be eliminated solely by women without the continued commitment of men who are prepared to reject the old model of a male-only clergy. Who are we to get in the way of what God has called women to do in ministry?

Male clergy need to prepare and promote women for ordination. Male clergy need to hire and promote women as part of their ministry team. Male clergy need to invite women to preach for all occasions in the life of the church, and not just for Women's Day or Missionary Sunday. Male clergy need to nominate women for consideration by church search committees looking for a new pastor. Male clergy ought to mentor and position women to be their successors as senior pastor, as J. Alfred Smith Sr. did with Jacqueline Thompson.

Male clergy ought to support women seeking positions within their denominational structure.

Male clergy ought to speak out whenever and wherever female clergy are being passed over, overlooked, pushed aside, or marginalized in local clergy associations, state conventions, national church bodies, and in major civic and liturgical events such as seven-last-word services on Good Friday, citywide revivals, Martin Luther King Jr. Day observances, and Emancipation Day or Juneteenth celebrations.

I say again, no woman has ever been elected to any of the top three offices of the Progressive National Baptist Convention, much less to the other more conservative Baptist conventions. All the Black Methodist groups have elected women as bishops in their church. What is wrong with Black Baptists? The only possible answer is that too many of us are clinging to gender bias rooted in an archaic interpretation of Scripture at a time when women are making great strides in every other area of national life.

Capable Black women in ministry are leaving their spiritual homes in the Black Baptist church to find open arms and ready appointments within the United Methodist Church, the United Church of Christ, the American Baptist Churches, USA, and the United Presbyterian Church. Tragically, their gain is our loss as Black Baptists.

Tonya Fields, of whom I spoke earlier, went to the United Methodist Church when we could not find a church in Greater Cleveland willing to call her as pastor. She was immediately assigned to St. Paul United Methodist Church, and within two years that church grew to one of the largest United Methodist congregations in the district. Gloria Chaney went to the American Baptist Church, where she now serves as pastor at Church of the Master in Cleveland Heights. Mylion Waite worked for an ecumenical agency called the Inter-Church Council of Greater Cleveland while continuing to work at Antioch with a focus on prison ministry. Monica Harmon went into hospital and hospice chaplaincy in Cleveland. It is not ability that women in ministry lack. It is opportunity.

I have intentionally devoted more attention to this issue than to the other forms of liberation theology. I am intentionally devoting the next chapter to a fuller discussion of womanist theology. I do this because Galatians 3:26-29 demands that I focus on this issue more than the other matters dealt with in that passage. None of the other areas of oppression and division listed in that passage are being resisted in the church. No one is arguing that slavery was good or that it should be reinstated. In Christ, "there is neither slave nor free." That is the issue of class. No one is still debating that God has a favorite nation out of all the nations of the earth. Whenever I hear someone singing "God Bless America," I invite them to follow up with another song: "He's Got the Whole World in His Hands." "In Christ there is neither Jew nor Gentile." That is the mater of ethnicity.

The passage includes one more call to let the oppressed go free. "In Christ there is neither male nor female." Galatians 3:26-29 is not a multiple-choice passage where we are free to embrace the categories with which we agree, while rejecting the categories with which we disagree. I offer this warning from 1 Samuel 8:7 to any and all persons who remain opposed to women in ministry no matter what their argument might be for their position. You are not rejecting the women who are announcing their call to ministry. You are rejecting the God who called them. "Who are you to get in the way of what God has called them to do?"

NOTES

1. Taylor Branch, *Parting the Waters: America in the King Years 1954–1963* (New York: Simon & Schuster, 1988), 505.

2. Courtney Pace, *Freedom Faith: The Womanist Vision of Prathia Hall* (Athens: University of Georgia Press, 2019), 188.

3. Article V, Section 2 of the Constitution of the Progressive National Baptist Convention.

4. Dr. Timothy Stewart, telephone interview by Marvin A. McMickle, September 16, 2020. His comments are included here with his knowledge and permission.

5. James Perkins offered these comments on September 16, 2020, and has granted permission to be quoted in this book.

6. Jena McGregor, "Southern Baptist Convention elects Fred Luter as First Black President: What This Leadership Moment Means," Washington Post.com, June 19, 2012.

7. Susan M. Shaw, "Should Southern Baptist Women Be Preachers? A Centuries-Old Controversy Finds New Life," ReligionNews.com, June 27, 2019.

8. Richard S. Newman, *Richard Allen, Freedom's Prophet: Bishop Richard Allen, the AME Church, and the Black Founding Fathers* (New York: NYU Press, 2008), 71.

9. Ibid.

10. Marvin A. McMickle, "Jarena Lee," in *An Encyclopedia of African American Christian Heritage* (Valley Forge, PA: Judson Press, 2002), 71.

11. Jarena Lee, "A Female Preacher among the African Methodists," in *African American Religious History: A Documentary Witness*, ed. Milton C. Sernett (Durham, NC: Duke University Press, 1999), 173. See also Jarena Lee, *The Life and Religious Experiences and Journal of Mrs. Jarena Lee: A Colored Lady Giving an Account of Her Call to Preach the Gospel* (n.p.: HardPress, 2019).

12. "Dorothy Height," biography.com, September 13, 2019.

13. Clarence B. Jones and Stuart Connelly, *Behind the Dream: The Making of the Speech That Transformed a Nation* (New York: Palgrave Macmillan, 2011), 100–102.

14. Jamie Eaddy, "Oppression, Privilege, and Spiritual Malpractice: A Psychological Approach to Understanding and Combating Gender Micro-aggressions in the Black Church," unpublished DMin thesis, May 2020, 79.

15. Johnetta B. Cole, *Gender Talk: The Struggle for Women's Equality in African American Communities* (New York: Random House), Kindle loc. 257.

16. Marvin A. McMickle, *Deacons in Today's Black Baptist Church* (Valley Forge, PA: Judson Press, 2010), 89.

17. Cleophus J. Larue, ed., *This Is My Story: Testimonies and Sermons of Black Women in Ministry* (Louisville, KY: Westminster/John Knox, 2005).

18. Ibid., 4.

19. Ibid., 1.

20. Ibid.

20. Ibid., 3.

21. Ibid.

22. Ibid., 4.

23. Ibid.

24. McMickle, *Deacons in Today's Black Baptist Church*. 78–101.

CHAPTER 8

Womanist Theology

In 2019, in recognition of Women's History Month, I wrote an essay in *Christian Citizen*, an online journal of the American Baptist Church, "Women's History Month, a Good Time to Focus on Womanist Theology."[1] I began that essay by saying:

> Womanist Theology is a critique of earlier approaches to biblical interpretation that may have separately addressed race, gender, or poverty, but never attempted to address them as inter-related realities . . . It is possible for some people to experience one of these realities without necessarily having had to experience the other two . . . Womanist Theology seeks to make church and society keenly aware of the conditions faced every day by Black women who are simultaneously impacted by all three forms of oppression.[2]

If we use Galatians 3:26-29 as the focal point for defining the various forms of oppression that have been examined up to now in this study, we would conclude that the broad issues are oppression based upon race or ethnicity, class or economic status, and gender. The text specifies these areas of division and distinction that must first be torn down within the church. Paul says, "In Christ Jesus you are all children of God through faith. As many of you as were baptized into Christ have clothed yourselves with Christ. There is no longer Jew or Greek, there is no longer slave or free, there is no longer male and female; for all of you are one in Christ Jesus. And if you belong to Christ, then you are Abraham's offspring, heirs according to the promise." These were the great social divisions of the ancient Greco-Roman world in general and within ancient Israel in particular. These are the forms of division that have resulted in centuries of oppression, marginalization, and denial of both human rights and vocational opportunity.

The divisions named by Paul in the first century CE remain with us in the twenty-first century CE as well. What is being argued in this book is that the church will not have any credibility when it seeks to tear down these dividing walls within the broader society as long as these walls of divisions remain in place inside the church itself. It has already been shown here how race, class, and gender continue to impact the church as well as the world.

This chapter will dig more deeply into what happens to people when they are the targets and victims of not just one of these categories of division, but of all three forms at the same time. For Black women in the church and within the broader society, their struggle is not just with being Black or being female. They are also heavily affected by economic factors driven by limited access to higher paying jobs, receiving less salary for doing the same job as their male co-workers, operating as single-parent heads of households, and too often forced into minimum wage jobs that offer no workplace benefits such as health insurance, the protection of unionized employment, or the chance to accrue any retirement income.

Judith Weisenfeld talks about these three connected forms of socially constructed boundaries and power divides. She uses as a point of reference Harriet Tubman, the nineteenth-century woman who escaped from slavery and then led hundreds of other slaves to escape from their condition and find freedom in free states in the North or ultimately in Canada. Weisenfeld says:

> Because Harriet Tubman for example, lived as a woman whose gender and sexuality were understood through the prism of her race and class as an enslaved person, her experience of gender, racial and class status necessarily differed from that of a white woman or man, an African-American man, an Asian-American woman, and so on, in her time. Moreover, her experience within these socially constructed categories differed from that of an African-American woman of free status.[3]

Here are the three categories of division set forth in Galatians 3, all of which are experienced by Harriet Tubman, and except for the factor of enslavement, by many Black women to this day. Her oppression was not solely the result of her race, class, or gender. Her oppression was defined by her exposure to and victimization by all three of these categories on a regular and sustained basis.

It was the fact that no previous forms of liberation theology had addressed this unique problem of threefold oppression and disadvantage that Black women scholars collaborated on the development of what has come to be known as womanist theology. Black theology focused on racism but not on sexism that was present in the Black church at the same time. Latin American liberation theology focused largely on poverty and economic exploitation but not with equal attention to race and gender questions. Feminist theology focused on matters of gender discrimination but never seemed sensitive to or especially interested in the unique experience of being a non-white woman in a white patriarchal society. For all three of these factors to be discussed as an interconnected experience it was necessary that the world hear from those women who lived that experience every day.

Katie Cannon and the Birth of Womanist Theology

In a 2019 article in *The Christian Century*, Eboni Marshall Turman of Yale Divinity School asserts that the origins of womanist theology can be traced to a lecture given by Katie Cannon at the American Academy of Religion in 1985. That lecture was entitled "The Emergence of Black Feminist Consciousness."[4] Turman says, "Together with four other Black women inquirers, she advanced the fundaments of a new form of discourse and emerged as a matriarch of theological womanism—a theology that affirms the significance of Black women's God-talk, survival, and flourishing for determining the substance of faithful Christian discourse and praxis."[5]

Turman continues by naming the other four "Black women inquirers." They were Jacqueline Grant, Delores Williams, Emilie Townes, and Renita Weems. She says they found themselves "welded between the masculine erections of Black liberation theology and the overwhelming white middle-class vexations of feminist liberation, both of which ignored the experiences of poor Black women in the United

States. But they inherited the wisdom of countless unlettered but responsible, in charge, serious Black women who knew the words and worth of prayer."[6]

According to Katie Cannon, the term "womanist theology" emerges from the term "womanish," used by Alice Walker to describe a young girl acting older that her age or being more aggressive than was expected by society where female conduct was concerned.[7]

As used by Walker, womanism or being a womanist involves four components, which do not necessarily define the work of womanist theology. However, it does set forth some broad parameters for the meaning of womanism itself. Those four components can be condensed to include the following:

1. Referring to outrageous, audacious, courageous or willful behavior. Wanting to know more and in greater depth than is considered "good" for one. Interested in grown-up doings. Acting grown up. Being grown up . . .

2. A woman who loves other women, sexually and/or non-sexually. Appreciates and prefers women's culture, women's emotional flexibility (values tears as a natural counterbalance of laughter), and women's strength . . .

3. Loves music. Loves dance. Loves the moon. Loves the Spirit. Loves love and food and roundness. Loves struggle. Loves the Folk. Loves herself.

4. Womanist is to feminist as purple is to lavender.[8]

Drawing variously from the term "womanism," Cannon says that term was then employed as a basis for Black women scholars to do theological reflection in ways and around issues that had been ignored by both white and Black male theologians. She says:

The chief function of womanism is not merely to replace one set of elitist, hegemonic texts that have traditionally ignored, dismissed, or flat-out misunderstood the existential realities of women in the African Diaspora with another set of Afrocentric texts that had gotten short shrift and pushed to the margins of the learned societies. Our objective is to use Walker's four-part definition as a critical, methodological framework for challenging inherited traditions for their collusion with androcentric patriarchy as well as a catalyst in overcoming oppressive situations through revolutionary acts of rebellion.[9]

Cannon asserts that there are three steps to doing what she also refers to as liberation ethics:

1. "Debunking, unmasking, and disentangling the ideologies, theologies, and systems of value operative in a particular society. That is accomplished by analyzing established power relationships

2. Analyzing the established power relationships that determine cultural, political and economic presuppositions and by evaluating the legitimizing myths that sanction the enforcement of such values.

3. These steps are taken so that Black women may become responsible decision-makers who envision structural and systemic alternatives that embrace the well-being of us all."[10]

In giving breadth and depth to the work of womanist theology, Cannon offers her own twist on a line made popular by W. E. B. Du Bois in *The Souls of Black Folk*. Du Bois said, "The problem of the twentieth century is the problem of the color-line."[11] Cannon says, "The problem of the twenty-first century is the problem of the color line, the gender line, and the class line."[12]

Turman refers to another founder of womanist rheology, Delores Williams, who in 1987 published *Womanist Theology: Black Women's Voices*. Turman says, "This trinity of essays developed the first scholarly assertions of womanist theology."[13] Together, these womanist theologians "knew that the consequences for Black women of living with multiple forms of oppression—based on race, gender, class, sexuality, and ability—can be brutal."[14]

Kelly Brown Douglas, another leading voice in the formation of womanist theology and a former student of James Cone, expands on these comments from Cannon and the other founders of womanist theology when she states:

Shaped by the Black Power/civil rights movement out of which it emerged; Black Theology focused only on one dimension of Black oppression—White racism. Its failure to utilize Black women's experience further prevented it from developing an adequate analysis of Black oppression. It did not address the multiple social burdens, that is, racism, sexism, classism, and heterosexism, which beset Black men and women.[15]

Douglas likens the need for a womanist theology today to the concerns raised by Black women during the antebellum era in this country. She refers to Anna Julia Cooper, who said, "The colored woman to-day occupies, one may say, a unique position in this country . . . She is confronted by both a woman question and a race problem, and is as yet an unknown or unacknowledged factor in both."[16] Douglas then notes:

> Unfortunately, the contemporary women's movement was no less characterized by a lack of concern for Black women than the nineteenth century suffrage movement . . . White women's narrow focus on patriarchy continued to reflect their disinterest in Black women's freedom. Their focus led some Black women to claim, "feminism is a white female thing that has nothing to do with Black women."[17]

Another leading scholar in shaping womanist theology was Jacqueline Grant, who offers another way of thinking about the way that womanist theology differs from both Black theology and feminist theology. She reflects on what she calls "the tri-dimensional experience of oppression based upon race, gender, and class."[18] She argues that Black women must speak for themselves in the liberation theology dialogue. While she recognizes the value of both Black theology and feminist theology, she also recognizes that both were flawed when it came to addressing the unique issues of those facing "tridimensional oppression." She states:

> This perspective in theology which I am calling womanist theology draws upon the life and experiences of some Black women who have created meaningful interpretations of the Christian faith. Black women must do theology out of their tri-dimensional experience of racism/sexism/classism. To ignore any aspect of this experience is to deny the wholistic and integrated reality of Black womanhood.[19]

Grant continues, "Class distinctions which have emerged even in the Black community, and sex differences, which have taken on new forms of institutionalization, must be addressed. For liberation to become a reality, race, sex, and class must be deliberately confronted. Interconnected as they are, they all impinge greatly on the lives of Black women."[20]

The preceding two chapters of this book have pointed to the limitations and obstacles faced by Black women because of gender bias in the Black church. While Black theology was birthed as a way to attack the racism that was at work in the church and the society as a whole, Black theology did not work to differentiate the ways by which Black men and women were affected by racism.

Similarly, while feminist theology sought to address the limitations faced by women in ministry, feminism did not fully embrace and likely could not comprehend the broader challenges associated with being a Black woman in this country. bell hooks makes this point when she says, "Racism abounds in the writings of white feminists, reinforcing white supremacy, and negating the possibility that women will bond politically across ethnic and racial boundaries. Past feminist refusal to draw attention to and attack racial hierarchy suppressed the link between race and class. Yet class structure in American society has been shaped by the racial politics of white supremacy."[21]

Renita Weems brings the skill and perspective of a biblical scholar to the shaping of womanist theology. Beginning with her 1988 book, *Just a Sister Away*, she allows the voices of nine women in the salvation narrative of the Bible to become a way to reconsider preaching and Bible study from a nonpatriarchal perspective. She defines two sources for her approach to doing biblical analysis. She states:

> *Just a Sister Away* attempts to combine the best of the fruits of feminist biblical criticism with its passion for reclaiming and reconstructing the stories of biblical women, along with the best of the Afro-American oral tradition, with its gift for story-telling and its love of drama. For this reason, the novelist Alice Walker's term "womanist"—best describes the critical perspective taken here.[22]

The unique thing about the nine biblical stories used by Weems is that they do not concentrate on how those women were treated, viewed, or valued by the men who appeared in those stories. Rather, Weems notes that "one of the best ways to get an idea of how a woman feels about being a woman is to take a look at how she treats other women. Hence, *Just a Sister Away* examines women's relations with one another."[23] We hear a story that stretches from Hagar and Sarah at the beginning of the salvation history story, to Elizabeth and Mary and the birth of Jesus and John the Baptist, to the many women who were followers of Jesus and underwriters of the ministry of Paul. This womanist reading of Scripture pauses to consider the voices and actions of women who were central to the biblical story but who have been kept unheard and unseen by too many preachers and expositors. As J. Alfred Smith Sr. once said, it was time to "Let Huldah Speak."

Emilie M. Townes introduces an important notion about womanism and womanist theology when she suggests that there is a confessional element involved. She says, "The confessional element of womanism means that it is a term that cannot be imposed but must be claimed by the Black woman who is engaged, from her own faith perspective and academic discipline, in the eradication of oppression. Therefore, the use of the term womanism to describe a theorist's or practitioner's work is one of avowal rather than denotation. This confessional stance is crucial." Townes continues, "Also, the womanist is not free to name others as womanist if this is not a term they claim for themselves. For example, describing Black women from the nineteenth century as womanists is inaccurate . . . At best, and most faithfully, these women embody nascent womanism that provides a rich framework for womanists of this era to flesh out."[24]

Early Voices in the Battle against Race and Gender Discrimination

Following up on those women that Emilie M. Townes refers to as embodying nascent womanism, it would be useful to consider four such persons: Sojourner Truth, Anna Julia Cooper, Nannie Helen Burroughs, and Ida B. Wells Barnett. Consistent with Townes' cautionary note that womanism is a term that a woman must choose and confess for herself, let me point to these four women as representative of Black women who addressed the themes of racism, sexism, and classism associated with womanist theology long before such a term had been conceived.

Anna Julia Cooper

Born into slavery in North Carolina in 1858 to an enslaved woman and her white owner, in 1892, Anna Julia Cooper wrote an essay entitled "The Status of Woman in America." It begins with reflections on the conditions faced by white women during the expansion and settlement of the United States. She says, "The dangers of wild beasts and of wilder men, the mysteries of the unknown wastes and unexplored forests, the horrors of pestilence and famine, of exposure and loneliness, during all those years of discovery and settlement, were braved without a murmur by women who had been most delicately constituted and most tenderly nurtured."[25]

She later turns her attention to the status of Black women at that point in history:

> The colored woman of today occupies, one may say, a unique position in this country . . . She is confronted by both a woman question and a race problem, and is as yet an unknown or an unacknowledged factor in both. While the woman of the white race can with calm assurance enter upon the work they feel by nature appointed to do, while their men give loyal support and appreciative countenance to their efforts . . . the colored woman too often finds herself hampered and shamed by a less liberal sentiment and a more conservative attitude on the part of those for whose opinion she cares most . . . The average man of our race is less frequently ready to admit the actual need among the sturdier forces of the world for woman's help or influence.[26]

"A woman question and a race problem" is compelling phrase to begin with as we look at the nascent womanist movement in the nineteenth century.

Sojourner Truth

It would be fair to say that Black men and women were equally impacted by the work requirements of the slave era, such as sharecropping, domestic service, and low-wage jobs. However, there were aspects of the slave experience that fell exclusively upon Black women: the constant reproduction of new slaves through their wombs. Isabella Van Wagenen, who would later change her name to Sojourner Truth, made that point in her 1851 speech delivered at a Women's Rights Convention in Akron, Ohio, where she used the phrase "And ain't I a woman?" She said, "I want to say a few words about this matter. I am a woman's rights. That man over there says that women need to be helped into carriages and lifted over ditches, and to have the best places everywhere. Nobody ever helps me into carriages, or over mud puddles, or gives me any best place. And ain't I a woman?"

She continues:

> Look at me. Look at my arm! I have plowed and reaped and gathered into barns, and no man could head me. And ain't I a woman? I have husked and chopped and mowed, and can any man do more than that? I have heard much about the sexes being equal. I can carry as much as any man, and can eat as much, too, if I can get it—and bear the lash as well. And ain't I a woman? I am as strong as any man that is now.[27]

Up to that point, Sojourner Truth was focusing on the things that both men and women experienced equally during the time of slavery, matters rooted solely in racism and ethnicity However, the speech then moved on to touch upon something that was unique to the experiences of Black women in slavery—namely, that the womb of a slave woman was as much a matter of exploitation by white and Black men as was her daily workload.

There were two driving factors that contributed to the sexual exploitation of Black slave women. First, they were used and abused through rape for the personal pleasure of white men.

M. Shawn Copeland recounted a harrowing tale of a Black woman who was the victim of brutal rape by three white men. She uses the words taken from a slave narrative in the voice of someone who observed that vicious assault. It says, "My mother's mistress had three boys—one twenty, one nineteen, and one seventeen. One day, Old Mistress had gone away to spend the day. Mother always worked in the house, and while she was alone, the boys came in and threw her down on the floor and tied her down so she couldn't struggle. One after the other used her as they wanted for the whole afternoon."[28] Copeland continued, "Slavery made Black women's bodies sexually vulnerable and available."[29]

The second thing that must be understood is that pleasure was not the only motivation when it came to the use and abuse of bodies of Black women during slavery. Profit was an equally powerful motive for the sexual assaults upon Black women. The bodies of Black women were the primary means of increasing and replenishing the number of slaves in this country. The bodies of Black women were monetized through their work in the day and were further monetized through their wombs as white men and sometimes Black men as well practiced a form of slavery based upon the forced reproduction of slaves via those sexual assaults on the plantation rather than through the purchase from a slave trader or importation from a slave port.

In that 1852 speech, Sojourner Truth also speaks to this aspect of slave life that was different for slave women than for men when she said, "I have borne thirteen children, and seen most all sold off to slavery, and when I cried out with my mother's grief, none but Jesus heard me! And ain't I a woman?"[30] Sojourner Truth reported that her womb was as much a part of her slave experience as was the work she did in the fields.

This is an important point, and essential to the eventual birth of womanist theology. Black women were victimized not only by race and by their status as slaves, but also by their gender in ways that did not apply to Black men. Here are the roots of "tri-dimensional oppression" in the form of race, class, and gender. Unlike Black male slaves, whose primary value was through their capacity to work and turn a profit for the slaveowner, the Black female slave was doubly valuable to the slave economy because she could not only turn a profit with her work but also give birth to new slaves through her womb.

Henry Louis Gates Jr. estimates that around 12.5 million people were shipped to the New World and sold into slavery. He estimates that half of that number (6 million people) went to Brazil. He estimates that Jamaica imported more than 1 million persons. Cuba and Haiti each accounted for nearly 780,000. Mexico received 550,000. He then estimates that 450,000 Africans were imported directly into the British colonies and later into the United States.[31] Most but not all of them entered through ports in Georgia, the Carolinas, and Florida.[32]

165

One of the reasons why the number of slaves imported into the United States was substantially lower than in the Caribbean or in South American countries was likely due to this practice of using Black women as the primary source for new saves. It was more cost effective to breed slaves than it was to buy them. In other active slaveholding regions throughout the Americas, slaves were essentially worked to death and then new slaves were purchased to replace them. In the United States slaves were replenished through reproduction on the plantation.

It is estimated that at the start of the Civil War in 1861, "4 million African Americans in the South lived in bondage, the chattel property of their masters."[33] In other words, the number of Black people living in slavery in 1861 was nine times higher than the number of Africans initially imported into this country. Add to that numerical fact this additional geopolitical fact. By order of the United States Constitution, Article 1, Section 9, the trans-Atlantic slave trade was ended in 1808. Of course, this allowed the importation of slaves to continue twenty years after the Constitution was ratified. But this also points to the fact that from 1808 onward, slave traders and slave owners were no longer focused on importing new slaves from Africa. The primary way by which slaves were secured was through birth inside the country. The domestic slave trade continued, as Sojourner Truth reported. She gave birth to thirteen children, and most of them were sold away. Her story was the story about how slaves were acquired in the United States. Slaves were born and bred in this country, and the sole method by which those births occurred was through the use and abuse of the bodies of Black women.

The life of women like Sojourner Truth and other women in the nineteenth century whose voices were captured in slave narratives was the earliest embodiment of what Black female scholars in the twentieth century would call tri-dimensional oppression, which serves as the basis for that form of liberation theology those scholars call womanist theology. The condition of Black women involved her race, her economic status or class, and her gender as an object of sexual exploitation. This tri-dimensional form of oppression has marked the experience of Black women over the years.

Nannie Helen Burroughs

A different point can be made by womanist theology as a critique of feminist theology that can be drawn from the life of Nannie Helen Burroughs. She focuses on gender distinctions between Black men and Black women. However, she also draws attention to "color consciousness" within the Black community so far as skin tone and the variety of skin colors among Black people are concerned. Finally, she offers a perspective from which to consider the racial distinctions between Black women and white women.

Nannie Helen Burroughs was born in Virginia in 1878. Having relocated to Washington, DC, for her own education at the M Street Preparatory High School, she aspired to be a teacher at that same school that was the first public school in the nation established in 1870 to educate Black youth. That opportunity was denied to her, because she was a very dark-skinned woman, and because of her complexion that school would not hire her to teach Black children.[34] Burroughs was therefore the victim of a double caste system that has haunted Black America for years, a system that differentiated between lighter and darker complexions among Black people, all of whom were collectively scorned by white people.

This fixation with light versus darker skin tones was brought home to me in a shocking way during a 1995 trip to research the trans-Atlantic slave trade at the Goree Island slave port off the coast of Dakar, Senegal. A young Senegalese woman was one of the persons guiding my group through that dreadful prison where white slave traders lived in luxury on one level, while captured Senegalese from the Wolof and Mandinka tribal groups were crammed into cells at the ground level. She revealed to me that part of her daily skin care ritual was the application of a skin-lightening bleach called Nadinola. Part of the painful effect of "whiteness" and the assumption of white supremacy on the world is that it caused that beautiful, dark-skinned African woman leading a tour at a slave prison on the African continent to bleach her skin in pursuit of a lighter complexion.

That fixation on skin tone has been alive and well throughout my lifetime. Burroughs referred to it as "colorphobia." She stated:

> What does wholesale bleaching of face and straightening of hair indicate? From our viewpoint, it simply means that the women who practice it wish they had white faces and straight hair . . . The fairer some Negroes are, the better they think of themselves, without any thought of an ounce of character to go along with it, and enough good common sense to know that color is no badge of superiority of mind or soul.[35]

I can remember attending public schools in Chicago where "the brown bag test" was applied. The test involved holding next to your hand a brown paper lunch bag (popular during my youth) to see if your skin tone was lighter than the color of the bag. As Burroughs went on to point out, there are Black churches across the country where it has long been understood that only a "fair-skinned person" could serve as senior pastor. There are some social circles where only a fair-skinned person can be accepted. She says, "The disease spreads from men to women, from women to families, from families to churches, and from churches to social circles."[36]

Dr. Joseph Lowery, a former president of the Southern Christian Leadership Conference, referred to this issue of skin tones in the Black community when he gave the benediction at the first inauguration of Barack Obama as president of the United States. Lowery said, "Lord, in the memory of all the saints who from their labors rest, and in the joy of a new beginning, we ask you to help us work for that day when Black will not be asked to get back, when brown can stick around, when yellow will be mellow, when the red man can get ahead, man, and when the white man will embrace what is right."[37]

Delores Williams, another womanist theology founder, gives great attention to this issue of skin color and pigmentation when she also references Alice Walker. Williams begins her essay by referring to a section in Walker's book, *In Search of Our Mothers' Gardens*.

> DAUGHTER: Mama, why are we brown, pink, and yellow, and our cousins are white, beige, and Black?
>
> MOTHER: Well, you know the colored race is just like a flower garden, with every color flower represented.[38]

Williams then points out that "Walker's allusion to skin color points to an historic tradition of tension between Black women over the matter of Black men's preference for light-skinned women."[39] Burroughs was a Black woman when being too "Black" was considered a negative trait. In the language of Joseph Lowery, Nannie Helen Burroughs, with her very dark skin, was told that because she was too Black, she would have to "get back." Her battle as a Black woman was first among other Black people of lighter complexion.

However, her second battle was a matter of gender as a Black woman within the confines of Black church life. In 1900 she joined with Virginia Broughton to organize the Women's Convention as an auxiliary of the National Baptist Convention. At the first gathering of that women's convention she gave a speech entitled "How the Sisters Are Hindered from Helping."[40] She pointed out what a loss it was to the Black Baptist church that the talents of women were not being fully utilized. She said:

> We come not to usurp thrones nor to sow discord, but to so organize and systematize the work that each may help through a Woman's Missionary Society and not be made poorer thereby. It is for the utilization of talent and the stimulation to Christian activity in our Baptist churches that prompt us to service. We realize that to allow these gems to lie unpolished longer means a loss to the denomination.

She continued:

> For a number of years there has been a righteous discontent, a burning zeal to go forward in his name among the Baptist women of our churches, and it will be the dynamic force in the religious campaign at the opening of the 20th century . . . We come now to the rescue. We unfurl our banner upon which is inscribed this motto, "The World for Christ. Woman, Arise, He calleth for Thee."[41]

That phrase, "righteous discontent," became the tile of a book by Evelyn Brooks-Higginbotham about the history of women within the Black Baptist church.[42]

The third battle for Nannie Helen Burroughs moved beyond her own skin tone and her gender. She also focused on the different ways in which Black women and white women were treated in American society. Thus she wrote a letter in 1902, "An Appeal to the Christian White Women of the Southland," in which she appealed to white women to use their influence within the white community to help bring an end to the segregation and color discrimination being imposed upon Blacks in the South.[43] Here is an early form of womanist theology. Nannie Helen Burroughs battled gender discrimination within the Black Baptist church and simultaneously encouraged white women to join in battling racial discrimination in American society. She was pointing out that Black men do not have to deal with sexism and white women do not have to deal with racism. Meanwhile, Black women must deal with both racism and sexism on a daily basis.

In her letter she spoke to the indignities suffered by Black people due to the separate but equal policies that prevailed throughout the South as a result of the *Plessy v. Ferguson* ruling established just six years earlier in 1896. She wrote:

> We wish to appeal to you on behalf of the thousands of mothers in this land who have suffered in silence the unchristian humiliation to which they have been subjected in the Southland since the introduction of the separate coach laws . . . The honor of Black womanhood is at stake. Let those who will, cower before the crisis, but let us here, in this place, put ourselves on record as protectors and defenders of Christian womanhood, white or Black.[44]

Like many civil rights activists, Nannie Helen Burroughs was angered that American rhetoric about defending freedom in Europe during US involvement in World War I (1917–1918) did not translate into policies to defend the freedoms of Black people living in the United States, including the Black men who fought in Europe during World War I. She was especially outspoken about the growing problem of lynch mob justice that was being openly sanctioned by state governments through their silence and by the federal government through its failure to pass any anti-lynching legislation.[45]

Ida B. Wells Barnett

Nannie Helen Burroughs was not the only Black woman taking a stand against lynch mobs and unlawful white violence against Black people. Ida B. Wells was also outspoken on this issue. As Angela Sims points out, "Wells addressed the hypocrisy that fueled this American practice and understood, as Dora Apel rightly surmised, that lynching was used as a weapon to terrorize the Black community as a whole in both racial and gender terms."[46] Even though Wells, unlike Sojourner Truth or Nannie Helen Burroughs, did not operate primarily within a religious or church-based context, she still qualifies as one of the women Emilie Townes referred to as "a nascent womanism" that laid out the themes and framework for womanist theology.[47]

Ida B. Wells was born into slavery in 1862 in Holly Springs, Mississippi. She relocated to Memphis, Tennessee, in 1879, studied at Rust College, and then began her career writing for local Black newspapers. Between 1889 and 1892, she became editor of the *Memphis Free Speech and Headlight*. In her columns, she focused on the discrimination and lynching Blacks faced throughout the country. She used her newspaper column to urge Black people in Memphis to migrate to other locations outside of the former Confederacy in hopes of escaping racial discrimination.

In 1884, Wells was thrown off a railroad car after physically resist-ing all attempts to do so by the train conductor and other white passengers, because she refused to leave the "ladies" section and sit in the "colored section" of the train, which was also the smoking section. She filed a legal action against the railroad and was awarded a settlement of five hundred dollars for personal damages.[48] This was more than seventy years before Rosa Parks refused to give up her seat while sitting in the colored section of a bus in 1955.

In 1892, Wells urged the Black citizens of Memphis to boycott the city buses in protest of the lunching of three Black men: Thomas Moss, Calvin McDowell, and Lee Stewart. That boycott nearly bankrupted the city bus system. Her anti-lynching columns, which linked mob violence by whites against Black men with rape by white men against Black women, so enraged whites in Tennessee that her newspaper office was bombed and burned while she was out of town visiting friends in New York City.[49] She was encouraged by people in Memphis not to return there because death threats against her were posted in newspapers throughout the state. One such death threat appeared on the editorial page of the white-owned *Commercial*

Appeal newspaper. That editorial claimed that Wells' comments were an insult to the honor of white women and the chivalry of white men. It suggested that "the Black wretch who had written that foul lie should be tied to a stake at the corner of Main and Madison streets, a pair of tailor's shears used on him and he should then be burned at a stake."[50] It is interesting to note that the editorial writer did not know or did not care enough to get the gender right.

Wells spoke about the threats to her life this way:

> I received telegrams and letters informing me that trains were being watched, that I was to be dumped into the river and beaten, if not killed . . . It had been learned that I wrote the editorial and was to be hanged in front of the courthouse and my face bled if I returned. One prominent insurance agent publicly declares he will make it his business to shoot me on sight if I return to Memphis in twenty years . . . A leading white lady remarked that she was opposed to the lynching of those three men in Memphis, but she did wish there was some way by which I could be gotten back and lynched.[51]

Wells shed a light on the sexual abuse and exploitation of Black women which would be part of the tri-dimensional oppression that would be voiced by womanist theologians. In doing so, she not only focused on the behavior of white men that had been going on virtually unchallenged since the days of slavery. She also targeted the hypocrisy of Black men, and especially Black preachers, regarding their sexual conduct. Here again, Black women were the victims of both racial and gender-based abuse which was not the experience of Black males or white women.

In discussing the sexual misconduct of Black preachers, she was able to demonstrate how preachers were more interested in protecting the reputations of one another than they were in ending the sexual abuse of Black women. She reports on a certain preacher who was caught in the act:

> A minister of the gospel who had gone from his church services one Sunday night to the home of one of the members had been surprised by her husband, who not only ran him out of the house in his night clothes but took possession of the new broadcloth suit which the sisters had given him, and also his shoes and hat . . . The minister

remained in hiding until a brother minister could furnish him some clothing and money with which to get out of town.[52]

Wells wrote a caustic editorial about that event in the *Free Speech and Headlight*. She reports that when the editorial appeared in Memphis, the Black clergy alliance condemned her for focusing on that issue and threatened to lead a boycott of the newspaper among their congregations. Wells responded to that threat from the Black clergy of Memphis. "We answered this threat by publishing the names of every minister who belonged to the alliance in the next issue of the Free Speech, and told the community that these men upheld the immoral conduct of one of their number and asked if they were willing to support preachers who would sneak into their homes when their backs were turned and debauched their wives."[53]

Wells was just as harsh when it came to the victimization of Black women by white men. She noted how many acts of lynching had occurred because a Black man was accused of sexually assaulting a white woman. Much of the variety of skin tone discussed under the section dealing with Nannie Helen Burroughs was directly related to the rape of Black women by white men. She states, "I found that this rape of helpless Negro girls and women, which began in slavery days, still continued without let or hindrance, check or reproof from church, state, or press until there had been created this race within a race—and all designated by the same inclusive term of 'colored.'"[54] Wells continued to point to racialized violence around sexual activity by saying, "I found that white men who had created a race of mulattoes by raping and consorting with Negro women were still doing so wherever they could, these same white men lynched, burned, and tortured Negro men for doing the same thing with white women; even when the white women were willing victims."[55]

Wells relocated to Chicago, where she continued her fight for racial justice. She established settlement houses to assist Black people who were moving to Chicago from places in the South. She called for economic boycotts of white-owned businesses that discriminated against Black employees or customers. She continued to travel to the sites of lynchings and race riots to focus national attention on those evils. All the while, she was active in the women's suffrage movement.[56]

From Nascent Womanism to
Twenty-First-Century Womanist Theology

The best way to conclude this chapter on womanist theology is not in my Black male voice, but rather the voice of a contemporary womanist theologian. Thus, I return to the 2019 article in *The Christian Century* by Turman. She provides the link between women who never claimed the term "womanist" for themselves—women such as Sojourner Truth, Nannie Helen Burroughs, and Ida B. Wells—and those contemporary Black female scholars who both coined the term "womanist theology" and who continue to give shape to its meaning. Turman says, "Long before Cannon brought womanist God-talk into the realm of academic discussion, it was flourishing in the faithful lives of Black Christian women. Womanism was born around Black women's kitchen tables, on front porches, in beauty shops, in women's clubs, in the varieties of Black women's prayer closets, and in various 'women's spaces' within the Black church."[57]

Turman continues:

> In these spaces, as Black women came to know the love, mercy, and justice of God for themselves, they forged a theology that affirms that Black women's lives are significant and valuable not only to God but also to the church and the world. In the social, political, and religious realms that so often erased Black women's experiences, Black women of faith had the courage to believe and assert, "I am": "I am here, I am fully human, and I am "fearfully and wonderfully" made in the image of God.[58]

Turman concludes with this powerful statement that sums up both the purpose and the power of womanist theology: "Black women do not have to wait for whites to not be racist and men not to be sexist in order to love their whole selves and community fully and deeply. It shows that womanist theology moves into the future fighting and dancing, recognizing that Black women's stories can be told many ways."[59]

NOTES

1. Marvin A. McMickle, "Women's History Month, a Good Time to Focus on Womanist Theology," christiancitizen.us/womens-history-a good -time-to-focus-on-womanist-theology, March 14, 2019.

2. Ibid.

3. Judith Weisenfeld and Richard Newman, eds., *This Far by Faith: Readings in African-American Women's Religious Biography* (New York: Routledge, 1996), 3.

4. Eboni Marshall Turman, "Black Women's Wisdom," *The Christian Century*, March 13, 2019, 30.

5. Ibid., 31.

6. Ibid.

7. Katie Cannon, *Katie's Canon: Womanism and the Soul of the Black Community* (New York: Continuum Press, 2002), 23. See also Alice Walker, *In Search of My Mother's Garden: Womanist Prose* (New York: Harcourt Brace Jovanovich, 1983), xi–xii.

8. Cannon, 22.

9. Ibid, 23.

10. Ibid., 138.

11. W. E. B. Du Bois, "Of the Dawn of Freedom," in *The Souls of Black Folk*, ed. David Blight and Robert Williams (Boston: Bedford Books, 1997), 45.

12. Cannon, 25.

13. Turman, 31.

14. Ibid.

15. Kelly Delaine Brown Douglas, "Womanist Theology: What Is Its Relationship to Black Theology," in *Black Theology: A Documentary History*, vol. 2: *1980–1992* (Maryknoll, NY: Orbis Books, 1993), 291.

16. Anna Julia Cooper, *A Voice from the South by a Black Woman from the South* (reprint from the 1892 original); New York: Oxford University Press, 1988), 134.

17. Douglas, 294.

18. Jacqueline Grant, "Womanist Theology: Black Women's Experience as a Source for Doing Theology," in *Black Theology*, vol. 2, ed. James Cone and Gayraud Wilmore (Maryknoll, NY: Orbis Books, 1993), 278.

19. Ibid.

20. Ibid., 287.

21. bell hooks, *Feminist Theory: From Margin to Center* (Boston: South End Press, 1984), 3.

22. Renita J. Weems, *Just a Sister Away: A Womanist Vision of Women's Relationships in the Bible* (San Diego, CA: LuraMedia, 1988), viii.

23. Ibid., xi.

24. Emilie M. Townes, "Ethics as an Art of Doing the Work Our Souls Must Have," in *Womanist Theological Ethics: A Reader*, ed. Katie Geneva Cannon, Emilie M. Townes, and Angela D. Sims (Louisville, KY: Westminster/John Knox, 2011), 36.

25. Anna Julia Cooper, "The Status of Woman in America," in *Women's Work: An Anthology of African American Women's Historical Writings from Antebellum America to the Harlem Renaissance*, ed. Laurie F. Maffly-Kipp and Kathryn Lofton (New York: Oxford University Press, 2010), 94.

26. Ibid.

27. Margaret Washington, *Narrative of Sojourner Truth* (New York: Vintage, 1993), 118.

28. M. Shawn Copeland, *Enfleshing Freedom: Body, Race, and Being* (Minneapolis: Fortress, 2010), 34.

29. Ibid.

30. Sojourner Truth, "Ain't I a Woman?", Modern History Sourcebook, Fordham University, https://sourcebooks.fordham.edu/mod/sojtruth-woman.asp.

31. Henry Louis Gates Jr. and Donald Yacovone, *The African Americans: Many Rivers to Cross* (New York: SmileyBooks, 2013), 37.

32. Henry Louis Gates Jr., *Life Upon These Shores: Looking at African American History 1513–2008* (New York: Alfred Knopf, 2011), 4–5.

33. James Ciment, *Atlas of African American History* (New York: Checkmark Books, 2001), 83.

34. Nannie Helen Burroughs, *Nannie Helen Burroughs: A Documentary Portrait of an Early Civil Rights Pioneer—1900–1959*, ed. and annotated by Kelisha B. Graves (Notre Dame, IN: Notre Dame University Press, 2019), xxii–xxiii.

35. Ibid, 32.

36. Ibid.

37. Joseph E. Lowery, benediction at the inauguration of President Barack Obama, YouTube, January 29, 2009.

38. Delores S. Williams, "Womanist Theology: Black Women's Voices," in *Black Theology: A Documentary History*, vol. 2: *1980–1992*

(Maryknoll, NY: Orbis Books, 1993), 265.

39. Ibid., 266.

40. Burroughs, 25–26.

41. Ibid.

42. Evelyn Brooks-Higginbotham, *Righteous Discontent: The Women's Movement in the Black Baptist Church, 1880–1920* (Cambridge, MA: Harvard University Press, 1993).

43. Burroughs, 156–58.

44. Ibid., 157.

45. Ibid., 104–7.

46. Angela D. Sims, "The Issue of Race and Lynching," in *Womanist Theological Ethics: A Reader*, ed. Katie Geneva Cannon, Emilie M. Townes, and Angela D. Sims (Louisville, KY: Westminster/John Knox, 2011), 205.

47. Townes, 36.

48. Ida B. Wells, *Crusade for Justice: The Autobiography of Ida B. Wells*, ed. Alfreda M. Duster (Chicago: University of Chicago Press, 1970), 1820.

49. Ibid., 66.

50. Ibid.

51. Sims, 258.

52. Wells, 40.

53. Ibid.

54. Ibid., 70.

55. Ibid., 71.

56. Marvin A. McMickle, "Ida B. Wells Barnett," in *Profiles in Black: Phat Facts for Teens* (Valley Forge, PA: Judson Press, 2008), 76–77.

57. Turman, 30.

58. Ibid.

59. Ibid., 34.

CHAPTER 9

Lessons from Barack Obama's Second Inaugural Address

I want to conclude this discussion about letting the oppressed go free by reflecting on a line that was spoken by President Barack Obama in his second inaugural address in 2013. While referring to the struggle involved in establishing the United States of America, he shifted his focus to the ongoing and unfinished struggles within this country in its pursuit of human rights and equality for all of its citizens. Bearing in mind that the rights of women, persons of African descent, and Native Americans or indigenous persons were not established in either the Declaration of Independence or the United States Constitution, President Obama said the struggle extended "from Seneca Falls, to Selma, to Stonewall."[1]

According to National Public Radio, "the president surprised many listeners by mentioning Stonewall in the same breath as Seneca Falls and Selma."[2] Seneca Falls was a reference to the struggle for women's rights, especially the right to vote that began with the first Women's Convention held in Seneca Falls, New York, in 1848. Selma was a reference to the 1965 march from Selma to Montgomery, Alabama. That, too, was an effort to achieve voting rights, this time for African Americans.

Stonewall was a reference to the resistance launched by LGBT persons following a police raid at the Stonewall nightclub in New York City in 1969 that gave birth to the gay rights movement in the United

States. While Barack Obama did not expand further upon either of those freedom struggles, he made it almost impossible to discuss any one of them without being mindful of the legitimate claims of the other two. All three movements involved people who sought liberation from oppression based upon gender (Seneca Falls), race or ethnicity (Selma), and sexual orientation (Stonewall).

What President Obama did was link together those three distinct human rights struggles that stretched over more than 120 years (Seneca Falls in 1848 and Stonewall in 1969) as the unfinished business of the American revolution. Like Moses standing before Pharaoh crying out "Let my people go," the leaders of these three human rights struggles were raising a similar cry. Initially, and perhaps to this day in some circles, those cries for liberation have gone unheard or unheeded. As mentioned earlier in this study, not everybody in this country wanted to grant full citizenship rights to women or African Americans. When President Obama presented those three human rights issues within the context of an inaugural address, he was attempting to elevate all three issues to national attention.

Seneca Falls

In *White Fragility*, Robin DiAngelo speaks about the slow pace at which white males decided what groups beyond themselves should or should not be allowed to vote. They were prepared to accept white women as full citizens by granting them the right to vote, as evidenced by the Nineteenth Amendment to the United States Constitution ratified in 1920. That was seventy-two years after Seneca Falls and forty-two years after Susan B. Anthony was arrested after attempting to vote in Rochester, New York, in 1878. DiAngelo writes, "The only way women could gain suffrage was for men to grant it to them; women could not grant suffrage to themselves. . . . And I would be remiss if I did not acknowledge the intersection of race and gender in the example of suffrage; white men granted suffrage to women, but only granted full access to white women. Women of color were denied full access until the Voting Rights Act of 1965."[3]

The complaint by womanist theologians that white women have shared in the presumption of white supremacy was no more clearly in evidence than with the passage of the Nineteenth Amendment, adopted and ratified one year before white mobs burned to the ground a thriving all-Black community in Tulsa, Oklahoma (1921) and three years before a similar massacre occurred in Rosewood, Florida (1923).[4] The intersection of sexism and racism continues to reveal that in the United States not all women are created equal.

There is one area where white and Black women share a similar experience, and that is with regard to sexual harassment and sexual assault. It should be noted that the #MeToo movement was initiated by a Black woman, Tarana Burke.[5] That movement is a reminder that while women in 2020 have gained voting rights and have made tremendous gains in terms of being elected to political office at every level of government, the problem of sexual harassment and sexual assault continues. Men like Harvey Weinstein, Bill Cosby, Matt Lauer, Bill O'Reilly, Donald Trump, Brett Kavanaugh, Clarence Thomas, Charlie Rose, Steve Wynn, Al Franken, Kevin Spacey, Mark Halperin, Louis C.K., Jerry Richardson, Bill Hybels, John Conyers, James Levine, Ben Vereen, Garrison Keillor, Donovan McNabb, Ryan Lizza, Tavis Smiley, Morgan Freeman, and dozens more have been in the news over the last thirty years on charges of sexual harassment and assault.[6] The name of Jeffrey Epstein can be added to this list since his case became public after a *New York Times* article was released. Obama was correct when he suggested that the work begun at Seneca Falls in 1848 remains unfinished so far as respecting women's rights is concerned. Let the oppressed go free.

Selma

Voting right for African American males was established by the Fifteenth Amendment to the US Constitution ratified in 1870. However, under the oddly named banner of "Redemption," the voting rights of African Americans were gradually stripped away until almost no Black persons were allowed to vote anywhere in the former Confederate states. This concept of "redemption" was a term that referred to the ways by which the Southern states were able to regain control of state governments and large portions of the federal government even though they were on the losing side of the Civil War. Nicholas

Lemann writes about it this way: "In the Southern states with the largest Black populations, the tradition of white vigilantism, which had persevered among Confederate veterans despite, or perhaps because of, their defeat at Appomattox, began to evolve into an organized, if unofficial, military effort to take away by terrorist violence the Black political rights that were now part of the Constitution."[7]

The right to vote continued to be denied to the vast majority of African Americans until the Voting Rights Act of 1965. For those who think the issue of racism was something consigned to the activities that occurred in the nineteenth century, I remind them that the right to vote for African Americans was established during my own lifetime. That being said, acts of voter suppression continue. More importantly, gaining the right to vote has not had the effect of ending other forms of racial discrimination in housing, employment, banking, and access to quality schools, access to quality fresh fruits and vegetables within their neighborhoods, access to quality medical care, and a lack of confidence that encounters with police and other law enforcement officials will not result in unwarranted harassment or even death.

Nothing better points to the unfinished business begun at Selma than the Black Lives Matter movement that was birthed in response to the acquittal of George Zimmerman, who had shot and killed Trayvon Martin in Sanford, Florida, on February 26, 2012. The phrase continued to gain traction as the number of deaths of unarmed African Americans at the hands of police officers continued to mount. One thinks of such instances as Eric Garner in Staten Island, New York, whose repeated cries of "I can't breathe" were ignored by a police officer using a choke hold on July 17, 2014. More recently was George Floyd, who uttered the same words while a police officer in Minneapolis, Minnesota, pressed his knee on Floyd's neck for 8 minutes and 46 seconds.

In between those two were Sandra Bland and Bothan Jean in Texas; Walter Scott in South Carolina; Ahmaud Arbery and Rayshard Brooks in Georgia; Breanna Taylor in Kentucky; Tamir Rice and Tanisha Anderson in Ohio; Freddie Gray in Maryland; Michael Brown in Missouri; Alton Sterling in Louisiana; Philando Castile in Minnesota; Aatiana Jefferson in Florida; Aura Rossier in Michigan;

Michelle Cusseaux in Arizona; Tanisha Fonville in North Carolina; Akai Garley in New York; and Gabriella Nevarez and Stephon Clark in California.[8]

The words Black Lives Matter have now been painted in large yellow letters on Pennsylvania Avenue in Washington, DC, leading up to the White House and on Fifth Avenue in New York City directly in front of Trump Tower. That is an appropriate response to Donald Trump's tweet that declared Black Lives Matter to be "a symbol of hate."[9] As CNN points out, "This is a description he's refused to use for Confederate emblems."[10] As with Seneca Falls and the rights of women, the work of Selma and the establishment of equal rights and protections for African Americans continue as well.

Selma may be a chapter in the civil rights movement of the 1960s, but it has amazing relevance to life in the twenty-first century. Selma opens the door to the outrageous birther movement launched by President Donald Trump that President Barack Obama was not born in the United States and thus was not qualified to serve in the office to which he was twice elected by the American people. It similarly points to Senator Mitch McConnell of Kentucky, who brazenly stated that his "number-one goal was to make sure that Barack Obama was a one-term president."[11]

Selma reminds us of Michelle Alexander's research about the staggering rate of arrest, conviction, and incarceration of African American and Hispanic people in this country.[12] When taken together, Seneca Falls and Selma are reminders of the poverty that works to limit the opportunities of single mothers and African Americans working every day on low-wage jobs.[13] It points to stunning rates of neighborhood segregation in cities across America as demonstrated in *Evicted* by Matthew Desmond that looks exclusively at the Northern city of Milwaukee, Wisconsin.[14] Given that the driving factor for the Selma-to-Montgomery march of 1965 was gaining voting rights for African Americans in Alabama, it is amazing to consider that chief among the political talking points of many elected officials in 2017 is how to suppress, not increase, the voting rights of many Americans.[15]

Selma reminds us of the rise of white supremacist organizations, often under the rubric of "the alt right," and their presence inside the White House in the person of an advisor to President Trump who had previously been the editor of Breitbart News.[16] It requires that we pay close attention to Richard B. Spencer and his National Policy Network; the Southern Poverty Law Center calls him "one of the country's most successful young white nationalist leaders—a suit-and-tie version of the white supremacists of old, a kind of professional racist in khakis."[17]

Selma reminds us of the tragic events in Charlottesville, Virginia, in the summer of 2015, when hundreds of white men carried torchlights, Confederate flags, and swastikas, and chanted the Nazi slogan of "blood and soil." It reminds us of Heather Heyer, a white woman who was killed in Charlottesville when a twenty-year-old white supremacist, James Alex Fields Jr., drove his car into a group of people who were protesting the presence of the Ku Klux Klan in their community.[18] Selma also reminds us of the comments of Donald Trump, who stated that there was violence "on both sides" and fine people "on both sides."[19] He repeated his view on September 14, 2017, suggesting that there was violence on both sides, thus equating the neo-Nazis and white supremacists with the peaceful protesters who had gathered to oppose a message of hatred and intolerance.[20]

Selma reminds us of Dylan Roof, who entered the Mother Emmanuel AME Church in Charleston, South Carolina, on June 17, 2005, and shot and killed nine people, including the pastor of that church who was also a member of the South Carolina State Senate. Roof, who was sentenced to death for his horrific actions, said his sentence was irrelevant since "white nationalists would free him from prison after an impending race war." Roof went on to say in a journal he kept in his prison cell, "I would like to make it crystal clear. I do not regret what I did. I am not sorry. I have not shed a tear for the innocent people I killed."[21]

Selma reminds us of the election of Donald Trump, who seems intent on undoing anything and everything established by Barack Obama—whose citizenship Trump questioned publicly for eight years without a shred of evidence. Trump finally had to acknowledge that he had been wrong when he made a five-second statement that was not accompanied by an apology during the 2016 presidential campaign.[22] Let the oppressed go free!

Stonewall

This brings us to the third struggle for human rights referenced by Barack Obama in his second inaugural address: Stonewall and the struggle to end discrimination against and the demonization of persons in the LGBTQ community. As with the issues of Black theology, feminist theology, liberation theology and womanist theology, my introduction to the issues that would give rise to what is called queer theology also began during my student years at Union Theological Seminary. When I arrived in New York City in 1970, there was a sizeable LGBTQ community within the Union student body and faculty. When I was hired as an associate minister at Abyssinian Baptist Church in Harlem, I quickly discovered that homosexuality was in no way limited to the white people I knew at the seminary or at Riverside Church, which was next door to Union. There was a sizeable group of Black gay men at Abyssinian. I was never sure about the number or even the identity of any Black lesbians in that congregation.

Prior to that time, I had little awareness of the issue of homosexuality. While there may have been friends or acquaintances of mine while I was growing up in Chicago who were homosexual, it was nothing to which I ever gave any thought. I did not know that a member of my family had married a gay man who was a renowned church musician in the Chicago area. She reported some years later that the wedding was never consummated. I later learned that he agreed only to the marriage in order to provide some cover for the lifestyle he preferred but that was viewed as sinful in the Pentecostal church settings in which he most frequently moved.

I knew all the songs by Motown artists that dealt with issues of race, class, or gender during the 1960s and 1970s. I knew that Berry Gordy had to insist that "Love Child" by the Supremes be performed on the *Ed Sullivan Show* in 1972 when the content about a child being born in poverty and out of wedlock was considered too controversial for Sullivan's primary audience.[23] I knew about Congresswoman Shirley Chisholm from Brooklyn, New York, running for the nomination of the Democratic Party to be president of the United States. I knew that Aretha Franklin was singing about "R-E-S-P-E-C-T" and about Dr. Feel Good in the same concerts. None of that early cultural exposure seemed to focus on the issue of homosexuality.

I was deeply influenced by the emergence of the Black Power movement and the civil rights movement during the 1960s and early 1970s. However, neither of those movements gave any attention to the issue of homosexuality or the oppression and harassment experienced by gay and lesbian persons because of their sexual orientation. That was the case even though Bayard Rustin, a key supporter of Martin Luther King Jr. and the primary organizer of the 1963 March on Washington, was an openly gay man. I was greatly informed by the novels, essays, and public appearances of James Baldwin. While he did focus much of his attention on racial justice and an end to racism, his novels such as *Go Tell it on the Mountain*, *Another Country*, *Giovanni's Room*, and *Nobody Knows My Name* forced his readers, especially within the African American community, to confront the evils of racism and homophobia. However, while I read the works of Baldwin, I was not particularly moved to take up any further interest in homosexuality as a practice or the people who were engaged in it.

I was shocked and disturbed by one of the great acts of hypocrisy and the double-standards about sexual activity that involved Congressman Adam Clayton Powell Jr. of New York. Powell was also the pastor of Abyssinian Baptist Church in New York City, a church with a considerable gay and lesbian constituency with whom I interacted when I worked at that church from 1972 to 1976. Nevertheless, Powell held great disdain for the involvement of Bayard Rustin in the civil rights movement on the grounds of Rustin being homosexual.[24] That was despite the fact that Powell himself was a well-known womanizer. It seems that adultery and fornication could be overlooked, but homosexuality could not be tolerated. That is the same double standard that haunts the church to this day.

Powell insisted that Rustin resign from the Southern Christian Leadership Conference (SCLC); and if Rustin refused, then Powell said he would publicly announce that Rustin and Martin Luther King Jr. were involved in a sexual relationship.[25] That Powell was prepared to make this false claim in 1960 is mentioned by Taylor Branch in *Parting the Waters* and by Charles Hamilton in his biography of Powell.[26]

As someone who worked at Abyssinian Baptist Church between 1972 and 1976 under Powell's successor, Samuel Dewitt Proctor, I am deeply ashamed over this shameful episode in the proud history of that great church. However, Powell's views about homosexuality were not at all uncommon among African American clergy and churches at that time. This was the climate within which I grew up, and these were the views about homosexuality I was taught.

In the Black church during this same time, there was little discussion about any matters of human sexuality in any form. Kelly Brown Douglas discusses that fact in *Sexuality and the Black Church*.[27] To the extent that such a discussion did occur, it always involved a judgmental tone regarding the evils of fornication and adultery. As mentioned regarding the views of Adam Clayton Powell Jr., there was a clear belief that homosexuality was an even greater sin than any form of heterosexual behavior. As such, that topic was never even considered outside the realm of it being deviant and sinful.

Horace L. Griffin reflects on his experience as a gay man battling for acceptance but meeting only resistance and condemnation in the Black church. The issue of race relations was always prominent. There was an intersection between race and gender around the issue of interracial sex and interracial marriage. Women's rights and women in leadership roles, especially in the Black church, had not yet become the topic of discussion, but that issue was front-page news in the broader society with the rise of the feminist movement in the late 1960s and early 1970s. Meanwhile, as Griffin writes, "Since most African Americans still consider homosexuality shameful and are unwilling to consider that their silencing and moral denigration of gay people could be at all similar to the historical racist attacks by white people on Black people's worth and moral legitimacy, they really are asking, why would you talk about people's sexual problems and the immorality of homosexuality?"[28]

Griffin continues by describing what it was like to face both racism and homophobia. He sees himself as "standing in the two worlds of racial and sexual oppression and experiencing similar responses of hostility, prejudice, and discrimination directed at me because of my skin color and because of my sexual orientation." He points out that white gay people continue to cling to racism, and Black people continue to cling to heterosexism:

> White gays' racism can be observed when they insist on ending homophobia while keeping their world white, resisting any contact with and equity for Black people in their gentrified neighborhoods, Euro-centric gay churches, private dance clubs, and television programs, for example, "Queer as Folk" and "Will and Grace." Black heterosexuals' homophobia and heterosexism are apparent when they continue ignoring the voices, concerns, interests, and sufferings of gay African Americans in their public forums, Black publications (namely, Ebony and Jet magazines), Black church organizations, community marches, and Black college campuses.[29]

In short, the issues of race, class, and gender were constantly before me, a heterosexual Black male, on television, in popular music, in political discussions, and in the blaxploitation films like *Shaft*, *Superfly*, and *Foxy Brown*. During the 1960s and 1970s, there was no urgency directed toward me to think about homosexuality as something to be considered alongside Seneca Falls and Selma. I was not aware of or made to feel the importance of being concerned about how the world and the church were treating gay and lesbian persons.

Cornel West points out in *Race Matters* that considerable attention was given to Black gay men in the media, but never in a positive way. West points out that gay men are often presented in the movies and on television in ways that seem to reject or conflict with what he calls "Black machismo" or Black men highly associated with sex appeal and physical strength. He says, "Black gay men are often the brunt of talented Black comics like Arsenio Hall and Damon Wayans. Yet behind the laughs lurk a Black tragedy of major proportions: the refusal of white and Black America to entertain seriously new stylistic options for Black men caught in the deadly endeavor of rejecting Black machismo identities."[30]

The message was that gay men were to be laughed at as they engaged in exaggerated manifestations of female behavior. That was certainly the case with the comedy segment on the television series *In Living Color* called "Men in Films" that featured Daymon Wayans and David Alan Grier. The message in such representations was never that such behavior should be emulated or admired by other men. Rather, it was presented as a behavior that was different from the norm at best and deviant at worst.

My worldview did not change during my college years, so far as my exposure to or awareness of homosexuality was concerned. There were, I later discovered, homosexual persons I knew and interacted with at Aurora University when I was a student there from 1966 to 1970. I was aware of rumors about a liaison that involved a male member of the faculty and one of the male students. However, there was also a rumor about a male member of the faculty and a female student who were involved in an ongoing affair. I chalked up both issues to being on a college campus in the 1960s. Neither activity involved me in any way, and I paid no attention to either of them.

However, I was early on made aware of the difference between being African American and being a homosexual in one particular way. During those college years I sang in the college choir, which went on tour to different parts of the country each year as a fund-raiser and recruitment tool for the university. The first year, which was January 1967, we took a tour that stretched from West Virginia to Florida with stops in Virginia, both Carolinas, and Georgia. This was at the height of the civil rights movement, at the dawn of the Black Power movement, and in the midst of the urban uprisings going on in cities like Los Angeles, Detroit, Cleveland, and Newark, New Jersey, among others.

I was the only African American student in the touring choir, and the student who I came to know was homosexual was also along for that trip. There could have been other homosexual students in the choir as well. What I know is that posters advertising our concerts were sent to the churches where we were to perform. Since I was in both the choir and a male quartet that performed separately at every stop, my picture appeared twice on that poster. As a result, I was called into the office of the university president only to discover that my mother was already seated in his office. We were told that word had reached the school that there were some stops along the way where no family was willing to host me, because I was an African American. In fact, the school was concerned that some attack might be directed at me if I went on this trip. The university president did not suggest that I not go on the trip. He just wanted my mother and me to be aware of the dangers that might await me.

We both agreed that I should go on the trip, and we trusted God that I would return home safely. That being said, the trip was not without incident. One of the homes that was willing to host me had planned to have me share a bed with another person in the choir from West Virginia. This student had a poster on his wall in the college dormitory that featured a Confederate flag and a Confederate soldier saying, "Hell no, we'll never give up." He asked the host for a separate place to sleep because, as was reported to me later, he was concerned that my skin color might rub off on him.

In Brunswick, Georgia, I had to stay on a naval base with password protection to reach me, because the Ku Klux Klan had threatened to bomb any house that hosted me overnight. In Ocala, Florida, I was denied service at a Woolworth's because they did not serve "colored people." In Jacksonville, Florida, I was warned to get off the beach where the whole choir was relaxing, because that section of the beach was reserved for "whites only." While I was allowed to stay in a hotel in Jacksonville, I could not share a room with a white member of the choir, because that would violate the segregation ordinances of the city.

None of this, or any other inconvenience, warning, threats, or meetings with the university president was experienced by the choir member(s) who were known to be or might have been homosexual. This experience greatly increased my awareness of racism and the assumptions of white supremacy as evils that need to be resisted and defeated. That experience also left me with the feeling that being Black was in any way commensurate with being homosexual in American society. I was guilty on sight. My homosexual choir mate(s) suffered no such stigma, and his (their) identity went largely unnoticed within the choir and unknown by the churches we visited in 1967. That would remain the case on our college campus unless and until their sexual orientation became known by them or by someone else.

I have not experienced the pain and anguish expressed by gay and lesbian people as they strive for recognition of their humanity and their human rights. I cannot identify with Horace Griffin when he says, "I internalized shame and self-hatred because the Black church taught other gays and me that same-sex sexual attraction is sin."[31] Given the fact that I had been conditioned to view racism as something that is not the sociopolitical equivalent of sexual orientation, I was deeply moved by Griffin's observation on this topic when he writes, "Those leading the verbal attack on lesbian and gay lives often have high status within the nation's churches. They include many Black heterosexual ministers and congregants across the country who join with their white counterparts to do to Black lesbians and gays what was at one time done to them. And like white racist Christians, they do it in the name of God, the Bible, and the Christian tradition."[32]

This book has relied upon Galatians 3:26-29 as the point of reference for the appeal to let the oppressed go free. I had to think carefully about how to discuss Stonewall in this present study, since it does not seem that the LGBTQ struggle flows as easily out of Galatians 3:26-29. Obviously, Galatians makes no mention about matters of sexual orientation. In fact, if I had attempted to write this book based upon my thinking in the 1970s, I might have initially agreed with those people who thought that the Bible condemns homosexual conduct through passages such as Leviticus 18:22 and Romans 1:28. I do not think I would ever have initiated a theological movement designed to link Seneca Falls, Selma, and Stonewall. I repeat that I was not hostile to such matters. I was unaware, uninformed, and thus disinterested in anything having to do with the concerns of the LGBTQ community.

NOTES

1. Barack Obama, second presidential inaugural address, January 20, 2013.

2. "Remembering Seneca Falls, Selma, and Stonewall," npr.com, January 22, 2013.

3. Robin DiAngelo, *White Fragility: Why It's So Hard for White People to Talk about Racism* (Boston: Beacon Press, 2018), 21.

4. Alicia Lee and Sara Sidner, "99 Years Ago Today, America Was Shaken by One of Its Deadliest Acts of Racial Violence," CNN.com, June 1, 2020; History.com editors, "Rosewood Massacre," History.com, June 8, 2020.

5. "#MeToo Is at a Crossroads in America. Around the World, It's Just Beginning," WashingtonPost.com, May 8, 2020.

6. Audrey Carlsen, Maya Salam, Claire Cain Miller, Denise Lu, Ash Ngu, Jugal K. Patel, and Zach Wichter, "#MeToo Brought Down 201 Powerful Men. Nearly Half of Their Replacements Are Women," NewYork Times.com, October 29, 2018.

7. Nicholas Lemann, *Redemption: The Last Battle of the Civil War* (New York: Farrar, Strauss and Giroux, 2006), xi.

8. "George Floyd: Timeline of Black Deaths Caused by Police," BBC.com, June 26, 2020; see also Alia Chughtai, "Know Their Names," Interactive .aljazeera.com.

9. Kevin Liptak and Kristen Holmes, "Trump Calls Black Lives Matter a 'Symbol of Hate' as He Digs in on Race," CNN.com, July 1, 2020.

10. Ibid.

11. Glenn Kessler, "When Did McConnell Say He Wanted to Make Obama a 'One-Term President?'", WashingtonPost.com, September 25, 2012, 1.

12. Michelle Alexander, *The New Jim Crow: Mass Incarceration in the Age of Colorblindness* (New York: The New Press, 2012).

13. David Rolf, *The Fight for $15: The Right Wage for a Working America* (New York: The New Press, 2016).

14. Matthew Desmond, *Evicted: Poverty and Profit in the American City* (New York: Crown Publishing, 2016).

15. Marvin A. McMickle, "The Real Issue Is Voter Suppression," DemocratandChronicle.com, blog, February 27, 2017, 1.

16. Sarah Posner, "How Donald Trump's New Campaign Chief Created an Online Haven for White Nationalists," MotherJones.com, August 22, 2016, 1.

17. "Richard Bertrand Spencer," SouthernPovertyLawCenter.org.

18. "Charlottesville Mourns Woman Killed in a Rally That Turned Violent," WashingtonPost.com, August 16, 2017, 1; Marvin A. McMickle, "A Climate for Hatred to Grow," *Democrat and Chronicle*, August 20, 2017, 31A.

19. Michael D. Shear and Maggie Haberman, "Trump Defends Initial Remarks on Charlottesville; Again Blames Both Sides," August 15, 2017, 1.

20. Tamara Keith, "President Trump Stands by Original Charlottesville Remarks," npr.com, September 14, 2017, 1.

21. Eric Levenson and Tina Burnside, "Dylan Roof Believed He'd Be Freed from Prison after a Race War, Attorney Says in Appeal," CNN.com, January 29, 2020.

22, Stephen Collinson and Jeremy Diamond, "Trump Finally Admits It: President Barack Obama Was Born in the United States," CNN.com, September 16, 2016, 1.

23. "Love Child by the Supremes," musicaficianado.com.

24. Jervis Anderson, *Bayard Rustin: Troubles I've Seen: A Biography* (New York: HarperCollins, 1997), 229–30.

25. Ibid., 230.

26. Taylor Branch, *Parting the Waters: America in the King Years 1954–1963* (New York: Simon & Schuster, 1989); Charles V. Hamilton, *Adam Clayton Powell Jr.: The Political Biography of an American Dilemma* (1991; New York: Cooper Square Press, 2002).

27. Kelly Brown Douglas, *Sexuality and the Black Church: A Womanist Perspective* (Maryknoll, NY: Orbis Books, 1999), 99–102.

28. Horace L. Griffin, *Their Own Receive Them Not: African American Lesbians and Gays in Black Churches* (Eugene, OR: Wipf & Stock, 2010), xi–xii.

29. Ibid., xii.

30. Cornel West, *Race Matters* (Boston: Beacon Press, 1993), 89.

31. Griffin, 3.

32. Ibid.

CHAPTER 10

A Substantive
Gay Rights Movement
Is Underway

It all began on June 28, 1969, when patrons of the Stonewall bar and nightclub in New York City, frequented by a largely gay and lesbian clientele, were being harassed by New York police officers. At that time, New York City refused to grant operating licenses to bars that served a gay and lesbian clientele. That is what allowed the police to enter the bar and attempt to close it down. It was considered an unlicensed enterprise. Such harassment had been routine for gay bars and clubs for years. This time, to the surprise of the police, the patrons resisted.

In June 2000, President Bill Clinton named June as Gay and Lesbian Pride Month. In June 2009, President Barack Obama expanded the commemoration to become LGBT Pride Month in recognition of bisexual and transgender persons as well. This is an important point to make for this study, since a Black transgender woman named Marsha P. Johnson was an active part of the Stonewall riot in 1969.[1] Here is a link between Seneca Falls, Selma, and Stonewall of which most people are unaware. The fact that President Obama could reference and celebrate that linkage in 2013 is an indicator of how much legitimacy that gay rights movement has gained in the intervening forty-four years from the Stonewall Inn in New York City in 1969 to the steps of the US Capitol in Washington, DC, and the swearing-in of an American president in 2013.

Much Has Changed in the United States for LGBTQ Persons

During those years between 1969 and 2013, much has changed in the United States. In 1973, the American Psychiatric Association voted to remove homosexuality as a mental illness resulting in deviant behavior. In 1992, the World Health Organization removed homosexuality from its classification as a mental disorder.[2] In 1994, the US military instituted a policy called "don't ask, don't tell" that prohibited military personnel from discriminating against or harassing "closeted homosexuals or bisexual service members or applicants."

It should be noted that persons already serving in the armed forces who were open about their homosexual status even after 1994 could be dismissed from the armed forces. The don't ask, don't tell policy was challenged in federal court and abandoned in 2011. It was reinstated in 2016.[3] The change in policy continued in 2017 as President Donald Trump issued an executive order banning transgender people from serving in the military.[4] Despite the order being challenged in federal court, the US Supreme Court overturned a lower court ruling and reinstated a ban on transgender troops in the armed forces.[5] This is even though more than sixty-six hundred transgender persons have been openly living and have been bravely fighting and dying in this country's wars in both Iraq and Afghanistan for years.[6] Aaron Belkin, who is the director of the Palm Center, which advocates for transgender troops, described Trump's actions by saying, "What happened is the commander-in-chief ordered a purge of transgender troops."[7]

This was not Trump's only resistance to the emergence of a gay rights movement. In the July 7, 2017, issue of USA Today, an openly gay Justice Department lawyer expressed deep disappointment that President Trump chose not to issue a statement of support during Gay Pride Month in June 2017. It was pointed out that Trump did issue a statement in support of National Home Ownership Month, African American Music Appreciation Month, and Great Outdoors Month.

In his speech at the 2016 Republican National Convention, Trump seemed to offer support to the LGBT community when he said, "As your president, I will do everything in my power to protect our LGBT citizens from the violence and oppression of a hateful ideology."[8] Those remarks were made in the aftermath of the terrorist attack on a nightclub in Orlando, Florida, that was popular with LGBT persons. However, less than one year later, Trump chose silence during the month devoted to the LGBT community. In response to that intentional snub, Adam Chandler wrote, "The White House appears to be sending a painful message that we don't deserve the progress we've made, and that it's still not OK to be who we are."[9]

There Has Been Progress on the Political Front

Despite Trump's attempts to derail gay rights in this country, much progress has been made in terms of LGBTQ persons being elected to political office. Openly gay persons such as Lori Lightfoot, who is mayor of my hometown of Chicago; Jared Polis, who is governor of Colorado; Kate Brown, who is governor of Oregon; Tammy Baldwin, who is a United States senator from Wisconsin; and Krysten Sinema, who is a United States senator from Arizona now serve in political office. The intersection of race and homosexuality was in clear view in 2020 when two openly gay Black men won Democratic primaries in heavily Democratic districts and will certainly be elected to Congress from the fifteenth and seventeenth districts in New York City.[10]

This is something Congresswoman Barbara Jordan of Texas was not able to do when she represented a district from Houston, Texas.[11] She had to hide the fact that she was a lesbian. Her biographer, Mary Beth Rogers, wrote:

> Having experienced many battles along racial and gender lines, and knowing the religious and social bigotry against lesbian and gay people, Jordan was straightforward about her sexual orientation in private but did not think it should be fodder for public consumption. Jordan never denied who she was, but she knew her political career would be over if she were outed as a lesbian congresswoman in the 1970s, as supporters of her opponent, Curtis Graves tried to do in 1972.[12]

During the years that persons like Barbara Jordan had to spend hiding their sexual orientation, it would have seemed impossible to imagine that the day would come when there would be nationwide events that would allow LGBTQ persons to gather together in parades, festivals, film viewings, book discussions, lectureships, and other public occasions at which LGBTQ identity could be celebrated instead of being closeted.

Gay Marriage Is Now Legal

The most remarkable change in this nation's treatment of LGBTQ persons may well have occurred on June 26, 2015, when the United States Supreme Court ruled in a 5-4 decision that same-sex marriage was being legalized in all fifty states. Writing for the majority, Justice Anthony M. Kennedy said, "No longer may this liberty be denied. No union is more profound than marriage, for it embodies the highest ideals of love, fidelity, devotion, sacrifice and family. In forming a marital union, two people become something greater than once they were. Marriage is a keystone of our social order. The plaintiffs were seeking equal dignity in the eyes of the law."[13]

President Obama, who had not embraced same-sex marriage when he was running for president in 2007-2008, welcomed the Supreme Court ruling in 2015. He said in a Rose Garden celebration that "this decision affirms what millions of Americans already believed in their hearts. Today, we can say, in no uncertain terms, that we have made our union a little more perfect."[14]

The Bible Is Being Used to Support Homophobia

As with challenges to racism and sexism, the Bible has and is still being used to frustrate the aspirations of LGBTQ persons in their search for human rights and equal protection under the law. Since I have begun speaking about Stonewall and the struggle for human rights and equal rights for LGBT persons, I have been told on more than occasion that my views on this matter are contrary to the teachings of Scripture. More often than not, one of the Scriptures mentioned is Leviticus 18:22, which says, "Do not have sexual relations with a man as one does with a woman; that is detestable" (NIV).

Romans 1:26ff. is the other text used to make the case that LGBT issues are more about human sin than they are about human rights. That passage says, in part, "Because of this God gave them over to shameful lusts. Even their women exchanged natural sexual relations for unnatural ones. In the same way, the men also abandoned natural relations with women and were inflamed with lust for one another." (vv. 26-27a NIV) Some may even extend their argument to include 1 Corinthians 6:9-10, which says, "Neither the sexually immoral nor idolaters nor adulterers nor men who have sex with men nor thieves nor the greedy nor drunkards nor slanderers nor swindlers will inherit the kingdom of God."

I had a shocking conversation at the biennial convention of the American Baptist Church in Portland, Oregon, with a person who was deeply committed to the issue of racial equality but unabashedly focused on 1 Corinthians 6, at least the part that dealt with men having sex with other men. This person seemed far less interested in the rest of the behaviors mentioned in that passage: thieves, the greedy, drunkards, slanderers, and swindlers. For this person, the whole focus of the passage was on human sexual conduct, with far more ferocity on same-sex behavior than on adultery.

There was no subtlety to the person's position. There was no openness to the ongoing discussion about whether sexuality is as much a matter of biology as it is about a chosen behavior. "All homosexual are going to be banned from the kingdom of God." Moreover, I was criticized for suggesting anything to the contrary. This person boasted about holding views that reflected true Christian holiness. I guess that means that my views reflected my acceptance of what this person believed to be human sinfulness.

That encounter reflected what I always find so amazing about many people who approach LGBT issues from the position of sinfulness. They are unfailingly selective in the verses or portions of verse in Scripture they are reading. Such persons can be outraged and outspoken about same-sex activity which is referenced in all three of the verses mentioned above. However, they are either tolerant of, mute about, or wholly disinterested in other behaviors that either appear elsewhere in Leviticus or in the verses immediately after Romans 1:27 and 1 Corinthians 6:9.

If they kept reading Paul in the two passages they love to quote, they would encounter thieves, the greedy, drunkards, slanderers, and swindlers, who are similarly being barred from the kingdom of God. They would discover Paul's additional references to envy, murder, strife, deceit, malice, gossip, arrogance, and boastfulness, as well as a lack of fidelity and love and mercy.

There can be little doubt that all our churches have members who are involved in all the behaviors and attitudes mentioned by Paul in these two passages. But it is also true that very little sermon time is devoted to theft, gossip, slander, jealousy, boastfulness, envy, arrogance, or deceit. What is even more amazing is to hear preachers who are publicly known for their own acts of adultery displaying righteous indignation on the single issue of same-sex activity. There are preachers who have no shortage of boastfulness or arrogance about the success of their own ministry. There is also no shortage of preachers who envy the successes and achievements of some of their clergy colleagues. Yet, they can look past all of that, which is so clearly present in Romans 1 and 1 Corinthians 6, and bring laser focus to the one behavior they want to vilify.

This is nothing short of homiletic hypocrisy where preachers are willing to engage in bold speech on one topic mentioned by Paul which involves a small percentage of their listening audience, while saying little or nothing at all about the other matters mentioned by Paul in the same verses of Scripture which likely affect everyone present, including the preacher. One of the reasons persons may be walking away from the church is because they are walking away from this kind of hypocrisy and intolerance and judgmentalism that is all too prevalent in the pulpit and the pews.

The same point could be made about Leviticus 18:22. There are many more practices to be considered in that tenth-century BC holiness code to which modern readers could hold themselves accountable. Leviticus calls upon men to abstain from sexual contact with their wives during their wives' menstrual cycle. I have yet to hear a sermon about that; and that is also in Leviticus 18. I wonder how many people who point to Leviticus as the basis of their condemnation of same-sex relationships also abstain from eating shellfish (Leviticus 11:10) or wearing clothing made of more than one fabric

(Leviticus 19:19). One cannot wear a linen and wool suit to Red Lobster where you enjoy lobster or crab or shrimp and use that meal as an occasion to condemn the LGBT community. Leviticus 19:28 prohibits putting a tattoo on one's body. In this age of tattoos all over people's bodies, I have yet to hear a sermon on that. How odd that conservative evangelical Christians who seem to be among Donald Trump's core supporters have not condemned Trump's ally, Roger Stone, who has the face of Richard Nixon tattooed on his back.

Where Can the Church Go from Here?

Stonewall points to a series of current concerns about which the twenty-first-century church cannot be silent and should not approach solely based on smug self-righteousness. Stonewall reminds many people that their anti-gay views can suddenly and dramatically be challenged if not changed when their son or daughter announces that they are gay. Stonewall is at the heart of a current sociopolitical debate that involves whether business owners and service providers can deny their services to same-sex couples (wedding cakes, photo and video services, limousine services, banquet halls) because the owner of those services objects to same-sex couples on religious grounds. Stonewall forces us to address the question of who can and cannot be ordained to Christian ministry.

Most important of all, Stonewall challenges the church to realize that it is not fair to expect that the only voices addressing these issues are those in the LGBT community who are advocating for themselves. There is another letter in the LGBTQIA term, and that is the letter A that stands for Allies, though I sometimes use the term "advocates." Allies or advocates of the LGBT community are neither homosexual, bi-sexual, nor transgender themselves. Rather, they are persons who reject the notion that any person ought to be denied any human right or is deserving of any form of discrimination solely because of their sexual orientation.

Is the only option the church holds out to the LGBT community that they repent of their sins and come back to a "normal heterosexual lifestyle"? Surely, heterosexuals who suffer with a more than 50 percent divorce rate in their marriages, and who are at the heart of domestic abuse and the brutalization of women, should walk more softly on this ground. The hypocrisy of the church concerning LGBT issues is not unlike the hypocrisy of the Roman Catholic Church and the pedophilia that infected the ranks of what the world presumed was a celibate priesthood.

When I was a pastor in New Jersey, I participated in an ordination service for a young person. Somehow, the preacher for that occasion stumbled onto the issue of homosexuality. In his sermon, he said "the only place for a homosexual in the church is on the mourner's bench" (a term used in the Black church as a place of repentance from sin). There was not a person in the church that night who did not deserve a place on the mourner's bench for one sin or another, and that certainly included the preacher himself. Instead of saying that, this preacher singled out homosexuals for a special place in hell if they did not repent of their sins.

There was no subtlety in his position. There was no hint that societal views about homosexuality might have evolved since the tenth-century BC holiness code had been written, in which Leviticus 18:2 is found. We no longer stone persons caught in adultery. We no longer tell slaves to obey their masters. We no longer omit women from the national census. We as Christians no longer observe Passover, Hanukkah, Purim, or Pentecost as an agricultural observance. Nor do most Christians even observe a Sabbath rest from sundown Friday to sundown Saturday. Why do some people cling so tightly to Leviticus 18:22 and the condemnation of homosexuals?

We no longer make animal sacrifices at the temple of Jerusalem. We no longer practice kinsman redeemer marriages, as with Ruth and Boaz. We no longer declare people to be unclean because they have skin infections. We no longer require a man who has a discharge of semen to bathe his whole body and be considered unclean until he does. We no longer practice the Year of Jubilee when all debts are forgiven and all prisoners are set free. We no longer tear down houses that are infected with mildew. We no longer prohibit persons with physical disabilities (labeled defects, Leviticus 21:18 NIV) from serving in the ministry. Why are some people so determined to retain homosexuality as an unpardonable sin while acknowledging that most other parts of the holiness code in Leviticus 17-26 are relics of an ancient past?

In more recent years, we no longer wage religious wars over the legitimacy of infant versus believers' baptism. We no longer convene inquisition panels to force Jews and Muslims to renounce their faith and convert to Christianity under penalty of death. We no longer tax persons to support religious institutions to which they do not belong and in which they do not believe. We no longer have blue laws that require certain businesses to close during Sunday morning. We no longer require a religious test for those seeking to serve in political office. We no longer ban Jews and Roman Catholics from voting or holding political office, as was the norm in the colonial era in this country. Given these changes in societal norms, what is it about the practice of homosexuality that causes the views of ancient Israel and the early Christian church to remain in force? Why is the sexual orientation of any person of any interest to other persons who are not themselves LGBTQ, and why are those who are quick to condemn homosexuality slow to condemn, or worse, continue to practice racism and sexism?

How Can Our Stonewall Discussion Begin?

There is no mistaking the fact that many Christians still fail or refuse to draw any connection between the civil rights movement and the fight against racism, and gay rights and the fight against homophobia. Even after same-sex marriage was legalized in 2015, many denominations, including the National Baptist Convention, the Assemblies of God, the Roman Catholic Church, the Southern Baptist Convention, the American Baptist Churches USA, and the United Methodist Church, refused to sanction such unions and did not permit their clergy to perform same-sex marriages. The same prohibition also existed among Orthodox Jews and Islam.[15]

I recall the furor that erupted at American Baptist College in Nashville, Tennessee, in 2015 when the college president, Forrest Harris, invited Yvette Flunder, a United Church of Christ pastor who is in a same-sex marriage, to deliver a lecture on that campus. The school is affiliated with the National Baptist Convention

USA, Inc. The National Baptist Fellowship of Concerned Pastors, a group also affiliated with the NBCUSA, Inc., was quick to condemn the school for issuing that invitation. In their formal statement of opposition, they said, "For a Baptist college president to invite a lesbian bishop legally married to a woman, to be a guest speaker and worship leader on a Baptist college campus is irresponsible, scandalous, non-biblical, and certainly displeasing to God."[16] When the college president refused to rescind the invitation, he stated that "we can't be guided and dictated to by a first-century world view."[17] That response brought this rebuke from those who opposed the invitation to Flunder: "We believe the Bible and its teachings. We believe homosexuality—as a matter of fact all the Bible talks about as sin—is sin."[18]

What Does the Bible Say and How Should We Read It?

How can churches begin a discussion about LGBT-related issues? How can churches see the importance of Stonewall no less than the struggles associated with Seneca Falls and Selma? It can begin with doing better biblical exegesis that studies the texts mentioned above through the lens of twenty-first-century sensibilities, and not through the noncritical lens of biblical literalism and fundamentalism. More importantly, the church can resist and reject those preachers who cherry-pick the text they will focus on, while ignoring or passing over a great many other matters also set forth in Scripture. The level of hypocrisy that has always been associated with those who have used the Bible to promote and preserve sexism, racism, and homophobia is staggering.

The church has been waging this war around the use of the Bible for millennia. That is precisely what the church had to do with the issues associated with Seneca Falls and Selma. Things that seemed so certain about the role and status of women and ethnic minorities in earlier eras in human history have been reconsidered and largely reversed in law, if not in the hearts of all people. Time and time again, society has shifted its views and come to the realization that it was time for a change. It was time to let the oppressed go free.

NOTES

1. David Oliver and Rasha Ali, "Why We Give Pride to Black Transgender Women Who Threw Bricks at Cops," USAToday.com, June 24, 2019; Christina Maxouris, "Marsha P. Johnson, a Black Transgender Woman, Was a Central Figure in the Gay Liberation Movement," CNN.com, June 26, 2019.

2. Neel Burton, "When Homosexuality Stopped Being a Mental Disorder," PsychologyToday.com, September 18, 2015.

3. Nicole Puglise, "Don't Ask, Don't Tell: Military Members Out and Proud Five Years after Repeal," TheGuardian.com, September 27, 2016.

4. Katy Steinmetz, "President Trump's Transgender Ban Was Just Blocked. Here's What That Means for Troops," TIME.com, October 30, 2017.

5. Julie Moreau, "Years after Trans Military Ban, Legal Battle Rages On," NBCNews.com, April 11, 2020.

6. Tom Vander Brook, "Trump Takes on Gender Policy," USA Today, July 26, 2017, B 1-2.

7. Ibid., 2.

8. David Weigel, "Trump's LGBT Rights Promises Were Tied to the War on Radical Islam," WashingtonPost.com, July 26, 2016, 1.

9. Adam D. Chandler, "Donald Trump Just Sent a Painful Message to Me and Other LGBT People," USAToday.com, July 7, 2017, 10.

10. Eugene Scott, "In a First, Two Openly Gay Black Men Are Probably Headed to Congress," WashingtonPost.com, June 25, 2020.

11. Horace L. Griffin, *Their Own Receive Them Not: African American Lesbian and Gays in Black* Churches (Eugene, OR: Wipf & Stock, 2010), 131–34.

12. Mary Beth Rogers, *Barbara Jordan: American Hero* (New York: Bantam Books, 1998), 354.

13. Adam Liptak, "Supreme Court Ruling Makes Same-Sex Marriage a Right Nationwide," NewYorkTimes.com, June 26, 2015.

14. Ibid.

15. David Masci and Michael Lipka, "Where Christian Churches, Other Religions Stand on Gay Marriage," PewResearchCenter.com, December 21, 2015.

16. Jordan Buie, "Pastors Oppose Lesbian Bishop Speaker at Baptist College," Tennessean.com, March 11, 2015.

17. Ibid.

18. Ibid.

CHAPTER 11

From Seneca Falls, to Selma, to Stonewall, to Standing Rock

Representatives and direct Taxes shall be apportioned among the several States which may be included within this Union, according to their respective Numbers, which shall be determined by adding to the whole Number of free Persons, including those bound to Service for a term of Years, and Excluding Indians not taxed, three fifths of all other persons.

With these words in Article 1, Section 3 of the Constitution of the United States, the framers and the founding fathers of this country determined that from its inception the United States of America was to be governed by and on behalf of its white citizens, free and indentured. The enslaved population fell subject to the three-fifths clause, which meant that those persons would be counted as only 60 percent of a whole person. Five slaves would be counted as only three. Ten slaves would be counted as only six. Twenty slaves would be counted as only twelve, and so forth. This was done at the urging of the northern states that were concerned that if all the slaves in the southern states were counted as whole persons, it would give a numerical and therefore a political advantage to the South when it came to Congressional seats.

As bad as the three-fifths clause was, what will concern us in this chapter are the words "excluding Indians not taxed." What these words mean is chilling when one considers that they were written and ratified by people who had demanded freedom from oppressive taxation by Great Britain on the basis of taxation without representation. In its founding documents, the United States relegated people of African descent to a lifetime of slavery and second-class status as human beings. Even worse, it determined that Native Americans (Indians) had no future in this country as citizens.

In *Caste*, Isabel Wilkerson offers the concept of class rather than the concept of race as the basis upon which certain societies are organized and preferential treatment is determined. She looks at Jews during the Nazi era in Germany (1933–1945), the Dalit or the "untouchables" in India over the last many centuries, and at African Americans in the United States from the inception of the country. She referred to a racial creed especially in force in the Southern United States that said, "Let the lowest white man count for more than the highest negro."[1] She then makes reference to the conclusions of the Swedish researcher Gunnar Myrdal, who in 1944 had done an extensive study of the issue of race in the United States. Myrdal concluded, says Wilkerson, "America had created a caste system and that the effort to maintain the color line has, to the ordinary white man the function of upholding that caste system itself, of keeping the Negro in his place."[2]

If the three-fifths clause of the US Constitution established the intended place of African Americans in society, then article 1, section 3 of the Constitution states that there would be no place for Native Americans in the United States, the very land upon which those indigenous persons had lived for centuries before the arrival of Europeans explorers and settlers. That exclusion from the ranks of US citizenship would remain in effect until 1924, with the passage of the Indian Citizenship Act. However, voting rights that are a hallmark of true citizenship were not granted all Native Americans until 1962. On certain reservations where there are no distinguishable street addresses, many Native Americans are still not able to register and vote. This is one of many forms of voter suppression.[3]

The Consequences of Caste for Native Americans

Everything that has happened to Native Americans in the United States can be traced to these four words in the Constitution: "excluding Indians not taxed." In point of fact, the eighteenth-century language in the Constitution only ratified decisions made by seventeenth-century British colonists in Jamestown, Virginia, that determined that Native Americans were not going to be part of the future of their colony. In *1619*, James Horn points out that beginning in 1622, "For the mass of Indian and African people, of course, even the faintest glimmer of hope of personal improvement was denied them. Slavery and inequality thus arose as synchronic opposites of liberty and opportunity, products of the same political and economic forces."[4]

In order to deny citizenship rights to African and Native Americans, the colonists first had to dehumanize them and cut them off from any sense of having equal status with whites. As regards the Native Americans, that came with this statement from Sir Edwin Sandys, who wrote on behalf of the Jamestown colony, "Man was a political and sociable creature. [Indians] therefore are to be numbered among the beasts who renounce society; whereby they are destitute of laws, the ordination of civility. By this standard, there was no longer any place for Indian peoples in the English colony."[5]

After the Powhatan tribe of Native Americans attacked the Jamestown settlement in 1622 because it was encroaching on their land, Horn states that "racial stereotypes demonizing the Indians were quickly adopted by settlers to justify the slaughter of Indian peoples and the appropriation of their territory. Huge areas of prime agricultural lands were taken up by settlers, creating the first English land rush in America. Some Powhatan captives were enslaved and joined Africans in bondage; other Indian peoples moved out of the region beyond the reach of settlers."[6]

During a subsequent encounter in 1623, a group of settlers offered to enter into a peace treaty with the Native Americans. Horn described what happened at the signing ceremony:

> Captain William Tucker passed around bottles of sack [fortified wine] to drink to the end of hostilities and the new peace. Tuck-

er and his interpreter tasted the wine to show no treachery was intended, but drank from a different bottle, while the Indians . . . were given poisoned wine. How many died is uncertain, but many suddenly became sick, giving Tucker and his men the opportunity to open fire, killing approximately fifty. As trophies, or perhaps to claim the bounty . . . Tucker returned to Jamestown with pieces of the Indians' heads.[7]

The oppression of Native Americans began before the country was founded and continues in various forms to this day. Nothing illustrates the painful experience of Native Americans in the United States more than the Indian Removal Act of 1830. Under the direction of President Andrew Jackson, who was himself a slaveholder, all Native Americans living on the east side of the Mississippi River in states including Georgia, Alabama, Tennessee, and Mississippi were forcibly relocated by the United States Army to a region in the country now known as Oklahoma.[8]

The underlying reason for that forced removal was not simply to marginalize the Native Americans through an unprecedented land grab. The larger reason, driven by economics, was to allow for the expansion of growing cotton and the increase of slave labor that was essential to the regional economy. Those states would become the center of cotton production for the next one hundred years. Charles Mills wrote about the general attitude of indifference held by Jackson toward Native Americans when he observed that "Jackson, the U.S. president who oversaw the forced removal of indigenous people from their ancestral homelands during that Trail of Tears, used bridle reins of indigenous flesh when he went horseback riding."[9]

As a result of the Indian Removal Act, more than forty-six thousand of the Cherokee and Choctaw tribal groups were relocated—and more than four thousand of them died along the way.

The Horror of Life on Native American Reservations

Native Americans of many different tribal groups would eventually be moved onto government-sponsored reservations in the Southwest and Upper Midwest portions of the country. Today, people living on those reservations experience staggering levels of alcoholism, depression, drug addiction, domestic violence, infant mortality, and unemployment, and the highest rates of suicide and teen suicide in the United States.[10]

There are 326 Indian reservations across the country. One of them, the Pine Ridge Reservation in South Dakota, has been in the news for two different reasons in recent years. In 2016, it was the site of a massive influx of drugs known as methamphetamines. That reservation is home to more than twenty thousand Ogala Lakota Sioux Indians. The increase in drug usage has resulted in a spike in murders and homicides. The murder rate doubled over the previous year. That placed the reservation on par with the deadliest US cities in terms of gun violence.[11]

The second reason for being in the news is the COVID-19 pandemic. Given that there were upwards of eighteen thousand positive cases of COVID-19 in South Dakota in May of 2020, tribal elders set up checkpoints on all roads leading onto the reservation to prevent the further spread of the virus. They issued a mandatory shutdown of all businesses on the reservation and mandated stay-at-home orders that lasted for thirty-six hours. That reservation includes Mount Rushmore, a national landmark where President Trump participated in a large, outdoor rally that did not mandate wearing masks.

The Native Americans opposed that event on July 3, 2020, on the basis of spreading the virus or the possibility that fireworks might contaminate or destroy sacred sites. Needless to say, that event was held even though the people on whose land the event was being held "did not give their permission."[12] Another mandatory lockdown was imposed the week after the event at Mount Rushmore in an attempt to prevent COVID-19 from spreading among the Ogala Sioux.[13] One elder in that community stated why the tribe was being so careful:

> Reservations have been the deliberate recipient of genocidal policies that would degenerate our health. We've been extremely fortunate and lucky and chosen by God to survive this ongoing threat to our very existence. Biological threats freak us out. Any Euroasian disease that doesn't have permission to be here, we have to repel that somehow through divine inspiration, through science, and through action.[14]

"Reservations have been the deliberate recipients of genocidal policies." From the decapitation of Powhatan chiefs in 1623, to the intentional exposure to COVID-19 of a 2020 Trump-led political rally on land set aside for the Ogala Sioux nation, the words "excluding Indians not taxed" has been the attitude of the United States toward Native Americans.

George Tinker points out, "When they first encountered European peoples, the indigenous peoples of the Americas must have numbered, according to current demographic research, well in excess of 100 million people."[15] However, with Christianity and the conquest by Europeans that followed, came diseases like smallpox that wiped out more than 90 percent of the indigenous population, beginning as early as the 1600s. William Loren Katz offers a lower number of indigenous people living in the Americas before the arrival of Europeans, but the impact on that population was the same. He writes:

> The estimated 80 million Native Americans alive in 1492 became only 10 million left alive a century later . . . These figures are even more striking within local areas. In 1519 when the Spaniards arrived, Mexico had a population of 25 million Indians. By the end of the century only a million were still alive. The invaders calculated that more profit would be made if laborers were worked to death and replaced. In their plans, pain and suffering did not count, and no cruelty was considered excessive.[16]

In 1634, John Winthrop, who has long been revered due to his leadership in the establishment of the Plymouth Colony in Massachusetts, gave an early indication of what the future of Native Americans would be in that and other parts of what would become the United States of America. Seeing the effect of European disease on the Native Americans, Winthrop wrote, "The Indians are nere all dead of the Small Poxe, so as the Lord hathe cleared our title to what we possess."[17] Winthrop was linking the horrific deaths of Native Americans with the will of God making it possible for white colonizers to lay claim to Indian lands. It appears that the earliest large-scale form of genocide was the mere presence of Europeans in the new world.

Bury My Heart at Wounded Knee

The Pine Ridge Reservation was the site of one of the most extreme acts of genocide when a group of Lakota Sioux were surrounded and massacred at a place called Wounded Knee on December 29, 1890. As reported on in *God's Red Son*, Louis S. Warren describes the scene that unfolded while a group of Lakota Sioux were on their way to surrender themselves at the reservation. The killing started after one Sioux warrior insisted that he be paid for his weapon, rather than surrender something he deemed to be of great value. When two soldiers tried to take his gun, the gun fired into the air. No one was injured, but Colonel James Forsyth ordered his men from the Seventh Calvary to return fire. Here is how an onlooker described the scene:

> The massed firepower of the troops shredded the council circle. Most of the men were killed or wounded in the first volley, but those who could grabbed guns and fought . . . The army opened up with its dreaded Hotchkiss guns, slaughtering groups of huddled Lakotas, most of them women and children. When soldiers on the high ground to the north unleashed another Hotchkiss gun, exploding shells destroyed a great many Lakotas fleeing along the road, including nine women trying to escape in a wagon. Back in the ravine, a few survivors managed to straggle out of the fight and flee, escaping the soldiers who stood watch and shot anything that moved, anybody that breathed, twitched, or raised a hand to surrender . . . Those who had managed to escape to the hills or ravines of the surrounding country now became prey for the calvary. Unarmed children and women were shot at point-blank range. For hours the horse soldiers took no prisoners at Wounded Knee. The bloodletting did not end until noon.[18]

The Massacre at Sand Creek

Another infamous act of genocide against Native Americans occurred on November 29, 1864, when nine hundred soldiers under the command of Colonel John Chivington attacked a village of Cheyenne and Arapaho Indians at Sand Creek, Colorado. That village that was not engaged in any hostilities against the government or white settlers and had been promised the protection of the US Army. Jim Beckworth—an African American who was born to a slave woman with a Native American legacy, and who himself had been adopted into the Crow Nation and had been an army scout in the wars against the Seminoles—was on hand to observe the attack at Sand Creek. He had been invited to share in the attack, but had refused to do so. He described it this way:

> At dawn Chivington's army reached Sand Creek, where Black Kettle's six hundred people—mostly women and children—were gathered under an American flag. Black Kettle raised a white flag and told everyone to "not be afraid." Beckworth stared with horror as Chivington's men began to fire wildly with howitzers and rifles. He saw people shot dead as they held up their hands. Then men charged in to finish the job with pistols, swords, and knives. Their seemed to be indiscriminate slaughter of men, women, and children . . . I saw quite a number of mothers were slain; still clinging to their babies . . . A white lieutenant, James Connor, described children and babies butchered or mutilated with swords and left to die while others were scalped. Hundreds died before the day was over.[19]

The Washita Massacre

Just four years after the massacre at Sand Creek, a massacre of Native Americans occurred at the Washita River near Cheyenne, Oklahoma, on November 27, 1868. This attack was led by Lieutenant Colonel George Armstrong Custer and the US Seventh Cavalry. This unprovoked attack was described this way:

> Custer did not attempt to identify which group of Cheyenne was in the village, or to make even a cursory reconnaissance of the situation. Had he done so, Custer would have discovered that they were peaceful people and the village was on reservation soil, where the commander of Fort Cobb had guaranteed them safety. There was even a white flag [flying] from one of the dwellings, indicating that the tribe was actively avoiding conflict . . . 103 Cheyenne were killed and the village (on a reservation) was destroyed.[20]

This is the same George Armstrong Custer who has been celebrated for so long in Custer's Last Stand at the Little Big Horn River in

Montana on June 25, 1876. There is a glamorous portrayal of Custer in the film *They Died with Their Boots On* featuring Errol Flynn as Custer. The historical facts around that massacre are much more closely followed in a later film, *Little Big Man*, with Dustin Hoffman as an observer of the attack.

According to the historical record, the Lakota Sioux and Cheyenne refused to be relocated to a reservation overseen by the Bureau of Indian Affairs, and they were living peacefully on their ancestral homeland. When gold was discovered in the Black Hills, which stretch from South Dakota to Montana, the US Army ignored previous treaty arrangements and invaded the region. As with the land grab in 1830 in order to expand the cotton industry, white prospectors poured into Native American lands hoping to strike it rich. Having divided his forces, Custer led his troops into another poorly planned assault—only to be met by more than three thousand Cheyenne and Sioux warriors. Within an hour, Custer and all his men were dead.[21]

Forgetting how many times U.S. Calvary troops had attacked and massacred Native Americans, this defeat of a cavalry unit sent the nation into a frenzy for revenge and for further assaults on Native Americans. "The demise of Custer and his men outraged many white Americans and confirmed their image of the Indians as wild and bloodthirsty. Meanwhile, the U.S. government increased its efforts to subdue the tribes. Within five years, almost all of the Sioux and Cheyenne would be confined to reservations."[22]

Native Americans and the Right to Self-Defense

Part of Native American liberation involves being liberated from two things tied to the events listed above. The first is the stereotype that Native Americans are savage and bloodthirsty; that their only instinct was to kill white settlers. The second, closely tied to the first, is that white people are always the ones who are the victims in any attack by Native Americans on persons trying to settle or exploit the indigenous people's ancestral homelands. Few white historians have ever made the case that Native Americans had the right to defend themselves and their homelands from what they viewed as an invasion and a conquest of their territory.

The Southern states of the United States seceded from this country, formed a separate country, and waged war against the United States on the grounds of "northern aggression" or "states' rights." It was acceptable for white people to defend their homes and families through force of arms. However, when slaves attempted an uprising, or when Native Americans fought back against whites who laid claim to their land and slaughtered their families, the same rule did not apply. When the U.S. government purchased land from France in the Louisiana Purchase, that transaction was viewed as a way to expand US territory. What went unnoticed then, and now, is that five major Native tribes had been living on that land for centuries. They were the Cherokee, Choctaw, Chickasaw, Creek, and Shawnee. When the land transferred from the French to the United States in 1803, no thought was given to the continuing land rights of the Native American tribes. The only concern was the fulfillment of what came to be known as America's Manifest Destiny—to have a nation that stretched from the Atlantic Ocean in the east to the Pacific Ocean in the west. Since "excluding Indians not taxed" was the national policy, there was no need to consult with them on what should happen to their lands and their culture.

Genocidal Policies at Standing Rock

I am certain that if Barack Obama had given his inaugural address in 2017, he would have said "from Seneca Falls, to Selma, to Stonewall, to Standing Rock." That reservation near Bismarck, North Dakota, was the reservation to which the Sioux were confined after the defeat of Custer. However, in 2017, it became the sight of a protest by the Lakota Sioux and thousands of their supporters over the construction of the Keystone oil pipeline that would run through the ancestral burial ground of the Sioux. It would disrupt hunting and fishing rights for the Sioux, who depend upon those activities for their survival. Moreover, it would likely leak oil into the ground and pollute the water supply for six neighboring states.

In 2015, in response to an appeal by the Lakota Sioux to President Obama over the environmental hazards associated with the pipeline, a freeze was placed on any further construction until all possible environmental dangers could be identified and resolved.[23] However, four days after he was inaugurated, President Trump lifted that freeze and allowed the construction of the pipeline to continue without the ownership or environmental issues being resolved.[24] Once again, a Native American reservation was the deliberate recipient of a genocidal policy. Michael Brune, the executive director of the Sierra Club that monitors environmental hazards across the country, said this about Trump's decision: "Donald Trump has been in office for four days, and he's already proving to be the dangerous threat to our climate we feared he would be."[25] Once again, the chance of economic gain by white, corporate interests resulted in a willingness to ignore treaties and grab land assigned to Native Americans by the federal government.

Standing Rock is private land owned by the Lakota Sioux Nation with the agreement of the federal government. However, like so many agreements and treaties between Native Americans and the US government, ownership rights always seem to lose out to corporate interests and the exploitation of natural resources.

The Scope of Oppression Experienced by Native American

It is necessary to review these historical details in order to lay out the basis for Native American sovereignty theology. After nearly four hundred years of being socially marginalized, forcibly relocated, racially stereotyped, physically assaulted, and economically deprived, is it any wonder that Native Americans joined the chorus of voices that said, "let the oppressed go free"? It was this history of oppression, genocide, and economic exploitation by the U.S. government, often supported by representatives of various branches of the Christian church, as well as by private entities operating without any government restraint or regulation, that has resulted in what is variously called American Indian liberation theology or a theology of sovereignty.

This approach to theology was created as a way to work for an end to the cruel conditions under which so many Native Americans are living, and to explore and explain a return to traditional forms of living and thinking that predate the arrival of Europeans into the Americas.[26] What makes Native American liberation theology different from all the other forms of liberation theology examined thus far in this book is that it is not necessarily attached to or limited by any form of Christian theology. In fact, it could be argued that what Native Americans want is liberation from a form or version of Christianity that had been used as a tool by those whose real agenda was the conquest and exploitation of their land its and natural resources.

George Tinker writes:

American Indians, the aboriginal residents of the Americas, entered European consciousness in1492 with the Columbia misadventure. The subsequent European invasion of the Americas resulted in untold devastation to these indigenous residents and owners of the American territories. The intentional destruction of their cultures and massacres of their communities were often perpetrated in the name of the invaders' christian religious convictions and their attempts to impose their religion on those whose land they came to steal.[27]

Tinker argues that earlier forms of liberation theology made reference to the words of Jesus and other aspects of the biblical story as the basis for their claim that "God was on the side of the poor and the oppressed." Even when certain biblical texts were used by some people to justify slavery, or the marginalization of women, or the conquest of land as part of God's plan for Manifest Destiny or of the United States as "The Redeemer Nation,"[28] liberation theologian would work to correct faulty and biased readings of Scripture in order to make their case to end racism, sexism, poverty, and homophobia.[29]

It must be understood that American Indian sovereignty theology does not start with Exodus, or Moses, or Jesus, or any other part of the biblical narrative. Like Africans who came from other countries and cultures, Native Americans had sophisticated cosmologies that connected them to their land, to their community, to the natural world around them, and to the spirits they viewed as dwelling in all things. They had religious rituals and ceremonies that were central to their identity. However, with the coming of Europeans, the traditional religions of Africans and Native Americans were deemed to be heathenish and backward, and both groups, Africans and Native Americans, needed the benefit of being "Christianized and civilized." However, the true ultimate objective was not saving the souls of those groups. The ultimate objective was to exploit their labor and/or their land in every way possible.

Tinker argues:

> The radical interpretation of Jesus would be an unproductive and even counterproductive starting point for a liberation theology because the first proclamation of Jesus among any Indian community came as the beginning of a colonial conquest that included the total displacing of centuries-old religious traditions and the replacing of those traditions with the one-size-fits-all euro-western Jesus.[30]

The Core Tenets of Native American Religion

The religious traditions may have varied from tribe to tribe or region to region in certain details, but there were core values that seemed to run through all Native American identity. Clara Sue Kidwell and others begin by saying that Native American religion revolves around the concept of "spatiality." This means that rather than living in a linear worldview, where history is a straight line moving forward, Native American religion follows the cycles of nature. Life is tied to seasons, harvests, movements of the sun and stars. "Where Christianity is oriented toward an ultimate end in heaven, Native time is oriented to the repetition of events . . . The importance of cycles in nature is paramount in Indian communities."[31]

Second, Native Americans are "communitarian" in that that they place more value on the group than on the individual. Kinship is of greater importance than what is accomplished by any single person. "In Indian communities, people are valued not for what they achieve for themselves, but for what they contribute to the stability and continuity of the group."[32] The concept of salvation is fundamentally different as well. For Native Americans, spiritual practices are engaged in for the sake of the people and not for the sake of individual salvation or personal spiritual empowerment.

Third, "in the indigenous world there is a firmly established notion of the interrelatedness of all the created/natural world." "In Indian cultures, people live and experience themselves as part of creation for instance, rather than living as separate from creation with the freedom or even the responsibility to consume it at will." "In the indigenous world, the community does not just consist of the human beings associated with any one tribal group." "This larger community consists of animals (four-leggeds), birds, and all the living, moving things (including rocks, hills, trees, rivers, and so on). Along with all the other sorts of two-leggeds (humans of different colors) in the world."[33]

Finally, individual ownership of land is a concept foreign to Indian peoples. There is a firm sense of group filial attachment to particular places that comes with a responsibility to relate to the land in those places with responsibility.[34] A wonderful article appeared in *Sojourners* in 2019 that focused on Native American and other indigenous cultures in relation to what we might call "the care of the earth" or environmentalism.[35]

Planet Earth is facing a climate crisis defined by rising temperatures, melting glaciers, increased flooding, droughts, mudslides, more powerful hurricanes, and more intense fires. The forests of the world are being decimated. Entire species are being endangered, if not being made extinct. Air pollution is blocking out the sun in places in India and China. Smoke from raging fires recently blocked out the sun over San Francisco. Much of this can be explained by human activity that is driven by corporate profits, human greed, blatant disregard for the land rights of poorer nations and communities, and a foolish disregard for warnings coming from scientists about how our behavior is endangering the future of the planet and the people who dwell on the earth.

Randy Woodley writes:

Indigenous peoples understand their relationship with creation as paramount to the abundant life God intends for all humanity. In other words, to be human is to care for creation. If we want to live our lives together in abundance and harmony, and if we want future generations to live their lives together this way, we must realize we are all on a journey together with Christ to heal our world. Earth healing will take cooperation from all of us to solve the problems . . . Instead of a relationship where nature is below us, we should be stewarding with or co-sustaining all creation.[36]

The American culture has celebrated a man named William F. ("Buffalo Bill") Cody. He earned that name due to the massive number of buffalo (bison) he killed largely for their skins, which were sold as souvenirs. What goes unmentioned is that those same buffalo were an essential part of the cycle of life for scores of Native American tribes living in the plains states of this country from Iowa to Colorado to the Dakotas and into Montana and Wyoming. In a world based upon the care of the earth, Native Americans hunted only for food and not for sport. More importantly, as regards the buffalo, that animal was not just a source of food. Every part of the buffalo was used for clothing, lodging, medicine, and religious ritual.

Why would Native Americans want to embrace the religion of those who were decimating their culture, destroying their villages, desecrating their burial grounds, exploiting their natural resources, and demonizing their very existence? It is easy to see why Native Americans were so reluctant to be removed from their ancestral homelands; their entire identity was tied to being a member of a community that is bound together by the land on which they lived and for which they cared and respected. The claim of "personal salvation" and life on reservations was contrary to their belief system. When missionaries and local clergy attempted to convert them to Christianity, they were often met with either resistance or disregard. What was even more problematic was when white Christians would attempt to suppress certain forms of Native American religion such as playing the drum and ritual dancing.

The massacre at Wounded Knee was discussed earlier in this chapter. What must be added to that story is that at its core the action against the Sioux was part of the suppression of an aspect of Native American religious practice. Most of those killed by the U.S. Army engaged in the Ghost Dance.

This ritual was based upon the belief that Native Americans could be rescued from the agonies of American conquest on a newly restored earth teeming with buffalo and horses. It drew believers into dance circles where some fell into unconscious trance visions in which they encountered their deceased kin and, sometimes the Creator himself. Late in 1890, the US Army arrived among the Western Sioux to suppress the religion on the orders of President Benjamin Harrison. At Wounded Knee Creek on the morning of December 29, the army veered into massacre.[37]

"Conversion" to Christianity

It is true that a great many Native Americans did convert to Christianity over the centuries since the arrival of white missionaries and settlers. Assimilation into the dominant culture worked in the same way it did for African Americans when they were introduced to the Christian faith. What is painful to consider is that much of that conversion was not entirely voluntarily.

Clara Sue Kidwell writes, "Through acculturation, abetted primarily by boarding schools which took young people out of their own cultural milieux to expose them fully to Christian values, Indian students' native value systems were replaced by the teachings of missionaries . . . The purpose was not only to convert Indians to Christianity, but to imbue them with the basic attributes of white American society."[38] Kidwell references the motto of the Carlisle Indian School, which was the most famous (infamous) of the boarding schools designed to "Americanize" the Native Americans. The slogan was, "Kill the Indian to save the man."[39]

The embrace of a new faith tradition often came at the expense of traditional religious practices that were either suppressed or were so drastically disrupted as a result of forced relocation that they could not survive. None other than William T. Sherman, who would become one of the leading generals during the Civil War, spent some time in the West working on maintaining peace between Apache Indians and white settlers. As a result of that experience he wrote, "There are two classes of people, one demanding the utter extinction of the Indians and the other full of love for their conversion to civilization and Christianity."[40] What seems never to have been an option was that the Native Americans would be left alone to live on their own land, embracing their own religion, and maintaining a way of life that had developed over hundreds of years.

To let the oppressed go free for Native Americans is to remember, celebrate, and perpetuate ways of life that continue to provide them with an identity that offsets those four horrific words in the U.S. Constitution: "excluding Indians not taxed."

Freedom from Stereotypes

Freedom from Hollywood

Letting the oppressed go free for Native Americans also includes breaking free from the demeaning stereotypes and images that have been offered up by Hollywood western movies and by the dehumanizing practice of having their images and tribal groups offered up as mascots for sports teams. I grew up in the 1950s and 1960s on a steady diet of movies involving "cowboys and Indians" in which brave white settlers were clearing the western plains so that "decent white people" could start a new life. There was never any serious consideration given to the morality of that westward progress. Indians were simply an obstacle that needed to be removed.

What made those films even more concerning is that in many instances, speaking roles for Native Americans were assigned to white actors wearing costumes and face paint to darken their appearance. I can still see Jeff Chandler as Cochise, Anthony Quinn as Crazy Horse, and Burt Lancaster as Jim Thorpe, the great Native American Olympic athlete. As recently as 2013, Johnny Depp was cast as Tonto in a new version of the 1950s television classic *The Lone Ranger*." At least with the original show, the role of Tonto was played by Jay Silverheels, who was a Canadian-born Mohawk Indian. Of course, he was still presented as a barely articulate person who was subjected to racial slurs in almost every episode.

This practice of white actors playing Native American characters reminds me of the practice of white actors like Al Jolson who put on black grease paint in order to appear on stage or screen in what was called blackface. What was especially egregious in that instance was that for many years African American performers had to wear blackface in order to appear on stage. Such is the insanity of white supremacy.

There have been a few films that have tried to offer a different view of Native American life. Most notable is *Dances with Wolves*, starring Kevin Costner, that points out the humanity within a Lakota Sioux tribe and the brutality and disregard for Native Americans lands and rights by white settlers and the U.S. Army. However, films like that are greatly overwhelmed by a string of John Wayne movies like *Fort Apache* and *She Wore a Yellow Ribbon*, in which Native Americans were presented as people who had to be conquered and subdued.

Freedom from Being Sports Mascots

The issue that seems to keep the plight of Native Americans in the news well into the twenty-first century is their demand that sports teams stop using Indian names and images as mascots. Some progress has recently been made in that effort. The National Football League team once known as the Washington Redskins has dropped that term and is now called the Washington Football Team. They will keep that name until they can settle on a new name. However, in terms of professional sports teams there is still the Golden State Warriors in basketball, the Kansas City Chiefs in football, the Atlanta Braves and Cleveland Indians in baseball, and the Chicago Blackhawks in hockey.

Imagine a sports team called the New York Negroes or the New Jersey Jews. Such a thing would be unthinkable for most people in this country. But otherwise justice-minded people happily attend sporting events featuring teams named after Native American tribal groups, and they buy and wear jerseys and caps featuring the images of Native Americans. Some who do such things think they are honoring Native Americans in this way. They are obviously not listening to Native Americans, who find the team names and the logos degrading and dehumanizing.

I think it is safe to say that with respect to the Washington Redskins, that name was not changed out of any sudden sensibilities about

Native American concerns. In 2013, Dan Snyder, who is the owner of the team, said, "We will never change the name of the team." However, the team plays in FedEx Field, and that corporation threatened to end its partnership with the team if the name was not changed.[41] In a quintessentially American moment, it was the money associated with corporate sponsorship and not the justifiable concerns of an aggrieved people that made the difference.

Donald Trump and Andrew Jackson

On November 27, 2017, President Trump hosted a gathering in the White House to honor the surviving members of a group of Navajo Indians who became known as the Code Talkers during World War II. As members of the United States Marine Corps fighting against the Japanese in various locations in the Pacific region, these Navajo Indians sent and received radio messages to and from the battlefield. The Japanese could not intercept and translate those messages, because they did not know the Navajo language that was being used. A great many battles were won and a great many American lives were saved because of the work of the Navajo Code Talkers. Their valor is presented in a film entitled *The Windtalkers*.

When the event to honor them at the White House began, Trump stood in front of a portrait of Andrew Jackson. Did he not know—or did he not care—that Jackson was the American president responsible for the Indian Removal Act of 1830 that resulted in the Trail of Tears and the deaths of thousands of Cherokee, Choctaw, and other tribal groups on that forced journey? Not only that, but those heroic Navajo warriors were dumbfounded when Trump used that occasion to refer to United States Senator Elizabeth Warren of Massachusetts as "Pocahontas."

He was taking the name of a young Powhatan Indian who had married John Rolfe of the Jamestown, Virginia, colony in the early seventeenth century. She had done so in hopes that it might result in peace between the colonists and the Native American group that had originally welcomed Europeans into their ancestral home. I wonder if Trump knows the origin of the name. Whatever his knowledge of the name or the tribal group might or might not have been, he was turning a historical figure into a derogatory term meant to demean one of his political adversaries.[42] Here again, at a time when genuine American heroes were being celebrated, a portrait of Jackson and the demeaning of Warren were reminders of the words "excluding Indians not taxed." All of this is involved when I suggest that Native American liberation theology rightly stands with all the other forms of liberation theology in saying, "let the oppressed go free."

NOTES

1. Isabel Wilkerson, *Caste: The Origins of Our Discontent* (New York: Random House, 2020), 25.

2. Ibid., 24.

3. Peter Dunphy, "The State of Native American Voting Rights," brennan center.org, March 13, 2019.

4. James Horn, *1619: Jamestown and the Forging of American Democracy* (New York: Basic Books, 2018), 9.

5. Ibid., 162.

6. Ibid., 8.

7. Ibid., 168.

8. Donald A. Grinde Jr., "The Indian Removal Act," *The Oxford Companion to United States History*, ed. Paul S. Boyer (New York: Oxford University Press, 2001), 378–79.

9. Washington, 153.

10. Julian Brave Noisecat, "13 Issues Facing Native People Beyond Mascots and Casinos," Huffingpost.com, August 31, 2015.

11. Ian MacDougall, "Should Indian Reservations Give Local Cops Authority on Their Land?" Atlantic.com, July 19, 2017.

12. Shannon Marvel, "Pine Ridge Reservation Holds Strong during COVID-19 Pandemic," mitchellrepublic.com, June 10, 2020.

13. "COVID-19 Lockdown for Ogala Sioux Tribe until Thursday," Blackhillsfox.com, July 7, 2020.

14. Marvel.

15. George E. ("Tink") Tinker, *American Indian Liberation: A Theology of Sovereignty* (Maryknoll, NY: Orbis Books, 2008), 6.

16. William Loren Katz, *Black Indians: A Hidden Heritage* (New York: Atheneum Books, 1986), 31.

17. Roy Harvey Pearce, *Savagism and Civilization: A Study of the Indian and the American Mind* (Baltimore: Johns Hopkins University Press, 1964), 19.

18. Louis S. Warren, *God's Red Son: The Ghost Dance Religion and the Making of Modern America* (New York: Basic Books, 2017), 288–89.

19. Katz, 139.

20. "This Day in History, November 27, 1868: Colonel George Custer Massacres Cheyenne on Washita River," History.com.

21. "Battle of the Little Big Horn," December 2, 2009, History.com.

22. Ibid.

23. Robinson Meyer, "The Standing Rock Sioux Claim Victory and Vindication in Court," TheAtlantic.com, June 14, 2017.

24. Peter Baker and Coral Davenport, "Trump Revives Keystone Pipeline Rejected by Obama," NewYorkTimes.com, January 24, 2017.

25. Ibid.

26. Tinker; Clara Sue Kidwell, Homer Noley, and George E. ("Tink") Tinker, *A Native American Theology* (Maryknoll, NY: Orbis Books, 2001).

27. Tinker, 5.

28. Ernest Lee Tuveson, *Redeemer Nation: The Idea of America's Millennial Role* (Chicago: University of Chicago Press, 1968).

29. Tinker, 128–29.

30. Ibid., 129.

31. Kidwell, Noley, and Tinker, 13.

32. Ibid., 15.

33. Tinker, 9.

34. Ibid., 8–9.

35. Randy Woodley, "The Fulness Thereof: How Indigenous Worldviews Offer Hope to a Besieged Planet," *Sojourners*, May 2019, 15–19.

36. Ibid., 18.

37. Warren, 2–3.

38. Kidwell, Noley, and Tinker, 8.

39. Ibid., 137.

40. Terry Mort, *The Wrath of Cochise: The Bascom Affair and the Origins of the Apache Wars* (New York: Pegasus Books, 2013), 65.

41. Kevin Draper, "Washington and the NFL Might Change the Redskins Name. Why Now?" NewYorkTimes.com, July 16, 2020.

42. Jessica Taylor, "Trump Brings Up Pocahontas at Event Honoring Navajo Code Talkers," npr.org, November 27, 2017.

Conclusion

When I started thinking about this book, I wanted to explore more thoroughly my own early introduction to Black theology and to my late friend and mentor James Cone. What I discovered was that Cone himself was open to the idea that liberation theology was not meant to be limited to the experiences of African Americans struggling with the problems associated with racism and race-based violence. God was certainly on the side of the oppressed, but the designation "the oppressed" was not in any way meant to limit God to only one liberation struggle or to rule out the other forms of oppression experienced by other people around the world based on things other than slavery and racism and its many offspring in the United States.

While I was a student at Union Theological Seminary in New York City from 1970 to 1973, I also became aware of Gustavo Gutiérrez and others whose focus was on Latin American liberation theology and the global problem of poverty. At the same school and at the same time, there were voices, both professors and other students, calling the church to reconsider the role that women could play in the work of ordained ministry. This resulted in a deeper inquiry into feminist theology as it affected all women aspiring for careers in ministry and affirmation by the church of their call by God to serve in ways that required that they be ordained.

I also became aware that African American women at Union and elsewhere were discontent both with Black theology and with feminist theology. It was shocking at first to hear Black women critiquing James Cone because he had initially discussed race without discussing the unique experiences of Black women. Black women wanted to hear the church publicly wrestling with the intersection of race, class, and gender. That gave birth to womanist theology. It was at this point that I began to discover that many, if not most, of my Black male colleagues thought we were approaching "a bridge too far." While Black male clergy were willing to embrace the reality of racism as an evil the church must oppose, they seemed less open to the argument that sexism was a form of oppression that deserved their attention, and that the fight to end sexism in the church was something that deserved and even required their advocacy. I can still hear my mother's voice in 1984 as she reported on the leader of the search committee for a new senior pastor at her local church in Chicago: "I would rather have the least qualified man than the most qualified woman."

It was easy enough for me to consider racism, poverty, and sexism as matters of biblical and theological relevance. After all, in Galatians 3:26-29, Paul declares that within the community of Christ-followers there is neither Jew nor Gentile (race and ethnicity), slave nor free (class and social standing), or male and female (gender). What I had to do was find a way to give voice to calls for an end to oppression from groups that did not easily fall within the framework of Galatian 3.

That was the case with the LGBTQ community and their oppression rooted in sexual orientation and same-gender loving relationships. I must confess that I did not end up in this book where I started out at the beginning of my ministry. Once again, James Cone was my teacher, pushing me beyond racism as my singular focus, to see that homophobia was a form of oppression for many, especially in and by the church. I suspect that many of my Black male colleagues that might go with me on feminist theology and womanist theology may find the embrace of queer theology to be a step they are not yet ready to take. I got an early sense of that when I gave a lecture at United Lutheran Seminary in Philadelphia in 2019 that linked the legacy of racism, sexism, and homophobia as evils to be attacked. The feedback I received from some in attendance that day was "I was with your man until he got to the 'gay stuff.' Then I had to leave him."

I remain grateful to President Barack Obama who, in his second inaugural address on January 20, 2013, lifted Seneca Falls, Selma, and Stonewall as seminal milestones in ongoing freedom struggles that require the nation's continued attention and support. What prevents this nation from moving forward on any of these issues is deep-seated bias falsely cloaked in the garb of honoring biblical teachings, using texts that are not considered with any degree of critical reflection. The same people who would vigorously oppose the use of the Bible to justify racism and slavery seem prepared to trust completely those interpretations of the Bible that leave women and LGBTQ persons as undeserving of advocacy and support. Bad and biased theology and hermeneutics (interpretation of biblical texts) are at the root of so much that is wrong in the church and in the world today.

Finally, I have recently come to understand the value and urgency of Native American liberation theology as focused on the issue of Standing Rock, the Lakota Sioux reservation near Bismarck, North Dakota. While this form of liberation theology is neither grounded in nor seeking legitimacy from traditional Christian sources, it is a voice that all the other oppressed groups need to hear. In many respects, this form of liberation theology is the strongest rebuke of the behavior of Christian nations with the complicity of Christian churches, missionaries, and clergy. This theology has a view of the sovereignty of God over the whole of creation that puts most Christians to shame.

The genocidal assaults on Native Americans are beyond words. Whether through disease, displacement, or the destruction of populations through military assaults and federal legislation, it must be said over and over again that in the United States of America there are four words that sealed the fate of Native Americans: "excluding Indians not taxed."

From Seneca Falls, to Selma, to Stonewall, to Standing Rock is the subtext of American history. One cannot tell the American story without telling all these stories. Eurocentric, white newspaper columnists like George Will may never understand this point. In one of his columns he wrote, "Progressives have a practical objective in teaching the essential squalor of the nation's past. The *New York Times'* '1619 Project'—it preaches that the nation's real founding was the arrival of the first slaves; the nation is about racism—is being adopted by schools as a curriculum around the nation. If the past can be presented as radically wrong, radical remedies will seem proportionate."[1]

Such words flow easily from the pen and heart of a white male living in the United States who is possessed of the centuries-long narrative of American exceptionalism. Will is kept from seeing that the point he argues against is the very point that needs to be made if the nation's school curricula are to be useful in the twenty-first century. There is no need to leave out the story of 1776 or any significant American achievements that occurred thereafter. The issue is not about what one takes out involving standard US history. The issue is what one must add in if the story of US history is to be fully and fairly reported.

A member of Antioch Baptist Church in Cleveland, Ohio, showed me a copy of his US history textbook from his high school years in Alabama in the 1930s. He pointed out the name of Booker T. Washington in the index. The index said the entry would be found on page 138. One would expect an entry about Booker T. Washington with information about Tuskegee Institute (University) in a high school textbook in Alabama. However, when he told me to find page 138 in the book, I discovered that it was not there. It had not been torn out; it had been left out. There was nothing about Booker T. Washington or anything else that spoke about the experiences of African Americans in the state of Alabama or anywhere else in the country. All of that was left out.

This is what Will and so many other white people in this country cannot comprehend. Most of their own stories, to one degree or another, have been told. They have always been included. They learned about George Washington, but not about George Washington Carver. They learned about George Armstrong Custer, but not about Tecumseh, or Cochise, or Geronimo, or Crazy Horse, except as savages that needed to be eliminated from the American story. They learned about Betsy Ross and Dolly Madison, but not about Susan B. Anthony or Sojourner Truth or Harriet Tubman. They learned about Mayor Fiorella LaGuardia of New York City, but not about Harvey Milk of San Francisco. This country has put forward the motto *e pluribus unum* as its guiding principle "out of many, one. This is a phrase taken from Cicero, the 1st century BCE Roman statesman who said: *When each person respects the other as much as himself, we can accomplish many things together*. Following the Democratic and Republican conventions in 2016, one news commentator observed, "I see the pluribus, but where is the unum?"[2]

What is needed is a long, hard look at Seneca Falls. Selma, Stonewall, and Standing Rock. Only when viewed through those lenses can the full and truthful story of American history be told. No syndicated columnist—no matter how clever or widely regarded he or she might be—should seek to obscure, overlook, or justify these moments in our national history when our biases, our prejudices, our brutality, and even our inhumanity were on full display. Indeed, it is because the United States has sought to ignore or downplay these struggles for so long that in 2020 and beyond, we still need to say, "Let the oppressed go free!"

NOTES

1. George Will, "Progressives Are Inflicting Their Progress in California," *The Plain Dealer*, September 20, 2020, E1.
2. Linda Lou Burton, "E Pluribus Unum", https://capitalcitiesusa.org/?p=15845#more-15845, *Capitalcitiesusa.org*, July 31, 2016.

Bibliography

Batstone, David. *From Conquest to Struggle: Jesus of Nazareth in Latin America*. Albany: State University of New York Press, 1991.

Boff, Leonardo, and Clodovis Boff. *Introducing Liberation Theology*. Maryknoll, NY: Orbis Books, 1987.

Branch, Taylor. *At Canaan's Edge: America in the King Years 1965–68*. New York: Simon & Schuster, 2006.

Burroughs, Nannie Helen. *Nannie Helen Burroughs: A Documentary Portrait of an Early Civil Rights Pioneer: 1900–1959*. Edited by Kelisha B. Graves. South Bend, IN: Notre Dame Press, 2019.

Cannon, Katie Geneva. *Katie's Canon: Womanism and the Soul of the Black Community*. New York: Continuum Books, 2002.

Cannon, Katie Geneva, Emilie M. Townes, and Angela D. Sims. *Womanist Theological Ethics: A Reader*. Louisville, KY: Westminster/John Knox, 2011.

Carmichael, Stokely, and Charles V. Hamilton. *Black Power: The Politics of Liberation in America*. New York: Vintage Books, 1967.

Cheng, Patrick S. *Rainbow Theology: Bridging Race, Sexuality, and Spirit*. New York: Seabury Books, 2013.

Cobb, John B., Jr., and David Ray Griffin. *Process Theology: An Introductory Exposition*. Louisville, KY: Westminster/John Knox, 1976.

Collier-Thomas, Bettye. *Daughters of Thunder: Black Women Preachers and Their Sermons, 1850–1979*. San Francisco: Jossey-Bass, 1998.

Cone, James H. *Black Theology and Black Power*. New York: Seabury Press, 1969.

———. *The Cross and the Lynching Tree*. Maryknoll, NY: Orbis Books, 2011.

———. *Martin and Malcolm and America: A Dream or a Nightmare*. Maryknoll, NY: Orbis Books, 1991.

———. *Said I Wasn't Gonna Tell Nobody*. Maryknoll, NY: Orbis Books, 2018.

Cone, James H., and Gayraud S. Wilmore, eds. *Black Theology: A Documentary History*, vol. 2: *1980-1992*. Maryknoll, NY: Orbis Books, 2007.

DiAngelo, Robin. *White Fragility: Why It's So Hard for White People to Talk about Racism*. Boston: Beacon Press, 2018.

Douglas, Kelly Brown. *Sexuality and the Black Church: A Womanist Perspective*. Maryknoll, NY: Orbis Books, 1999.

Du Bois, W. E. B. *The Souls of Black Folk*. Boston: Bedford Books, 1997.

Duster, Alfreda M., ed. *Crusade for Justice: The Autobiography of Ida B. Wells*. Chicago: University of Chicago Press, 1970.

Epps, Archie, ed. *The Speeches of Malcolm X at Harvard*. New York: William Morrow, 1968.

Gafney, Wilda C. *Womanist Midrash: A Reintroduction to the Women of the Torah and the Throne*. Louisville, KY: Westminster/John Knox, 2017.

Gates, Henry Louis. *Life Upon These Shores: Looking at African American History, 1513–2008*. New York: Alfred Knopf, 2011.

Gilkes, Cheryl Townsend. *If It Wasn't for the Women: Black Women's Experience and Womanist Culture in Church and Community*. Maryknoll, NY: Orbis Books, 2001.

Glaude, Eddie S., Jr. *Begin Again: James Baldwin's America and Its Urgent Lessons for Our Own*. New York: Crown Books, 2020.

Graham, Lawrence Otis. *Our Kind of People: Inside America's Black Upper Class*. New York: HarperCollins, 1999.

Griffin, Horace L. *Their Own Receive Them Not: African American Lesbians and Gays in Black Churches*. Eugene, OR: Wipf & Stock, 2010.

Gutiérrez, Gustavo. *A Theology of Liberation*. Maryknoll, NY: Orbis Books, 1971.

Higginbotham, Evelyn Brooks. *Righteous Discontent: The Women's Movement in the Black Baptist Church, 1880–1920*. Cambridge, MA: Harvard University Press, 1993.

Bibliography

Horn, James. *1619: Jamestown and the Forging of American Democracy*. New York: Basic Books, 2018.

Johnson Cook, Suzan D. *Too Blessed to Be Stressed: Words of Wisdom for Women on the Move*. Nashville: Thomas Nelson, 1998.

Jones, Clarence B., and Stuart Connelly. *Behind the Dream: The Making of the Speech That Transformed a Nation*. New York: Palgrave Macmillan, 2011.

Jones, William Augustus, Jr, Jennifer Jones Austin, ed. *God in the Ghetto: A Prophetic Word Revisited*. Valley Forge, PA: Judson Press, 2021.

Joseph, Peniel E. *The Sword and the Shield: The Revolutionary Lives of Malcolm X and Martin Luther King Jr*. New York: Basic Books, 2020.

Katz, William Loren. *Black Indians: A Hidden Heritage*. New York: Atheneum Books, 1996.

Kidwell, Clara Sue, Homer Noley, and George E. ("Tink") Tinker. *A Native American Theology*. Maryknoll, NY: Orbis Books, 2001.

King, Martin Luther, Jr. *Trumpet of Conscience*. New York: Harper & Row, 1967.

———. *Where Do We Go from Here?* New York: Bantam Books, 1967.

Klein, Herbert S. *African Slavery in Latin America and the Caribbean*. New York: Oxford University Press, 1986.

Larue, Cleophus, J. *This Is My Story: Testimonies and Sermons of Black Women in Ministry*. Louisville, KY: Westminster/John Knox, 2005.

Lee, Richard G. *The Battle for the Soul of America and How Christians Can Win It*. Cumming, GA: There's Hope America, 2020.

Lemann, Nicholas. *Redemption: The Last Battle of the Civil War*. New York: Farrar, Straus, and Giroux, 2006.

Lipsett, B. Diane, and Phyllis Trible, eds. *Faith and Feminism: Ecumenical Essays*. Louisville, KY: Westminster/John Knox, 2014.

Mills, Zach. *The Last Blues Preacher: Clay Evans*. Minneapolis: Fortress, 2018.

McMickle, Marvin A. *An Encyclopedia of African American Christian Heritage*. Valley Forge, PA: Judson Press, 2002.

————. *The Making of a Preacher: 5 Essentials for Ministers Today.* Valley Forge, PA: Judson Press, 2018.

————. *Preaching to the Black Middle Class: Words of Challenge, Words of Hope.* Valley Forge, PA: Judson Press, 2000.

————. *Where Have All the Prophets Gone: Reclaiming Prophetic Preaching in America.* Cleveland: Pilgrim Press, 2006.

Moltmann, Jürgen. *Theology of Hope.* Minneapolis: Fortress, 1993.

Moore-Koiko, Cynthia. "Power Dynamics and Sexual Ethics: Even Bishops Get Sexually Harassed—and This One Is Not Putting Up with It." *Sojourners*, April 2019.

Morris, Aldon. *The Origins of the Civil Rights Movement: Black Communities Organizing for Change.* New York: Free Press, 1984.

Mort, Terry. *The Wrath of Cochise: The Bascom Affair and the Origins of the Apache Wars.* New York: Pegasus Books, 2013.

Newman, Richard S. *Freedom's Prophet: Bishop Richard Allen, the AME Church, and the Black Founding Fathers.* New York: NYU Press, 2008.

Oxford World History: The Desk Encyclopedia. New York: Oxford University Press, 2016.

Pace, Courtney. *Freedom Faith: The Womanist Vision of Prathia Hall.* Athens: University of Georgia Press, 2019.

Remini, Robert V. *A Short History of the United States.* New York: HarperCollins, 2008.

Resner, Andre, Jr., ed. *Just Preaching: Prophetic Voices for Economic Justice.* St. Louis, MO: Chalice Press, 2003.

Roberts, J. Deotis. *Liberation and Reconciliation: A Black Theology.* Philadelphia: Westminster Press, 1971.

Ruether, Rosemary Radford. *Liberation Theology: Human Hope Confronts Christian History and American Power.* New York: Paulist Press, 1972.

Smith, Christine A. *Beyond the Stained Glass Ceiling: Equipping and Encouraging Female Pastors.* Valley Forge, PA: Judson Press, 2013.

Smith, Christine M. *Preaching as Weeping, Confession, and Resistance: Radical Response to Radical Evil.* Louisville, KY: Westminster/John Knox, 1992.

Thurman, Howard. *Jesus and the Disinherited.* Nashville: Abingdon, 1949.

Tinker, George E. ("Tink"). *American Indian Liberation: A Theology of Sovereignty*. Maryknoll, NY: Orbis Books, 2008.

Townes, Emilie M. *In a Blaze of Glory: Womanist Spirituality as Social Witness*. Nashville: Abingdon, 1995.

Tran, Jonathan. "The New Black Theology: Retrieving Ancient Sources to Challenge Racism." *Christian Century*, February 8, 2012.

Trible, Phyllis. *Texts of Terror: Literary-Feminist Readings of Biblical Narratives*. Philadelphia: Fortress, 1984.

Tribble, Sherman Roosevelt. *Images of a Preacher: A Study of the Reverend Joseph Harrison Jackson*. Nashville: Townsend Press 1990.

Turman, Eboni Marshall. "Black Women's Faith, Black Women's Flourishing." *Christian Century*, February 28, 2019.

———. "Black Women's Wisdom: Womanist Theology and How It Evolved." *Christian Century*, March 13, 2019.

Tuveson, Ernest Lee. *Redeemer Nation: The Idea of America's Millennial Role*. Chicago: University of Chicago Press, 1968.

Vivian, C. T. *Black Power and the American Myth*. Philadelphia: Fortress, 1970.

Walker, John. *The Rise and Fall of Black Wall Street*. Reklaw Education Lecture Series 4. N.p.: Reklaw Education, 2010.

Warren, Louis S. *God's Red Son: The Ghost Dance and the Making of Modern America*. New York: Basic Books, 2017.

Washington, James M. *A Testament of Hope: The Essential Writings of Martin Luther King Jr.* San Francisco: Harper & Row, 1986.

Washington, Margaret, ed. *Narrative of Sojourner Truth*. New York: Vintage Books, 1993.

Weisenfeld, Judith W. *New World A-Coming: Black Religion and Racial Identity During the Great Migration*. New York: NYU Press, 2016.

Weisenfeld, Judith W., and Richard Newman. *This Far by Faith: Readings in African American Women's Religious Biography*. New York: Routledge, 1996.

West, Cornel. *The Radical King*. Boston: Beacon Press, 2015.

White, Andrea C. "God Revealed in Blackness: James H. Cone (1938–2018)." *Christian Century*, June 6, 2018.

Wilkerson, Isabel. *Caste: The Origins of Our Discontents*. New York: Random House, 2020.

Williams, Demetrius K. *An End to This Strife: The Politics of Gender in African American Churches*. Minneapolis: Fortress, 2004.

Woodley, Randy, "The Fullness Thereof: How Indigenous Worldviews Offer Hope to a Besieged Planet." *Sojourners*, May 2019.

Index

Index